# FREEDOM

Center Point
Large Print

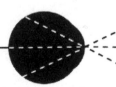

# FREEDOM

## The OVERTHROWING
## of the SLAVE EMPIRES

# James Walvin

CENTER POINT LARGE PRINT
THORNDIKE, MAINE

*For Byron Criddle,*
*a friend of fifty-eight years.*

# Contents

# FREEDOM

# Introduction

ON THE EVE of the French Revolution, all of Europe's major maritime powers, and a number of thriving colonies in the Americas, were keen to have a share of the transatlantic business of slavery. Shipping Africans to the Americas and using them (and their offspring) to labour mainly in agricultural work was a lucrative concern, which no one seemed able to resist. A century later, those same nations had banned the slave trade, had freed all their former slaves and were now vehemently opposed to slavery. Not only was their antipathy expressed in the upper echelons of power (in formal politics, government and diplomacy) but it had also caught the imagination of millions of ordinary people: people who were increasingly well informed via the explosion of literacy and the world of cheap print. To make the point more crudely: in the late eighteenth century, most Atlantic slave owners and slave traders felt confident that they could ride out any criticism of slavery; by the late nineteenth century, they had all vanished and only an eccentric would have felt confident to defend slavery publicly in the West.

At its height, the Atlantic slave system formed a massive international industry that linked

Europe, Africa and the Americas. For all its crude violence, it was a finely tuned commercial enterprise that generated prosperity at all points of the Atlantic compass (and beyond). It was a matter of major commercial and strategic concern for all of Europe's maritime powers, and for the emergent economies of the Americas. Equally, it became a source of economic importance in Africa itself, to the merchants, traders and heads of state who pandered to the demands of the slave ships. From the earliest days when Iberians shipped Africans to Spain and Portugal, to the last days of the trade to Brazil and Cuba, it was a commerce that attracted entrepreneurs and speculators (both large and small) and it seduced governments who were keen to enhance their nations' power, wealth and status.

But slavery was a commercial system fraught with human and natural dangers. European powers fought each other for slave colonies, for essential trading posts on both sides of the Atlantic and for control of the shipping routes that bound the system together. In addition to the great risks of oceanic travel and settlement, Europe's slaving powers faced the unavoidable dangers of African diseases *and* the threats posed by their maritime and strategic rivals. Above all, however, all faced the inescapable dangers posed by the slaves themselves.

Europe's Atlantic trade scattered millions of enslaved Africans across the Americas. From the Chesapeake Bay to the River Plate, a string of American colonies disgorged a host of lucrative commodities (sugar and rum, tobacco and cotton, coffee, timber and many others), which transformed the taste and consumption habits of millions of people. In the process, new economies emerged in Europe, Africa and the Americas. The entire system rested on the Africans, taken from their diverse homelands, shipped to the Americas and finally turned over to a lifetime's arduous toil mainly in tropical and semi-tropical settlements. The numbers involved are astounding. Between the early sixteenth century and 1866 more than twelve million Africans were loaded onto Atlantic slave ships, and more than eleven million survived to land-fall in the Americas. That oceanic journey—the 'Middle Passage' of popular parlance—was a unique and hellish experience, which left deep-seated physical and personal scars on every African who stepped ashore in the Americas. It was a brutal transportation, the memory of which lay at the heart of all slave communities, and was refreshed, year after year, by new groups of Africans joining existing slave communities, fresh from the Atlantic crossing.

The Africans, and their descendants born in the Americas, were kept at work by a system of control and management that was ruthless, callous and extremely brutal. Those who stepped out of line—slaves who resisted or refused to comply—were subject to a range of draconian punishments. There was, moreover, nothing secret about how the slave system worked. What happened on the slave ships and plantations was openly discussed both in the American colonies and in the European heartlands. Yet the severity and cruelties of slavery went largely unchallenged for much of its history. There were, it is true, occasional doubts raised about slavery from the early days, but criticisms of cruelty, or about whether slavery was an efficient labour system, were isolated voices drowned out by the commercial success of the system. Morality and religion counted for little when weighed in the balance against the huge commercial benefits generated by slavery.

The wellbeing and development of Western societies from around the seventeenth century was in large measure paralleled by their involvement with slavery. For more than two centuries, slavery marched in step with Western material progress, though other factors were also at work, notably the West's ability to tap possessions and trading systems in Africa, India and Asia. But slavery stood out as the dominant form of labour that, alone, seemed capable of bringing the luxuriant lands of the Americas to profitable cultivation. It was a form of slavery—chattel slavery—like no other.

The Africans toiling in the Americas had been bought and traded, each with a price on his or her head, from Africa to the slave ships, from the quaysides of the Americas to auction blocks and sales rooms clean across the Caribbean and the continental mainlands. They found themselves inherited and bequeathed, exchanged and bartered, just like other items of trade in any commercial transactions. The surviving paperwork of slavery provides stark evidence of this at every turn. In slave ships' logs, the ships' masters tabulated Africans by number—not by name. In plantation ledgers, sugar planters listed their slaves alongside the beasts of the field. Nor was this merely the march of impersonal economics: the slave's status as an object, as an item of trade, was supported by the law. Legislation and courtrooms on both sides of the Atlantic gave legal shape to slavery. The essential heart of this range of legal transactions—from papal law, through diplomatic agreements to a multitude of statutes—was the status of the African slave as an item of trade: as things.

Just as the law had shaped the origins and development of slavery, it also pronounced the formal death sentence on slavery. When the slave trade was banned, and when slaves were emancipated, each step involved changes in the law. Legislation, proclamations, court cases and constitutional changes conferred formal freedom—but that tells only one side of a complex story. When black freedom was viewed in this light, it was even possible to regard emancipation as a gift, conferred on the slaves, by others. But what we need to know is *why* those changes came about. Behind the various legal enactments of freedom lay deep-seated changes in attitudes towards slavery. And at the heart of those changes were the actions of the slaves themselves.

If we focus not on the emancipators and their political backers, but on the slaves—if we consider slave emancipation as an aspect of slave activity, as something that took place because of what the slaves *did*—the story of emancipation begins to look quite different. What follows, then, is an attempt to explore how slaves were the critical element in securing their own freedom. The intention is to place slaves centre-stage in explaining why the massive and previously unchallenged slave empires of the Americas were overthrown.

To understand how that happened, and to see more clearly the role slaves played in overthrowing slavery itself we need first to come to terms with two major issues. Firstly, why and how were so many millions of Africans shipped into the Americas? Secondly, what role did those

Africans play in the remarkable development of the Americas? When we grasp the enormity of both those issues—the transatlantic trade in Africans and the impact of African slave labour in the shaping of the early Americas—we are in a better position to assess the role of Africans in bringing slavery to an end.

# I

## People as Things: The Slave Trade

MORE THAN ELEVEN million Africans landed in the Americas as slaves. All of them had endured the torments of enslavement in Africa followed by many months of agonies on the Atlantic slave ships. This experience, of capture and transportation, was the seminal and defining experience of every single African shipped to the slave colonies between the late fifteenth century and 1867 (when the last Africans landed in Cuba). Each carried with them not only memories of the world they had left behind— their lives in Africa—but what had happened to them (and others who did not survive) as they were forcibly moved, by land and then by sea, to the bewildering world of America. The millions of survivors of the Atlantic slave trade were the people who formed slave communities that quickly proliferated from the colonies of North America to the River Plate—and most places in between. Even before settling into the rigours of American slavery, they had undergone a traumatic experience that had no real precedence in human history. There had, of course, been many previous slave trades. But none like this.

Civilisations that made extensive use of slave labour often had to rely on the arrival of fresh slaves to replenish the enslaved communities. These human supplies came from slave traders who pillaged societies across whole continents in search of human plunder. Conquered peoples were force-marched, shipped and traded from one end of Europe to another. Victorious Roman armies, for instance, marched their captives ahead of the legions as they entered Rome. Vikings moved slaves from western Europe to the Black Sea and beyond to central Asia: Arab and African traders shifted captives across the hostile vastness of the Sahara to the slave markets of the Mediterranean and Cairo. Wherever slavery thrived, there we find slave traders happy to supply enslaved peoples.

There was, however, little in the history of slavery that approached slave trading in the Atlantic world between the fifteenth and nine-teenth centuries. This oceanic trade was unique in its size, its geographic reach and its global influence. It lasted for four centuries in which time more than twelve million people were loaded onto ships destined for the Americas; one million would not survive the journey. It also created an increasingly complex social and economic network that linked Europe, Africa and the Americas, and involved, in varying degrees, all the major maritime nations of Europe and the Americas.

Of all the people (Europeans and Africans) who landed in the Americas before 1820, the Atlantic slave ships transported 80 per cent. African slaves were *the* major pioneers of great expanses of the Americas. The misery and suffering on the slave vessels, first widely exposed in the late eighteenth century, have haunted the public imagination ever since. Yet, despite the slave ships' fearsome death rate, and despite the damage they inflicted on the survivors, the Atlantic slave trade laid the foundations for an astonishing commercial success. The survivors of the Atlantic crossing, in the words of David Brion Davis, 'became indispensable in creating the prosperous New World that by the mid-nineteenth century began attracting millions of voluntary European immigrants'.[1] African slaves were the foundations on which later societies were built.

Europeans had been familiar with Africans long before the Atlantic slave trade, and with enslaved Africans, mainly via ancient trading links across the Mediterranean. They had also long been curious about the riches of Africa itself, especially the spices and precious metals—gold above all else—that were so valued in Europe and which came overland from Africa. The rise of Islam, however, created a barrier and prompted the need to find new maritime routes to Africa's riches, so, in the fifteenth century, the kingdoms of Portugal and Castile embarked on those exploratory maritime voyages that gradually established sailing routes along Africa's Atlantic coast, round the Cape and thence to the riches of India and beyond—and across the Atlantic.

The Portuguese led the way, establishing trading posts and new societies on the Atlantic islands and along the African coast. By the end of the fifteenth century, they had rounded the Cape and opened up the seaborne routes to Asia. They began trading with Africa at the northern trading post of Arguin, which had inland links all the way to Ethiopia. There, and at the multitude of settlements and trading posts dotted along the Atlantic coast, they found Africans keen to trade for the variety of European and Asian goods on offer. In return, they provided numerous goods— including African slaves.

From the first, Africa seemed a commercial cornucopia, but it was also dangerous. Sailing there, and exploring the treacherous coastline, posed a multitude of hazards, but most dangerous of all were Africa's diseases. The men sent to work at the European posts died in great numbers—many within months. The survivors found themselves wedged between the threats of Africa and the dangerous enormity of the Atlantic. Yet for four centuries, those settlers and traders, and the men who sailed in and out on the Atlantic vessels, thought it worth the risks. Trade with Africa was lucrative, and in time nothing was more lucrative than the trade in African humanity. At first, however, other prizes beckoned, especially the gold (hence the Gold Coast). The potential rewards began to outweigh the natural risks, and by the end of the sixteenth century, Europe's major maritime powers all sought their share of trade on the African coast, each nibbling away at what the Portuguese claimed was their monopoly.

The first slave traders shipped Africans from one coastal region of Africa to another; from the Niger Delta, from the Portuguese bases in Congo and Angola, to bases on the Gold Coast. There the slaves were traded for local gold. In time, Europeans constructed sixty forts along that stretch of coast to provide a defence against Africans, against European foes and, increasingly, as holding pens for the slaves awaiting transfer to the Atlantic ships. Today, the major forts are tourist sites, visited by tens of thousands of people every year.

The major forts became the local commercial HQs for European trading companies, which were initially monopoly 'charter companies' designed to secure the vital flow of African slaves to their slave colonies in the Americas, and to keep other Europeans out. The initial attempts to provide slaves via national monopolies proved inadequate: the slave colonies wanted more Africans than the companies could provide and, eventually, this led to a more open trade. The forts survived, often changing hands as European powers jostled and fought for strategic and commercial dominance on the slave coast (and in other parts of the world). As the slave trade expanded, so too did the major forts. The original Portuguese fort at Elmina, for example, was transformed into a major fortification, with resident and local staff of skilled craftsmen, clerics and administrators. Soon it had its own local community of Africans, Europeans and their mixed-race descendants—all dependent on work in and around the fort. In time, the fort became the massive castle we are familiar with today—a building that seems more suited to a medieval European kingdom. Successive generations of European owners—by turns Portuguese, Dutch and British—nonetheless found it well-suited to their colonial and trading presence on the Gold Coast.

All the early European traders followed this pattern. Portuguese, Dutch, British, French, Danish, Germans—all constructed fortified trading posts and HQs along the Gold Coast. They also developed fortified positions at other spots on or near the coast: at Bunce and James Island (Gambia), at Sherbro (Sierra Leone), on Goree Island (Senegal), at Accra (Ghana), Ouidah (Benin) and São Tomé. Some soon faded, others were little more than temporary and quickly became overgrown.[2] Of course, this type of development was not unique to West Africa and major fortifications sprouted in all corners of the world where European imperial powers put down military or commercial roots. They were (and are still) visible in the Caribbean and North America, in India and south-east Asia. But on Africa's Atlantic coast the forts offered Europeans a unique mix of advantages: they were defensive and strategic sites (in a world of global conflict), trading posts (for a massive Atlantic economy)—and they were prisons for armies of Africans destined for the slave ships.

The larger forts were indeed European castles transplanted to the African coast. The design, construction and defences were European in style. The designers and craftsmen were European, and so was much of the fabric—the building materials. Vast quantities of bricks to construct the forts were shipped from Europe as ballast. The yellow/greenish bricks used at Elmina can be seen in many Dutch courtyards. The Danes, Germans and English did the same, constructing key features of their own forts with bricks, lime, mortar, tiles and metalware imported from their homelands.[3]

As demand for slaves in the Americas

increased, Europeans began gathering Africans from a wide range of African locations. By the end of the slave trade, in the 1860s, Africans had been rounded up at myriad points along a coastal expanse stretching from Senegambia in the north, to Angola, and even round the Cape to Mozambique. Slaving locations changed from time to time, as colonial powers waxed and waned in Africa, and as Europeans developed new bases on the coast—much depending on internal African events (such as warfare, famine and changes in state power). Some slave-trading positions were not even on the coast, but on offshore islands, on inland lagoons or even deep within Africa's massive river systems.

At first, the Portuguese delivered small batches of Africans from Congo to the Gold Coast, and some to Lisbon and Seville, where they worked as domestic servants or on agricultural projects. The story was completely transformed by the impact of sugar, transplanted first to Madeira (from Sicily) and the Canaries. Madeira first satisfied Europe's rising sugar demands—and it did so using African slaves, alongside people of mixed race, with a Portuguese managerial elite in charge. When Portugal colonised São Tomé and Príncipe in the Gulf of Guinea after 1471, sugar again transformed the entire story of the islands. São Tomé attracted settlers familiar with sugar cultivation, and backed by Italian finance. The African coast, only 200 miles away, began to provide slave labour. A pattern was quickly established that was to dominate the sugar industry for the next three centuries: sugar plantations, managed by experienced Europeans, supported by European financiers and their output eagerly devoured by a voracious European market for sweetness. Most critically, the strenuous labour in the sugar fields was undertaken by African slaves. By 1550 perhaps two thousand African slaves were working on São Tomé's sugar plantations. Though the numbers involved look miniscule compared to what followed, it established the blueprint. African slave labour more than proved itself in creating a lucrative export crop for the eager European demand. Sugar planters wanted ever more slaves, and the slave traders provided them—at a price. What emerged was an Atlantic slave system that has entered popular consciousness like no other aspect of slavery. When people think of slavery, they are likely to imagine a sailing ship packed with Africans.

Though the early Spanish conquerors in the New World concentrated on Central and South America, by the mid-seventeenth century, the real potential of the Americas was to be found in Brazil and the Caribbean. That meant sugar cultivated by slave labour, all provided by the

Atlantic slave ships. Two distinct Atlantic systems developed, each determined by prevailing winds and current. In the South Atlantic, the anti-clockwise system directed the maritime and commercial flow of trading ships between West-Central Africa and Brazil south of the Amazon. In the North Atlantic, a clockwise system saw the development of the European trade with the African coastline north of the Congo, thence to the Caribbean and North America.

Africans were taken from eight major regions: Senegambia, Sierra Leone, the Windward Coast, the Gold Coast, the Bight of Benin, Bight of Biafra, West-Central Africa (focused on the Congo) and south-east Africa (Mozambique). But the largest group—almost half of the twelve million total—was drawn from West-Central Africa. These millions of people were then scattered across the face of the Americas, from the Chesapeake Bay in the north, to the River Plate in the South. Although slave ships made landfall at dozens of locations, 95 per cent of all Africans were landed either in Brazil or the Caribbean; and fewer than 4 per cent landed in what became the USA.[4]

This oceanic trade in humanity quickly proved its commercial value and attracted a host of merchants and traders—from both sides of the Atlantic. Odd as it may seem to the modern eye, it was a business that attracted little moral

27

condemnation throughout much of its history. What to us seems an ethical and religious outrage passed largely unnoticed, not least because slave trading became so widespread and pervasive among all the maritime nations in the Atlantic world. The initial coastal trade in Africans gave way to a transatlantic system, feeding Africans into Spain's early settlements in the Caribbean and Central America. By 1641, 418,000 Africans had embarked on ships from Lisbon and Seville. By then, 340,000 had been shipped to Brazil, first in Portuguese ships, but later in Brazilian vessels. When the nations of northern Europe began their own colonial ventures, they too moved into the Atlantic slave trade. In little more than a century and a half after 1642, the Dutch, British and French carried more than five million Africans across the Atlantic. When, in the nineteenth century, these same nations turned their back on slaving, the trade was taken over by traders based largely in Brazil and Cuba, and the scale of African transportations eclipsed even the daunting figures of northern European traders before abolition in 1807; some two million Africans were transported in the fifty years to 1850.[5]

The slave trade was so profitable that other, smaller powers joined in: the Danes, Swedes, Germans (Brandenburgers). Although theirs was a minor contribution, this confirms that anyone able to organise a slaving voyage was keen to do so. We know of 188 ports that were involved in slave trading, but 93 per cent of all slave voyages originated in only 20 ports. Particular ports came to dominate their nation's slave trading though other, lesser and sometimes unlikely places dispatched a local vessel to the African coast for slaves. Ships from Rio de Janeiro and Salvador were the largest carrier of slaves (1.5 and 1.36 million); Liverpool was the third largest with 1.32 million. Port cities with well-established commercial foundations were suitably placed to enter the slave trade. Established ports were able to use existing financial systems and commodities traded from Asia (textiles, for example) to create new commercial connections to Africa. But there were plenty of newcomers keen to elbow their way into the lucrative market, if only for an occasional or infrequent venture. Who, today, would think of Cowes, Poole, Lyme Regis, Oulton, Whitehaven or Lancaster dispatching a ship to trade for African slaves? Merchants with existing links to other forms of trade in the Atlantic had no hesitation in turning their attention to the trade in Africans. Here were commercial riches, which lured all sorts of merchants and investors, including minor, local ones. Locations that offered good access to Atlantic sailing routes enabled previously small ports to become ascendant slaving cities (Liverpool and Nantes, for example).[6]

London was geographically well away from obvious shipping routes to Africa, yet ships from there carried more than one million Africans, primarily because the city was the hub of a thriving system of finance and insurance (which became increasingly important in the slave trade). In addition, London became the centre of global maritime experience and an entrepôt for a multitude of goods and commodities with which to tempt African slave traders. The city's outbound vessels were thus loaded with mixed cargoes of essentials and luxuries, all ideal to be exchanged for African slaves. Slave ships from Bristol transported half a million Africans, and that port (primarily serving Jamaica) had become Europe's second largest slaving port by the mid-eighteenth century. Thereafter it was eclipsed by the rapid emergence of Liverpool, which by 1807 had risen to a newfound civic and commercial prominence on the back of the Africans carried in Liverpool ships. It was well placed for the sailing routes to Africa, had good links to internal British markets and its slave captains quickly developed important networks of contacts among African traders.

Most of Europe's major ports responded to the commercial prospects of the slave trade. Le Havre was the first French port to develop a significant slave trade, carrying 135,000 Africans mainly to St-Domingue. Bordeaux carried a similar number to St-Domingue and to French islands in the Indian Ocean. But the dominant French slaving port was Nantes, whose ships carried almost half a million Africans destined to French possessions in the Caribbean.

Until recently, the study of the Atlantic slave trade tended to see the system as one dominated by Europe. We now know that, as port cities developed in the Americas, a number of them came to play a major role in the slave trade: 46 per cent of all slave voyages originated in ports in the Americas, dotted along the entire eastern rim from New England in the far north to Montevideo in the south. That said, most American slaving voyages originated from a small number of major ports, most of them in Brazil. Even before 1807, ships from Recife loaded more than a half million Africans, while another one and a quarter million embarked on ships that originated in Salvador. Almost 700,000 were embarked on ships from Rio. By the time the Cuban slave trade ended in 1867, slave ships from Havana had transported 683,000 Africans.

By comparison with these immense Brazilian figures, the numbers of Africans embarked on vessels from other American ports before 1807 seem small scale. Ships from the British Caribbean carried 125,000 while 33,000 were transported on French Caribbean ships and 131,000 on ships from Rhode Island.[7]

The first European slave voyages had been piratical ventures, with Africans seized and bundled aboard. Sir John Hawkins' first English slaving voyage described it perfectly. He acquired 300 Africans in Sierra Leone, 'partly by the sworde and partly by other meanes', and took them to Hispaniola.[8] Such piracy had obvious, natural limits (people would flee at the sight of an arriving sailing ship). The transactions for African slaves quickly developed into routine commercial dealings. For that, the European, and later the American traders, needed to offer attractive deals. They haggled for enslaved Africans using those imported goods preferred and valued by local African merchants and traders. It was, after all, a *trade*. The point of enslavement—the moment when Africans were actually seized or captured and enslaved—was clearly a moment of violent seizure. But in the great majority of cases that initial seizure was not the work of men from the slave ships. They had sailed to Africa to trade for Africans who were already enslaved. They acquired their cargoes of Africans from local traders, from people who were eager to get their hands on imported goods. Much like any other trading vessel, the ships heading to West Africa—from Europe or the Americas—arrived with their holds filled with items expected to be the basis of trade on arrival.

The slave ships' captains were critical players in the entire project. They had to be a master-mariner in dangerous, unpredictable waters, in charge of a generally difficult crew and, on the African coast, they became the main commercial negotiator. Once enslaved Africans came on board, the captain became head jailor of a floating prison. For their part, African traders and rulers quickly developed a keen sense of what to expect from masters of the slave ships. The days soon passed when Africans could be bought off with cheap trinkets; they learned how to judge and value the goods on offer against the worth of the slaves they provided in return. Soon, commodities from the wider world were traded. Both Lisbon and Amsterdam became the crossroads for cargoes of tempting goods: from the Indian Ocean, from India, China and Indonesia—in addition to the Americas—and many of those items, along with local and European goods, were shipped on outbound slave ships to West Africa.

Dutch slave traders to Upper Guinea offered textiles from Flanders, England and Spain, woollen goods from France, calico from Gujarat and other cloths from Bengal and Seurat. They offered satin from Persia, taffeta from China, woven goods from North Africa. They also traded beads and precious stones—coral, cowries and pearls—salt fish from Newfoundland, fruits and French brandy. All alongside more mundane items of clothing—hats, shoes, belts and cloaks. A similar pattern was repeated from one slave ship to another and, with variations, from one slaving nation to the next. The Bristol ship, *Fly*, on the Windward Coast in 1786-7, traded for slaves with a cargo that included brandy, Virginian tobacco, a range of Indian textiles, brass kettles and pans, pewter basins, firearms from France and Denmark, iron bars, linen from Ireland, knives, swivel guns, beads and earthenware.[9]

Like Amsterdam before it, London became the financial, commercial and political bedrock on which the nation's slave system developed and thrived. From the mid-seventeenth century the growing number of British ships heading to West Africa carried mixed cargoes from a range of British industries and from far afield: textiles of all kinds (from Yorkshire, Lancashire and India), metal goods—iron bars from Sweden—and firearms in enormous volumes. No single country could provide *all* the goods demanded by African traders and hence the British (and all the others trading on the African coast) had to assemble their cargoes from their homeland, from Europe, from Asia and the Americas. French brandies, Brazilian tobacco and Caribbean rum, all and more were eagerly awaited by

African traders along Africa's Atlantic coast.

When the early monopoly trading companies gave way to freer trade in Africans, London's initial dominance in the British trade gave way, first to Bristol, then, by the mid-eighteenth century, to the rapidly growing city of Liverpool. London's financial importance, however, remained a fixture in the subsequent history of British slave trading. What happened to Liverpool provides a glimpse into the importance of the slave trade not only in the development of that city but in the economic development of Liverpool's wider hinterland. The slave trade from Liverpool spawned a commercial and financial web throughout Lancashire and was important in the subsequent growth of the nearby city of Manchester and a host of regional towns. The trade between Liverpool and West Africa in search of Africans was to be an important element in the transformation of Lancashire's economy.

In 1709 only one Liverpool ship, of a mere 30 tons, traded to West Africa. A century later, that had grown to 134 ships. The cargoes carried to Africa were more valuable than cargoes on most other ships from Liverpool, because they consisted largely of the *manufactured* items sought by African slave traders. One Africa-bound slave ship after another carried similar cargoes: textiles, metal goods, firearms, pipes, luxury drinks. Many of those goods were manufactured by local craftsmen, who, along with the local shipbuilding trades, formed a workforce of some 10,000 people (from a population of 80,000) dependent on the trade to West Africa. Eventually, an estimated 40 per cent of Liverpool's income was derived from its slaving business to and from West Africa.[10] Liverpool is just one example of a phenomenon we can find at all points of the Atlantic slaving system. Each major slave port spawned trades and businesses within the city itself and its wider hinterland, which fed upon the Atlantic slave trade. This was also true of slave ships departing from American ports: fish from Canadian waters, rum from Barbados, tobacco from Brazil— all found their way to the bargaining sessions between sea captains and African slave traders. The latter often rejected out of hand goods they simply did not want. (There were times when slave captains returned home with cargo rejected by African traders.) As the trade evolved, the maritime slave traders developed a keen sense of which goods would suit their purpose. They even developed long-standing commercial dealings with particular Africans, nurturing their goodwill with valuable or much-sought-after gifts.

Slave ships themselves came in all shapes and sizes. The Liverpool ship, the *Brookes*, gave us perhaps the most famous image of a slave ship.

Launched in 1781, the 207-ton *Brookes* collected 5,163 Africans (of whom 4,559 survived) on ten voyages. The engraving of that ship, cleverly used as abolitionist propaganda after 1788, showed 482 Africans packed like sardines. Yet two years earlier, that same ship had crossed the Atlantic carrying 740 Africans, i.e. 258 more than we see in that pestilential drawing.

Overcrowding was a well-known problem, and there had been early efforts to control the 'packing' of slaves. The Spanish had limited numbers to one slave per ship's ton in 1586. By the late seventeenth century the Portuguese sought to establish a limit of 2.5 slaves per ton on their vessels. The *Brookes*, sailing at the peak of Liverpool's slave-trading success, carried five times that ratio. There was a marked deterioration in the shipboard condition of the Africans. Yet the data is confusing.

We know of one tiny vessel of a mere 11 tons, while another Liverpool slave ship was a massive 566 tons. The pioneering Dutch first used ships drawn from other areas of maritime trade and gradually came to rely on small frigates, which were adapted by the ship's carpenters to accommodate Africans as they were bought on the coast. By the late eighteenth century, when Liverpool dominated the North Atlantic trade, all of Europe's major slave ships were much bigger than earlier vessels. A substantial proportion of Liverpool's vessels had been built in the city itself, notably of the 'Guineamen' type built specifically to carry slaves. But as slave ships got bigger, the space provided for each person contracted. Even so, the level of 'packing' on slave ships was not the main cause of slave mortality. The key factor was the length of time Africans spent on board a ship: the longer they remained incarcerated there, the higher the mortality. As Atlantic crossings got swifter, the mortality rate dropped.

The exception to this was in the last 'illicit' phase of slave trading (post-1807) when crowded Cuban and Brazilian vessels, pursued by British and American naval patrols, packed in as many Africans as possible before making a seaborne dash for the Americas. It was then, on grossly overcrowded ships, that we find the most terrible of all transatlantic conditions. Excessive crowding, brutal treatment, bad provisioning, all creating a string of harrowing stories—of suffering and death rates at horrifying levels.

To modern eyes, all the slave ships—including the biggest ones used by the Brazilians in the nineteenth century—seem tiny; 200 to 300 tons, not much longer than a cricket pitch, and perhaps only 7 metres wide. But they were the floating prison, for months on end, for hundreds of Africans. At sea, the Africans were steeped in the filth below decks, not knowing where they were or where they heading: the sick and the dead chained together in a stew of violated humanity. There had been nothing like it, on this scale, before, and no other recorded or contemporary account of sea travel provides such horrifying data. But even the raw data of the Atlantic crossings fails to evoke the experience of life on a slave ship. The noise, the stench, the violent movement of a sailing ship in rough weather, the fears—all this and more was the everyday, commonplace experience of every one of the twelve million Africans who boarded a slave ship.

The Atlantic crossing was the latest stage of a prolonged journey, albeit the most punishing and brutal leg. Many Africans had reached the Atlantic coast after travelling from inland communities. As far as we can tell, most were driven there by a variety of factors; famine, poverty, but, overwhelmingly, by acts of violence. Moreover, the networks of enslavement expanded, geographically, as demand on the coast for enslaved Africans increased. Contemporary, mainly late eighteenth century, accounts and a few surviving illustrations reveal that the victims were force-marched and sometimes taken by river craft, in coffies, in pairs or small groups, and generally shackled in some way in metal or wooden fetters.

Although the trade was scattered along an

enormous expanse of African coastline, almost two-thirds of all Africans embarked on slave ships at a mere ten locations (Anomabu, Ouidah, Bonny, Old Calabar, Luanda, Benguela, Cabinda, Malembo, Loango and Quilimane), and an astounding 4.7 million left from just four of those places (Loango, Cabinda, Luanda and Benguela).[11] The centre of this trade also shifted across time, waxing and waning with the rise and fall of the colonial powers and of their maritime or trading strength.

Slave traders from particular countries, even from specific ports, had favourite locations for their dealing with African traders. What emerged, at many African trading locations, were well-established relations between the seaborne traders (or in some cases their local representatives) and African dealers. This created important commercial and trading networks that linked the slave ships to a deeper African economic hinterland. It also had the effect of funnelling large numbers of *particular* African peoples into certain regions of the Americas, with profound consequences for the development of American slave communities—from the languages they spoke and the food they ate to the gods they worshipped.

As if to make their torments worse, the enslaved Africans were guarded by sailors who were themselves often terrified. The crew of slave ships were always greatly outnumbered, and always worried about slave violence and revolt. Large numbers of the crew would become sick or die, especially on the African coast. Working a slaver was renowned for its dangers, and the crew were drawn from the bottom of the seafaring barrel: only the desperate, the ignorant or the drunk would sign up. Over the course of the British involvement in the slave trade, an estimated 350,000 men worked on the slave ships. In 1788, the abolitionist Thomas Clarkson proved that fewer than half the men who left Britain on slave ships returned. Far from being a nursery for the Royal Navy (as was often claimed), it was a graveyard. Though the crew consisted of a mix of nationalities (and ethnicities) the bulk of sailors were drawn from ports and communities within Britain's slaving system, so there could have been no secrecy about the deadly environment of the slave ships. And yet, it continued for centuries . . .

Perhaps the best-known feature of the slave trade—the image that remains to this day—is the misery of the Atlantic crossing: the Middle Passage. The experiences on the slave ships have entered popular folklore. Indeed, the imagery of a crowded ship has become part and parcel of a collective memory. It is vivid in the mind's eye because it has been so frequently portrayed in the mass media in recent years, with pictures of a crowded ship used in all sorts of advertisements, posters, flyers, dustjackets and billboards to portray an enormous range of issues—some tacky and tasteless—but all confirming the basic horror of the slave ships.

Although most contemporary images of slave ships display a human cargo dominated by men and boys, that was not always typical. Some carried more women than men, while the number of child slaves varied enormously. In time, the proportion of child slaves—and males—increased. What happened to all those people on the Atlantic crossing depended largely on the time it took to cross the ocean, and that depended on the weather—and good fortune.

Africans often spent longer on board a slave ship anchored off the coast of Africa than in crossing the Atlantic. The ships accumulated their human cargoes slowly, from place to place. Where there were no facilities for holding Africans on shore, the ship acted as a floating prison until the master decided that he had enough enslaved people to set out across the Atlantic. Some ships—little more than hulks—acted as permanent offshore prisons, passing on their captives to other ships ready to sail. In the seventeenth century, Dutch ships spent an average of 120 days on the coast; British ships 94. A century later, the Dutch spent an average of

200 days on the coast; French ships 143. In the mid- and late-eighteenth century, British ships spent 173 days on the African coast.

One stark fact stands out from this welter of information: millions of Africans spent months at sea *before* the Atlantic crossing began. As they waited (not knowing what was to happen to them, but hearing rumours that swirled around the slave decks and gossip that was sometimes gleaned from crewmen), many fell ill, some died—most of them were bemused or terrified. The ship's crew were now warders in a floating prison.

Africans boarded the ships stripped of their names and given numbers. Whatever they called each other, and whatever their original names, was lost to the accountancy of slaving. Slave captains entered the Africans as numbers in their logs: '1 woman, 2 boys, and 3 girls, all small, No. 38 to 43.' When they died, they were deleted as numbers. 'In the morning buried a boy slave (No. 66) who was ill with a violent flux.'[12] The Africans now became human cargo, at the mercy of the elements and the crew.

Careless sailors and slipshod management of tools and equipment could lead to a disastrous slave insurgency, as we shall see later. The slave ship was a human brew of fear and animosity, with Africans shackled below—though released in small batches, weather permitting, for exercise. The yards of chains and metal fetters, loaded at the ship's home port, now came into their own, shackling the Africans to prevent upheaval. Without the metal restraints there could be no guarantee of security. If the worst happened, strategically located guns covered the hatches to the slave decks.

Though the speed of an Atlantic crossing was largely dictated by winds and currents, navigational and other errors sometimes intervened. Sailing from Upper Guinea to the Caribbean or North America might be completed in six weeks. So too a journey from West-Central Africa to Brazil. Voyages that crossed from one prevailing weather system to another were more protracted, with their slaves having to endure a crossing of three months. Of course, *all* sailing ships were at risk from the unpredictable freaks of weather, of storms and doldrums, and of maritime errors that sometimes sent them to their doom.

Every slave captain knew that the key to a successful voyage was a quick passage and did what he could to speed the journey. There were times when a ship was reduced to a pestilential vessel. The filth of the slave decks, the contamination of eating and drinking in fouled conditions, created a perfect breeding ground for a string of ailments, none more virulent and commonplace than amoebic dysentery— the 'bloody flux'. Although Africans had been crudely inspected for obvious physical defects or unhealthy symptoms, before boarding, illness was often brought on board, spreading quickly among the crowded slaves. Despite the efforts to sustain the human cargo in reasonable condition until landfall, Africans succumbed to a series of complaints en route. The sick were documented in the master's log, and the dead were deleted from his list, their remains cast overboard to the following sharks.

All this poses a bizarre puzzle. It was in the slave traders' interests to maintain the Africans in a healthy state until they reached the American auction block. The foul conditions on a storm-tossed slave ship were not planned or intended, and the master and crew were struggling against conditions they could not always control. It is true that slave ships were marked by violence, often on a barbaric scale, and by sexual assaults and capricious cruelty. In addition, the crew themselves were subject to traditional shipboard physical punishment for any acts of personal violence against the slaves. Slave ships became a lethal brew of resentment and terror: among the slaves, between the slaves and the crew, and sometimes between the master and his men. The longer the voyage, the more severe the sufferings of the Africans, often made worse by the attrition among the crew. (Slave masters tried to conceal crew losses from the slaves. If Africans noticed the shortfall in sailors, they were more likely to take advantage of the diminished crew.)

Like all sailing ships, slavers were at risk of oceanic and coastal dangers. Storms could simply swallow the ship and all on board. We know of 148 cases of the total loss of slave ships—of crew and Africans. The doldrums caused enormous human damage. So too could bad planning before departure, or navigational errors en route. On unexpectedly prolonged journeys, food and water simply ran out—that was the cause in 1781 of the murderous disaster on board the *Zong*, when over a hundred slaves were thrown overboard. Most savage of all were the disasters when the crew abandoned the vessel in a shipwreck. Sailors struggling to save themselves rarely tried to save the manacled Africans (who might overwhelm them in the fight for survival). Africans remained shackled on a sinking ship driven onto rocks: one case in 1738 led to the death of 702 Africans.[13] A further 443 vessels were shipwrecked. Some slaves were rescued by other ships—only to be sold when they made landfall. In addition there was the danger of European warfare, played out in the waters of the Atlantic and the Caribbean, when slave ships were seized by enemy vessels, and the slaves then sold by different slave traders. The *Zong* itself had originally been a Dutch slave ship (the *Zorgue*) before falling into British hands during the conflict with the American colonies.

Long-distance oceanic travel was always a physical and sometimes a frightening ordeal, but nothing came close to the prolonged physical and mental torments of months on board an Atlantic slave ship. No other ship smelled like a slave ship. They were infamous, among their own men and even among fellow sailors on distant vessels, for their stink. They stank like a floating cesspit and could be detected miles away, downwind.

What did the enslaved Africans make of all this? Even when conditions allowed them to be brought on deck for exercise, what sense did they make of the watery vastness all around them? As far as the eye could see, for months on end, they saw nothing but the immensity of the Atlantic Ocean. Moreover, they were Africans drawn from *inland* regions who, in the main, had not seen the sea before they were marched to the coast. Now there was no escape from the sea. It was rarely silent. Even at night, or in those stormy fetid days when the Africans were incarcerated below, they could hear the sea, incessantly battering the vessel on all sides—only inches from where they lay.

One major problem facing historians is that the facts and figures of the crossings can easily appear sterile and devoid of human feeling. How do we create a human story from the abundance of data we now possess? How do we conjure forth any sense of what all this meant for the millions of Africans involved? The one million who died on the crossing, and all the survivors—every single one of the eleven million Africans—had endured an experience of such deep and abiding trauma that it remains difficult, even now, to convey the full horror involved. What memories of the crossing did these survivors carry with them as they settled into their new homes across the Americas?

The Africans landed as troubled people. Often sick, most were deeply distressed by the ordeal of their enslavement followed by months at sea. Slave owners buying Africans off the slave ships recognised they had to treat them carefully. Some had even lost the will to live. At first sight, then, the new arrivals looked like a defeated people: battered into physical and mental submission by a terrifying and violent experience. But that ordeal fostered embers of subsequent slave defiance. Every survivor drew their own conclusions from the slave ships, the most bitter being the knowledge of what happened to defiant slaves who resisted openly—and failed. But the Africans' determination was not so easily quelled, and the subsequent history of slavery throughout the Americas is a complex story of slave defiance. In time, that defiance became a key factor in the overthrow of slavery itself.

# 2

## Sinews of Empire: Africans and the Making of the American Empires

ALTHOUGH SPAIN HAD been the first colonial power to dabble with African slavery in the Americas, it was the Portuguese establishment of sugar plantations in Brazil that launched the westward flow of Africans. The Portuguese sugar plantations on São Tomé and Príncipe had employed perhaps two thousand African slaves by the mid-sixteenth century. What happened to those slaves was the apprenticeship for the millions who were to follow them—but on the far side of the Atlantic. They produced crude cane sugar, which was then shipped to the early refineries in Europe's major port cities, thence, once refined, to the fashionable tables of Europe's well-to-do elites.

The boundless prospect of Brazil persuaded sugar planters to quit the Atlantic islands and head west—accompanied by their slaves. Sugar was an obvious crop to transplant into the tropical lands of the Americas (Columbus had taken sugar cane with him on his second voyage in 1493) because it had already proved its commercial value in São Tomé and Príncipe. After initial experiments with various other export items (timber notably), from the 1530s Portuguese settlers in Brazil turned to sugar. Encouraged by royal support (in the form of land grants), Brazilian sugar entrepreneurs took hold around Pernambuco, then, more securely, in and around Salvador. São Tomé's sugar industry vanished almost as quickly as it had emerged, undermined by Brazilian sugar.

At first planters tried local Indian labour, but (in common with Indian peoples throughout the Americas) native people would not, or could not, bend themselves to the rigorous demands of sugar plantations. Thus, from the 1570s onwards, Brazilian planters turned to African slave labour. What followed was staggering. By 1600, 200,000 Africans had been shipped to Brazil. The critical link was between Brazil and Angola (which the Portuguese colonised, from their slaving post in Luanda, in 1575). Over the entire history of the Atlantic slave trade, an astounding 2.8 million Africans were shipped from Luanda, bound primarily for Brazil.

Brazil seemed to be a cornucopia that yielded a multitude of crops, but until the nineteenth century it was sugar that dominated. Growing volumes were shipped first to Portugal, and subsequently to the greedy markets served by the port cities of northern Europe: Antwerp,

Amsterdam, later Hamburg and London. The rise of sugar can be traced by the proliferation of sugar refineries in European cities, and by African arrivals in Brazil. Antwerp had nineteen refineries as early as 1550, Amsterdam had 110 in 1770, London 80 by 1753.[1] But all this was made possible by African labour, first in Brazil, and later in other European colonies. By 1600, 200,000 Africans had landed in Brazil and over the following century almost one and a half million had been transported there.

The Brazilian sugar economy was copied later in the Caribbean. It was brutal, regimented, and paid little heed to many of the human needs of its labourers, forced to work in the unforgiving tropical environment. Producing sugar was not merely rural work, but also partly industrial. Bigger plantations had their own factories where the cane was converted to crude sugar and molasses, their large factory chimneys belching smoke and steam into the tropical sky. The enslaved labour force failed to increase naturally, however, and sugar planters were permanently in need of fresh labour for their fields. Sugar proved to be (in the words of David Geggus) a 'barren mother' who consistently failed to provide the offspring we might expect from such vast numbers of transported people. It was as if sugar devoured its own, and had to turn, year after year, to Africa to replace the sick and the dead, or to fill the labouring ranks when new lands were opened up.

Brazil's enormous geography soon revealed how adaptable slavery could be. Slaves were put to a multitude of different tasks, notably in Brazil's increasingly large and sophisticated urban societies, where domestic slavery expanded hugely. As prosperous planters and other country residents developed more comfortable—sometimes lavish—lifestyles, they instinctively turned to slaves for domestic comforts. Slaves were widely used as symbols of status and wealth, and Brazilians became especially fond of being carried, in sedan-like arrangements, shielded from the sun by costly textiles, and cooled by fan-wielding slave domestics. Visitors (and graphic satirists) regularly remarked on the slave retinues attending Brazil's prosperous classes (and not so prosperous too). Slave labour was available for every conceivable task—housework, cooking, travelling, childcare, sexual favours—all and more were provided by slaves. They toiled everywhere, from the dockside and riverside, through to the isolation of ranching on remote frontier lands. Slavery took on a distinctive form in the urban areas, where they were rented out as porters (both of people and goods), or were set to work as street vendors, salesmen, craftsmen and musicians. Recent scholars reckon that Brazilian slaves worked in more than a hundred occupations in town and country.[2] They were to be seen at their most wretched as they stumbled from the slave ships, on the auction block or being driven, they knew not where, to a new place of labour.

African slaves found themselves used in every new Brazilian economic discovery and enterprise. Gold, discovered in Minas Gerais and Goiás, prompted an early eighteenth-century rush of speculators to the region—along with 80,000 slaves to do the hard work. The increasing world demand for cotton in the eighteenth century, and the expansion of cotton production in Amazonia, saw Africans shipped to the northern ports in Pará and Maranhão. In the late eighteenth century the most southerly regions of Brazil turned to slavery, with the development there of ranching, and an associated hide and beef economy. All these and other new industries, especially the coffee industry, required the enforced movement of Brazilian slaves from older, more established regions, and the importation of yet more Africans from the slave ships.

Until 1791 the French colony of St-Domingue had been the world's major coffee producer, but the Haitian revolution shattered that economy, allowing other tropical colonies, notably Jamaica, Sumatra and Brazil, to step into the commercial gap. The real expansion of coffee production, however, stemmed from the rise of coffee drinking in the USA. In their struggle against British colonial control, Americans had turned against their initial taste for tea, and by 1830 they drank six times as much coffee as tea; by 1860 nine times as much. The powerful coffee culture of the USA was nurtured first by European immigrants and then by the huge expansion of the US population. In 1800, the population stood at more than five million, but a century later it was seventy-six million. It was a nation of coffee drinkers, and cheap Brazilian coffee satisfied that thirst. In 1791, 1 million pounds of coffee were imported, but when the coffee import duties were removed in 1832, coffee imports increased massively, and by 1844 they were running at 150 million pounds. By then, on average, each American was consuming more than six pounds of coffee annually.[3] This had major ramifications on slavery in Brazil.

Brazil opened up new coffee-growing regions and huge numbers of slaves were relocated from the north-east of Brazil, where they had been settled on the sugar plantations. Just like the cotton planters of the US South at much the same time, Brazilian coffee growers (after the end of Brazil's slave trade, but not of slavery, in 1850) could no longer buy Africans, which created instead an *internal* slave trade. Huge numbers of Brazilian slaves were transported great distances from one part of that huge country to the new coffee frontiers, sometimes by ship along the Atlantic coast. It was a trade accompanied by acute human suffering. Most painful of all was the devastation caused by the break-up of slave families. It was a heartless reprise of the dislocation and seaborne horrors endured by their African forebears crossing the Atlantic.

Though sugar remained Brazil's most valuable export until the mid-nineteenth century, by the time slavery ended in Brazil in 1888, the coffee-producing regions were home to about 65 per cent of the nation's slaves.[4] There is a real paradox at the heart of this story, because at the very time Western opinion was turning against slavery in the nineteenth century, slavery continued to be sustained and strengthened by the massive Western demand for slave-grown produce, notably cotton grown in the US South and Brazilian coffee. Although Brazilian slavery expanded alongside the country's wider agricultural growth (in cattle, tea and grain cultivation, much of it for consumption by Brazil's growing population), above all it was the coffee industry that confirmed the continuing value of slavery in Brazil.

In the nineteenth century, Brazilian slavery was at its most visible in urban life. Slaves constituted a sizeable proportion of the local population in Brazil's major cities. In common with other Western societies, Brazilian cities grew apace.

By mid-century, Rio was home to more than 200,000 people, of whom 80,000 were slaves. In São Paulo, almost a quarter of its 31,000 people were slaves. In Porto Alegre, upwards of one-third of the 17,226 inhabitants were enslaved. In some urban areas, almost half the population were slaves.

Though the focal point of Brazilian slavery remained the plantation, this diversity of slave labour meant that slave ownership was widely diffused throughout Brazilian society. Planters and the wealthy may catch the eye, but there were substantial numbers of slave owners in all walks of life. Slavery was not restricted to the major industries, nor limited to wealthy elites, but permeated Brazilian society to a degree that was unusual in other parts of the Americas. Large numbers of people—even poorer sorts—owned two or three slaves, often relying on the income from their rented labour. In effect, slavery was part of the warp and weft of society at large. This meant, however, that ending slavery would have massive consequences, not merely for planters or major vested interests, but throughout Brazilian life.

Although African slaves and sugar had been introduced into the Caribbean islands by early Spanish settlers, both remained marginal until the 1620s. Spain's prime interest was Central and South America, and the apparently boundless riches disgorged by the collapse of the ancient Aztec and Mayan empires. Treasure fleets heading home to Spain, packed with the riches of the Indies (with all the temptations they dangled before privateers) seemed a better investment than the arduous involvement in agricultural commodities. The Portuguese and Dutch in Brazil, however, had proved otherwise. The rising power of Dutch mercantile interest (in all corners of the globe) had seen their growing involvement in Brazil. Though Dutch control of Brazil proved short-lived, they acquired the skills of sugar cultivation and production, and they had the money necessary to invest in sugar industries. It seemed natural that the Dutch should facilitate the transfer of sugar and Africans into the Caribbean itself.

Bit by bit, the French and English took command of the islands from local Indians or from the fading power of Spain. By turns, the English conquered Barbados (1627) and Nevis (1628), followed by Montserrat and Antigua. Finally, they took Jamaica from Spain in 1655 (a consolation prize, having failed to conquer Santo Domingo). Almost in parallel, the French seized Guadeloupe and Martinique, shared St Kitts with the English and finally took St-Domingue (the western part of the island of Santo Domingo). This was to become France's most valuable Caribbean colony, home to the largest number of African slaves and a major source of wealth to France. Ultimately, however, it was to be the cause of the collapse of France's slave empire and send terror throughout the enslaved Americas.

Like others before them, English settlers in the Caribbean and North America experimented with a number of crops—cotton, tobacco and sugar—and used various forms of labour: indentured whites, free labour, and both free and unfree local Indian labour. Everything changed with the rise of sugar, and the use of African slaves. It was not an inevitable progression; but, with the right mix of location, climate and crop, slavery emerged as the most viable and commercial labour system. Initially, it seemed that indentured labour might be the answer, but sugar was an extremely harsh taskmaster, and people simply refused to commit themselves to working in the sugar fields—even for a limited period. Slavery fitted the bill.[5]

It had been proved to work, profitably, in São Tomé and Brazil, and it soon took hold in the Caribbean. There was, moreover, no real moral issue at stake. With a few notable exceptions, African slavery had effectively gone unchallenged since its arrival in the Americas. Local Indian peoples had been enslaved, and small numbers of African slaves had been settled in the region from the early days. But it was the experience of Brazilian planters that clinched the argument: slaves worked until they died. Those born in the Americas worked from their early years until old age or decrepitude rendered them useless. The phrase 'old and useless' entered plantation ledgers as a heartless descant to the slaves' basic economic value. So it was, as British and French settlers in the Caribbean turned to sugar cultivation, they also turned to African slaves (the early success of tobacco there was undermined by the astonishing rise of tobacco cultivation—by slaves—in the Chesapeake). From the 1640s onwards, sugar crept through the islands; from Barbados onto Guadeloupe, Martinique, St-Domingue, St Kitts, Nevis, Antigua and Montserrat. It was never the sole export crop, even on the major sugar-producing islands (coffee was very important in some places). But it came to dominate the islands' exports, and enhanced their economic and strategic value to all of Europe's colonial powers.

Sugar began to pour eastwards across the Atlantic. By 1650, Barbados exported 7,000 tons of sugar. Fifty years later, when the British islands dispatched 25,000 tons to British refineries, they outstripped Brazilian production (of 22,000 tons). In 1700, the slave colonies were producing 60,000 tons of sugar, but even that huge amount was surpassed in the coming century. The total volume reached 150,000 tons in 1750, and 180,000 by 1770. By then, St-Domingue was producing an astonishing 60,000 tons, Jamaica, 36,000 tons. All this was produced by the gangs of African slaves. In the early 1600s some 7,000 Africans a year were being shipped to the Americas, rising to 18,000 by the 1660s. A century later, the numbers had risen to 80,000 a year, the great majority destined for Brazil or the Caribbean. Almost half a million landed on the small island of Barbados; twice that number in Jamaica.[6]

This new sugar economy rested on the backs of armies of African slaves. Yet there is a historical puzzle here. Europeans turned to African slavery when slavery in Europe itself had faded away. Although Europeans had used slave labour at home for centuries, by the time they were settling new colonies in the Caribbean, slavery had effectively died out in Europe. The British developed colonial and metropolitan laws to regulate their new slave system, and a complex web of maritime law evolved to juggle the complexities of shipping millions of Africans across the Atlantic. But the *justification* for holding humans in perpetual bondage was not really addressed until the late eighteenth century. Whatever moral issues were involved in this system, they lay relatively dormant and unaddressed for a century and a half. This silence involved a strange contradiction, because at the very time Europeans were concerned about the concepts of freedom at home, they were actively extending slavery to unprecedented numbers of people in the Americas. They could partly justify the process of enslavement because the people involved were not European—but African. Europeans came to think of Africans as people beyond the pale of civilised humanity: pagan, barbaric and devoid of the cultured characteristics that Europeans reserved for themselves.

The basic justification for African slavery was much simpler and more basic. Unlike Europeans, Africans were available in abundance, were bought and transported cheaply (despite the distances), and were readily replaced. African slavery offered the perfect economic solution to the endless hunger of American plantations for a cheap, malleable and durable (or replaceable) labour force. In the words of Barry Higman, 'Slave owners rarely doubted that slavery was the most profitable system of labour available to them.' What more justification did slavery require?[7]

Sugar thus shaped the justification for slavery. Indeed, one indication of the economic importance of slavery and sugar was the comparative wealth of the Caribbean and North American colonies. The sugar islands formed a much greater, and more valuable, part of British trade than the North American colonies. Similarly, the French islands, but especially the sugar and coffee industries of St-Domingue, were vital to France's overseas trade. The two major powers in the eighteenth-century Atlantic, Britain and France, were also deadly rivals, enviously eyeing each other's colonies and trade, battling each other for imperial and economic dominance, and pitching their military (mainly naval) power to protect their own possessions, or to seize those of their opponent. The Caribbean emerged as the engine of growth and prosperity in the Americas. It was the axis on which an enormous Atlantic economy turned, and a focal point of a huge maritime trade linking Africa, the Americas and Europe. The islands disgorged commodities and their related prosperity both to local owners and to metropolitan backers, and this generated North American colonial activity via the enormous volumes of foodstuffs and timber shipped from there to the Caribbean. It also transformed global dietary habits by flooding world markets with sugar, rum and coffee. Legions of working people, on both sides of the Atlantic, derived much of the energy they required for their labouring efforts from the sugar they consumed, notably in their hot drinks. And all this was made possible by the gangs of Africans in the sugar fields.

In the ninety years to 1790, slave numbers in the Caribbean increased by 2 per cent annually.

By that year, almost 1.5 million slaves lived in the region, with small numbers in Dutch, Danish and Swedish possessions, 9 per cent in Spanish islands, but the very great majority—83 per cent—in French or British colonies. On the eve of the French Revolution, St-Domingue alone was home to a third of *all* slaves in the Caribbean. In the early nineteenth century, there was another expansion of slavery in Cuba and Puerto Rico, and by 1830 (on the eve of British emancipation) there were more than 3.25 million slaves throughout the Caribbean.[8] These are, by any standards, startling numbers when we remember that the enslaved population had stumbled from the Atlantic slave ships.

The development of all slave colonies was closely linked, of course, to the policies of their mother country, though in time the emergence of colonial societies, with their own governing and economic elites, created inevitable friction and disputes with the metropolitan power. There emerged a divergence of interests and views between Europeans and their possessions across the Atlantic. That was at its most severe and obvious in the breakaway of Britain's North American colonies, and later the break-up of the Spanish and Portuguese empires in the Americas. The one factor that anchored the slave colonies most securely to the mother country was the slaves. Clean across the Caribbean, slaves greatly outnumbered the slave-owning classes, sometimes to a massive degree. On isolated sugar plantations, local management and white people might be outnumbered by fifty to one. Few Caribbean slave owners, from the humblest with only a handful of slaves to the wealthiest planters who owned hundreds, doubted that their ultimate security lay in the military strength of their mother country. They needed the military support provided by London and Paris.

Naval forces were vital, not only in safeguarding the islands and the shipping routes against European rivals, but especially as the ultimate safety net against the slaves. Colonists had their own militias, and there were military bases scattered across the islands. But it was the ability to move large military groups between the islands, and from one part of an island to another, that made navies so important. In periods of major European conflict, the French and British navies transported whole armies into the Caribbean. Of course, maintaining the security of slave colonies involved much more than military power. Indeed, the ability of slave owners to maintain control over huge numbers of disaffected slaves for long periods of time remains one of the great conundrums of slave history. But the threat and reality of physical and military action was the slave owners' last line of defence in societies where large numbers of recalcitrant slaves lived cheek by jowl with apprehensive slave owners.

Although the Spanish Crown had been the first to stake a claim to the Caribbean islands, in time their main colonial ambitions lay elsewhere. As power shifted in Europe, from the Mediterranean to northern Europe, the northern powers began to exercise growing control over the Caribbean. Spain based its regional power initially in Santo Domingo, then, from the early seventeenth century, in Havana, which became the waystation for Spain's vital maritime links to and from Central America. Havana was the refuelling post and defence for Spanish fleets bringing astonishing treasures, especially silver, back to Spain. That apart, Cuba had little to offer Spain: its population and economic output declined but Havana (home to 14,000 people by 1620) and its hinterland were the exception. By then, half of Cuba's population consisted of slaves, many of them Catholic, and there were large numbers of freed slaves. Cuba thus developed a distinctive social structure quite unlike the societies that evolved in the other slave islands in the region.

Spain's other main possession, Hispaniola, had a different experience, though it lacked Cuba's strategic importance. Sugar took hold there thanks mainly to settlers from the sugar industry in the Canaries. As the local industry boomed, so did the import of African slaves. But, from 1570, the island's sugar industry was undermined by the rapid growth of Brazilian sugar, and Hispaniola returned to a cattle economy.[9] Yet Hispaniola was nominally in control of Spain's thinly stretched Caribbean empire and by the early seventeenth century that scattering of Spanish islands had become ungovernable, made worse by the decline of Spain itself. Spain's islands proved a great temptation to the rising power of the Dutch, French and English, all now keen to develop their own colonies in the Americas, who began picking off Spain's exposed and undefendable islands in the eastern Caribbean. Spain effectively retreated to its well-defended port cities (Havana, Santo Domingo and San Juan). From the 1620s onwards, islands began to change hands, and acquired new European rulers and took on new economic identities. Fresh waves of northern Europeans, aided by state power and private capital, were seeking a foothold along the vast edge of the Americas, from Jamestown, Virginia, to Barbados. Like the Spaniards before them, they soon discovered that their various agricultural developments required more labour than they could muster from their own ranks. They tried a range of crops, notably cotton and tobacco, before in many areas the viability of tobacco was swept aside by the astonishing rise of the crop in Virginia and Maryland. Once again, however, everything was changed (though slowly in some islands) by the advent of sugar and the arrival of Africans to work the sugar fields.

This 'sugar revolution' failed to take root and thrive in Spain's surviving Caribbean islands. For a start, Spain's imperial interest remained focused on Central and South America, and its fading power was stretched merely to hang on to Cuba, Santo Domingo and Puerto Rico. In effect Spain backed itself into a defensive corner, happy to hold on to what it had, but allowing the rest of Europe to press on with its slave-based sugar economy.[10]

Cuba did not turn to sugar and African slaves to any major degree until the upheavals of the French Revolution and the collapse of the French colonial economy. Though original Spanish restrictions on slave imports had been removed in 1762 (in the period of brief British control of Havana), slave imports increased steadily thereafter. In 1774, there were perhaps 44,000 slaves in Cuba, doubling by 1792. The pattern previously familiar in St-Domingue now developed in Cuba, with sugar, coffee and slavery growing side by side. Though the sugar industry grew steadily during the late eighteenth century, that growth was outstripped by the exceptional expansion after the Haitian collapse. In 1792 there were 529 sugar mills in Cuba, but by 1827 that had increased to 1,000, and to 1,531 by 1862. In the same period—a matter of only seventy years—the number of slaves in Cuba increased from 197,415 in 1792 to 323,759 in 1863. This increase was due entirely to the importation of Africans. Between 1801 and 1825, 229,000 had landed in Cuba, and a further 318,000 followed in the next twenty-five years. Although Cuban slavery was (like Brazilian slavery) diversified and was to be found throughout the economy, and had a major presence in Havana itself, by the 1860s one-half of Cuba's slaves worked on sugar plantations—most of them in the west of the island.[11]

The Cuban story reprised what had happened in other Caribbean islands two centuries earlier; where the sugar economy took hold, plantations evolved and were worked by African slaves. But this nineteenth-century Cuban sugar industry was different. It was highly mechanised and it thrived at the very time when other empires were turning their back on slavery. What happened in Cuba was a reminder that slavery could prosper even in an era when modern capitalism was transforming the economies of the Western world. There was no evidence, from Cuba, that slavery was outdated or uneconomic—even in the modernising, industrialising world of the mid-nineteenth century.

As we shall see in Chapter 4, the revolution of 1791–1804 swept aside slavery and the slave economy in St-Domingue, and ousted the French colonial government, but perversely that led to the arrival of waves of Africans in Spanish America. The years of revolution and the demise of French control 'set off a frenzy for the expansion of the slave trade and tropical staple production'.[12] In Puerto Rico, for example, three times the number of Africans were landed between 1775 and 1807 than in the previous two centuries. This pattern was true from the River Plate to Spanish Florida, from Venezuela to Peru. All restraints on slave imports had been abandoned and Africans were shipped in to make the most of the economic opportunities created by the collapse of France's great exporting colonies. The end result was that Spain's slave-based economy in the Americas was more dynamic *after* 1800 than at any period in its history.

Puerto Rico's experience of slavery was, like Cuba's, a relatively small-scale affair until the late eighteenth century. San Juan was a port city which was a fortified part of Spain's Caribbean defences, but it concentrated on exporting agricultural produce to Europe. That changed with the expansion of sugar and coffee cultivation, helped by refugee planters and their slaves from St-Domingue, or Haiti as it became known. But it was the major expansion of sugar in the 1820s and 1830s that prompted Puerto Rico's growing demand for Africans. Compared to Cuba, however, the figures were small. In the years 1826–50, while Cuba imported 318,000

Africans, Puerto Rico received only 12,000. Even so, wherever sugar flourished in Puerto Rico, there we find the heaviest concentration of slaves. The island's sugar industry also employed many more free people than on other islands, but it was on a much smaller scale than Cuba's. It could not modernise and mechanise to the same extent, and it became much less competitive. From the mid-nineteenth century both slavery and sugar declined in Puerto Rico.[13]

The result was that the slave populations of these two major Spanish islands were very different. In Puerto Rico, slavery peaked at 51,000 slaves in 1846, but, by then, Cuba was home to 324,000. Equally, slaves never formed more than a small proportion of Puerto Rico's overall population: 12 per cent at most in the nineteenth century. In Cuba, the story was very different. In the 1840s, slaves formed 43 per cent of the population. In the nineteenth century, Cuba had become what its French and British neighbours had been since the late seventeenth century: a genuine slave society. This is hardly surprising when we look at the imports of Africans into Cuba.

Cuba had followed the pattern evident from São Tomé to Brazil, Brazil to Barbados, Barbados to Jamaica and St-Domingue. It was shaped by the advance of sugar as a major (though not always the sole) driving force in the transformation of an island and colony, and all made possible by astonishing numbers of African slaves. Spain, the first colonial power to experiment with slavery in the Americas, was still clinging to slave-based economies three centuries later, though by then most other empires had thrown in the slaving towel. There were, however, two major exceptions to this story: Brazil and the USA.

African slaves had begun to arrive in North America soon after the early European settlements, though by then Europeans were already accustomed to African slaves on the African coast and in other parts of the Americas. Early Dutch settlers in North America soon used slaves. By the 1660s, some 20 per cent of the (admittedly small) population of New Amsterdam (New York) consisted of African slaves. For the next century Africans continued to be a small presence in Vermont, Massachusetts, New Jersey, New York, Connecticut and Rhode Island, but they performed important work (generally of the most strenuous kind) in a string of urban and rural activities. By the mid-eighteenth century, slaves worked in every conceivable job in the northern colonies, from domestic service to road building, from cattlemen to skilled artisanal work, normally working alongside free white workers. But that huge northern region did not have dominant export crops—say, sugar or tobacco—on which slavery thrived and flourished elsewhere. What happened in Virginia and Maryland was quite different.

The arrival of poor Britons in that region seemed more than adequate at first for the fledgling colonies' economic and labouring needs, but that flow dried up by the late seventeenth century and local landowners began to turn to African labour, shipped in, almost to their doorstep, by Atlantic slave ships nosing their way along the rivers of the Chesapeake. As tobacco came to dominate the local economy, slaves began to dominate the labouring population, both in the fields and as skilled workers. Given the predominance of small tobacco farms, most slaves lived and worked on small properties, and slave masters owned relatively small groups of slaves: This was quite unlike the sugar planters in the Caribbean and Brazil with their massive gangs counted in their hundreds. Tobacco slaves lived and worked close to their owners, and to other white people, with all the complex social and cultural consequences such daily—and often intimate—proximity created. On the sugar lands, slaves lived in what contemporaries often called 'African' villages, physically and culturally distant from white people. Slavery differed greatly between the two regions.

From the 1720s North America's slave population began to diverge from Brazil and the

Caribbean. It had begun to expand by natural increase, while elsewhere it grew only because of ever more African imports. North American slave owners thus became less dependent on the Atlantic slave ships, but at the same time they began to worry about the expansion of the slave population. They feared being overwhelmed and overawed by their subject people, though that concern receded after 1820, when the new cotton economy of the South provided slave holders in the old territories with a blessed (and profitable) relief. Now they could sell slaves to American slave traders who moved them onto the new cotton plantations of the South.

South Carolina's slave system was founded by settlers and their slaves moving from Barbados. They arrived equipped both with a slave code and with a mentality about slaves that was markedly different from the tobacco planters further north. The development of rice cultivation—harsh, debilitating and severe—was closer to labour in sugar than in tobacco, and local slaves retained striking African cultural features (including language), which were lost in the Chesapeake. Africans dominated the rice fields, not only as labourers but as experienced workers in the peculiarities of rice cultivation. Others were to be found in all sorts and conditions of jobs, especially in the thriving port city of Charleston (which was the landing point for 40 per cent of all Africans shipped to North America before American abolition in 1808). Slaves also proved vital for the defence of the colony throughout much of the eighteenth century, mainly against the dangers posed by Spaniards (in Florida) and by local Indians. But the *real* threat to the system was to come from the slaves themselves. The Stono rebellion in 1739 proved to be the most severe in colonial North America. In many respects it was in keeping with the persistent dangers posed by slaves in the Caribbean and Brazil.[14]

The emergence of the USA from its British colonial status was significantly helped by a new form of North American slavery. It substantially helped to drive forward the material wellbeing of the young republic. It also gave birth to a new slave trade, though not, this time, from Africa. A new inland and coastal trade evolved in the USA, which saw slaves from the old slave states of the eastern seaboard transported to the rich lands of the American South.

This was the story of 'King Cotton', a story not only of the transformation of the institution of American slavery but also of the rapid conversion of the USA itself into an emergent industrial powerhouse. Like sugar before it, slave-grown cotton was to have ramifications on a global scale. And yet, it involved an astonishing irony. According to David Brion Davis, the US Declaration of lndependence (1776) 'showed that the very idea of slavery is a fiction or fraud, since liberty and equality are fundamental rights that no one can legitimately lose'.[15] The words are clear enough:

> We hold these truths to be self-evident, that all men are created equal, that they are endowed by their Creator with certain unalienable rights, that among these are life, liberty, and the pursuit of happiness.

Despite this ringing declaration, eighty years later, on the eve of the Civil War, the USA had more than four million slaves. The republic, which had staked out its identity as a land of freedom and rights, was home to the largest slave population anywhere in the Americas. It grew and thrived on cotton.

The invention of the cotton gin by Eli Whitney made possible the spread of short-staple cotton across an enormous expanse of the US South after 1791. Over the next seventy years, the cotton South evolved into one of the key engines in the astonishing growth of the US economy. In the 1780s the US produced less than 1 per cent of the world's cotton but by 1810 that has soared to just over 53 per cent. On the eve of the Civil War in 1861 it had increased to 80 per cent.

Although slavery continued in the states of the Old South (tobacco in the Chesapeake, rice in South Carolina), both were characterised by small slave holdings; groups of ten to twenty slaves for tobacco farms, fifty to a hundred for rice. Cotton, on the other hand, employed armies of people—free and enslaved—and by the time the war started, more than half of all US slaves lived in the cotton South.

Slave numbers also began to increase in a new US sugar industry in Louisiana, itself acquired only in 1803 from France. That fledgling industry was helped at first by emigres from Haiti. Louisiana's sugar estates doubled in the 1820s, increasing even faster in the 1840s, and by mid-century there were some 1,536 sugar estates in the state. By the time of the Civil War, some 125,000 slaves worked on the state's sugar estates, though by then cotton was the unrivalled employer of North American slaves.[16]

Slave-grown cotton was the lifeblood of the expanding textile industries of New England and Britain. Some 80 per cent of Britain's cotton imports came from the USA, and by the Civil War the US was exporting more cotton than all the world's other cotton exporters combined. Despite cyclical downturns, the overall pattern was of ever-increasing cotton production and exports, helped by the US government making cheap land available to adventurous settlers willing to make the move westwards (in the company of their slaves). It was also a result of the wider expansion of the US economy, with its improved internal and oceanic transport, the emergence of a sound banking system and the development of new and efficient heavy industries.[17]

Cotton and slavery spread inexorably across the US South: Alabama, Louisiana, Mississippi, Arkansas and extending into Texas. By 1850 the US was producing 2.5 million bales of cotton a year (each bale weighed 181 kg). A decade later that output had doubled again. Behind this data lay a new transatlantic commercial axis. American cotton was shipped to Liverpool, thence to the myriad cotton mills of Lancashire. They, in turn, re-exported their finished textiles through Liverpool, to provide the wider world with cheap clothing. Lancashire textiles flooded first into the USA, then into Latin America, the Middle East and India. In the process, Liverpool had undergone its own transformation. By the late eighteenth century, it had been the major port of the North Atlantic slave trade, but by the mid-nineteenth century it had become the great entrepôt for slave-grown US cotton and finished Lancastrian textiles. Exports from Liverpool had, by the 1820s, even outstripped exports from London.[18]

The cotton plantations of the US South absorbed huge numbers of slaves via the internal slave trade. Almost one million people travelled along the slave routes leading to the cotton belt: twice as many slaves as had crossed the Atlantic to North America from Africa. Often sold from hand to hand, they passed from owners in the east to the cotton planters. Sometimes, they journeyed with their original owners. Others travelled by ship from Norfolk to New Orleans, for example, thence up the Mississippi to their new homes. Often, these journeys involved those heart-breaking scenes of family break-up and separation, leaving a deep scar on the family and folk memory of African-Americans throughout the USA.

The migrations of enslaved (and free) people recast the populations of the South, which had previously been thinly populated. In forty years between 1810 and 1850, the population of Louisiana, for example, increased from 77,000 to half a million, Alabama from 9,000 to 772,000. And the majority of those people were slaves. What had emerged—in a very short period— was a pattern long familiar in the Caribbean and Brazil: societies where the great majority of people were black.

The popular image that springs to mind when thinking about the US South is of large cotton plantations. In reality, most slaves were owned in small numbers. In 1860, almost a quarter of Southern slave owners each had between 50 and 200 slaves. The converse of this pattern was the widespread ownership of slaves. More than a third of a million Americans owned slaves at mid-century, though the majority of slaves in 1860 worked in cotton, and it was the cotton planter who dominated the social and political culture of the South. They were among the wealthiest of contemporary Americans, a fact readily confirmed by a visit to their surviving homes on plantations and their town houses in New Orleans to this day.

Visitors to the US South were struck (as they were in Brazil at much the same time) by the inescapable presence of slaves—in towns, on rural properties and in domestic life. They were found wherever hard physical work was needed; labouring on construction sites (towns blossomed across the South), building railways, manning each and every local industry, and working on the thousands of steamboats that churned up and down the Mississippi. Above all, they worked the cotton fields that stretched across the South.

It was here that American slaves endured a harsh working regime, often brutally enforced by overseers who were largely unrestrained and whose capricious violence and malice com-pounded the miseries of work in an unforgiving environment. It was a cruel and remorseless system, but it yielded astonishing wellbeing and profits to planters and their backers. Moreover, cotton snugly integrated itself into the wider economy of the USA. The northern states benefited greatly from slavery, their heavy industries feeding the expansion of cotton while their banks sustained and profited from cotton's success. The cotton industry was not an isolated, regional phenomenon: it was a vital element in the expansive US economy and cotton's spokesmen were heeded in Washington. Within a single lifetime, cotton had become a golden crop, with customers begging for more. In 1820 it provided 32 per cent of all US exports. Less well known, the US South was as dependent on steam power (in the form of the steamboats) as the cotton mills of Lancashire.

The British demand for cotton was voracious, growing at 5 per cent a year to 1850. By then, 3.5 million people in Britain were employed, one way or another, in cotton. A decade later, 4,000 people owned cotton mills in Britain. The workers involved—slaves in the fields in the US, cotton operatives in the mills of northern England—worked at labouring disciplines that were new to human history. A new form of work discipline became an essential element in the way the entire system functioned. Although factory discipline has long been discussed among historians of the industrialising West, less well known and studied is the work discipline that had been fundamental to slavery for centuries.

By the mid-nineteenth century it was clear that Lancashire in particular would be lost without American cotton—and therein lay a major risk. What would happen to cotton, and to Lancashire, if slavery in the US was abolished? Slave holders throughout the Americas had traditionally raised this threat whenever slavery had been challenged. Who would do the back-breaking labour (in sugar/coffee/rice/cotton) if slavery were abolished, and when all attempts to find alternative forms of labour had proved fruitless? Cotton needed slaves in the USA in the nineteenth century, just as sugar had needed them in Brazil and the Caribbean a century before, and as Cuba did at much the same time. In the event, there were other forms of labour ready to fill any vacuum vacated by slaves freed from the plantations. Nonetheless, whenever emancipation was discussed, the simple necessity of slavery had been a powerful card played by slave holders and their backers before the world's consumers of slave-grown produce.

Cotton in 1850, like sugar in 1750, was at the centre of a massive global empire, with millions of people, on both sides of the Atlantic, employed in its cultivation, refinement and manufacture, and with many millions more consuming the final outcome in all corners of the globe. And the entire system hinged on the slavery of Africans and their offspring born as slaves in the Americas.

• • •

The slave system that had evolved, so quickly, around cotton in the US South seemed a sharp break from the slave systems that had previously characterised North America from the seventeenth century: it was more pervasive, harsher, more powerful—and more rewarding to the nation at large—than any earlier forms of slavery. But it came at a terrible price.

It constituted a gross violation of millions of people. The forced migrations, sale and marshalling of millions of slaves were made possible by astonishing levels of violence. Slave narratives—slave voices—which provide a haunting descant to this story, return time and again to the personal and communal violence that accompanied slave life in the South. Yet had not this always been true of the story of African slavery from its earliest days? The history of slavery in the Americas is one of violence inflicted on millions of people: on the coast of Africa, on the Atlantic ships, and in slaves' workplaces across the Americas. Modern students, when confronted by this depressingly miserable history, often ask a simple and obvious question. Why did the slaves—normally in the majority—not rebel, overthrow their masters and secure their freedom? Why did so many people languish for so long in such miserable slavery? This same question lay at the heart of the slave holders' worst nightmares. Slave owners slept uneasily because they lived not merely on the fruits of slave labour, but also in the midst of slave defiance.

# 3

## Slave Defiance

BEGINNING IN 1791, a convulsion of violence swept away slavery and all it produced in the French colony of St-Domingue (see Chapter 4). Haiti emerged from the ruins. It was an exceptional event and nothing comparable happened in the entire history of slavery in the Americas. Yet both before and especially after 1791, slave owners everywhere could not escape the fear that they might be overwhelmed by their slaves. What happened in St-Domingue sent shockwaves throughout the Americas, and struck, tsunami-like, thousands of miles away, against the European foundations of the Atlantic slave system.

Despite having its origins and development in the particularities of French revolutionary politics, the Haitian slave revolt seemed to prove that slave owners had been right all along. From the first days of Atlantic slavery they had feared their slaves, had worried about slave unrest and, even in peaceable times, rarely felt at ease in the colonial exile of slave societies. Some slave owners deluded themselves that they enjoyed the trust of their slaves, but most recognised that, whatever benefits were derived from slavery, they were more than counterbalanced by an inescapable anxiety. The most hard-headed and realistic of slave owners accepted the dangers: theirs was a volatile and unpredictable world, which could turn troublesome or violent at a moment's notice—and without warning or signs of danger. This is not to claim that slaves were in a state of permanent rebellion, but rather that their owners could never fully trust them and lived in a pervasive climate of uncertainty.

This was not unique to the Americas. The problems of keeping slaves in their place, of maintaining some semblance of control and discipline over them, had been recurrent features of any number of ancient slave societies. Slaves ran away, plotted, struck their masters, sometimes killed them, and even, in extremes, schemed to rebel. There is, for instance, ample evidence from antiquity of Roman slave owners advertising for the return of runaway slaves, and regular accounts of slave violence against their masters. It ranged from simple, angry blows (normally after one indignity too many) through to murder. Most spectacular of all, of course, were slave revolts, perhaps the best remembered being the Spartacus slave revolt, and its spectacularly gory suppression, of 74 BC. We learn of plots or vague rumours about slaves planning to take revenge, though often such plots were merely false alarms, more a result of slave owners' febrile imaginations than of slave realities. Add all this together, and we begin to glean some sense of the persistent worries of people who owned slaves. However close their physical or social proximity, slaves lived beyond the understanding of their owners. The millions of slaves of the Americas loathed their bondage and lived out their lives trying to mitigate its worst features. They bore an enduring resentment against the people who held them in such miserable servitude.

Africans had known a different life, before enslavement, however impoverished or simple it may have been. Those born into slavery in the Americas also knew about a life other than slavery: they heard about it from Africans, and they saw it enjoyed by free people in the world around them, from the poorest of labourers to the grandest of landowners. Slaves saw how free people lived. It was perhaps free people working most closely to slaves who highlighted the slaves' bondage. However humble the lives of free people, and however mean their rewards, they were not treated like slaves. Their families and loved ones were not taken from them at the whim of a master—to disappear, for ever, when sold to another slave owner. The children of free people were also free, but children born to slave mothers were slaves. These were only the most obvious differences the enslaved could *see* between their own lives and the lives of others. Slaves lived in a world built around their uniquely inferior station: different at all levels from free people at large.

At its simplest, but most crucial, slaves were the material possessions of their masters. They were objects inherited and bequeathed, items of trade both in daily commerce and in legal status. They always had a price on their heads. That had been their status from the moment of African enslavement, or from their birth into American slavery, and it grated painfully against their obvious humanity. While others may have viewed them as objects, they regarded themselves differently. They were people anxious for a different life. Long before the Western world adopted the language of the rights of man and the vernacular of equality in the late eighteenth century, slaves yearned for something different. They wanted to be like others. Instead, they were forced to devise means of coping with the burdens of slavery imposed by their masters. Slaves needed a protective coating against life's indignities and injuries, and that protection took the form of slave defiance. At all points of Atlantic slavery, from Africa to the American frontier and even into Europe's heartlands, slaves offered defiance. It was a defiance that evolved into a complex slave culture of coping with, deflecting and challenging their bondage.

Long before the friends of African freedom began to agitate for black freedom, the enslaved themselves had created their own strategies of resistance. In time, their defiance was to prove the crucial final factor in bringing down slavery itself.

Slave owners everywhere recognised that slaves detested their bondage, and would do what they could to challenge, change or cope with it. They knew that their slaves would try to escape, plot, flare up in anger, drag their feet at work, deceive—and even rebel. And throughout the history of slavery in the Americas—from the African coast to the American plantations—slave owners tried to cover all those eventualities.

Violence lay at the heart of Atlantic slavery. Africans were enslaved through acts of violence, in warfare, slave raids and kidnapping. They were prisoners in Africa and as they were force-marched to the Atlantic coast, they were normally restrained, their every move scrutinised in case they attempted to escape. When herded into the barracoons on African beaches, in the gloom of a cell in an African slave fort, and finally below decks on board a slave ship, the Africans' initial experiences of slavery was as a prisoner to alien people. None were more alien than the white people they first encountered on the coast.

Some tried to escape as they were moved to the coast, from the canoes that took them out to the slave ships, or even overboard (if they dared) from the slave ship itself. Such escapes were always daunting and dangerous: daunting when the slaves were removed from their native region, and dangerous when confronted by armed jailors or sailors—not to mention the perils of the sea itself. However fierce the determination to flee, Africans faced enormous risks. Despite all this, many persisted.

Violence, from first to last, was the lubricant of slavery. Every slave had entered the Atlantic slaving system via a series of terrifying acts of brutality, and the reality and threat of violence continued to hang over them long after they stumbled ashore in the Americas. They were seized, incarcerated and transported via an overlapping sequence of violent experiences, and they faced capricious, individual acts of violence, from captors, merchants and sailors. This was their baptism into the world of slavery. The slave ships provided the manpower required for agricultural work in the Americas, but they also taught the harshest of lessons for the Africans. Not one of the eleven million African survivors of the Atlantic crossing could have been left in any doubt about the power of their oppressors. Nor could they doubt what happened to those who sought to dispute or challenge that power. *Every* African survivor entered the Americas— whether it be Brazil, the Caribbean or North

America—familiar with the violent power of the men who now controlled their lives. Life on a plantation might seem, at first glance, to have been an improvement on the torments of a slave ship. But the first lessons of enslavement, in Africa and at sea, had already taught the Africans what they faced: what they could and could not do—and what would happen to them if they tried and failed to challenge their masters. It was a brutal apprenticeship for what was to follow.

Although the slave ships functioned as tightly run prisons, they were regularly beset by slave uprisings. Perhaps one ship in ten had slave upheavals, especially on the African coast. When revolts failed, however, the punishments were exemplary and public. Executions and dismemberment of the victims took place so that others could see what happened to rebels. The Atlantic slave ships developed their own 'bloody code' to rival the most savage of European penal systems, all in addition to the terrifying daily experience of being on a crowded slave ship. Such reprisals were to be repeated across the slave colonies in the aftermath of slave revolt. Yet, time and again (and despite knowing what might happen to them), Africans on the slave ships resisted: attacked their tormentors, killed individual sailors, sought to take over the vessel—lashing out as best they could against the hellish world that took them (they knew not where) across the ocean for months on end. Most of this seaborne slave resistance was crushed—or ended in disaster—and only a handful of such revolts succeeded. At first sight, the millions of Africans landed in the New World may have looked like a defeated people: cowed, battered and forlorn. Yet their subsequent resistance was remarkable and their defiance, which had periodically flared on their recent travels, was to recover and come to characterise slave life across the Americas. But it was a defiance tempered by the awareness of what was possible.

Slavery varied enormously across the Americas, from one region and from one occupation to another. In addition, slaves did not live a static working life, but generally changed jobs as they passed from childhood, to maturity, to old age. The same person might experience a variety of different roles during their working life: from a child picking up stray cane, through to an old man guarding the animals, or an old woman looking after a gaggle of slave children. For all that, slaves everywhere at all ages and in all types of labour developed their own ways of coping with the indignities that came with their daily toil. Some jobs seemed easier—better—than others. Working in a master's household might seem an improvement on being a member of a field gang, but, even there, life had its tribulations:

the sexual approaches of the resident males, the inescapable vigilance of the mistress of the house. Slaves working in towns and cities were exposed to the random and unpredictable insults and assaults of others. These, and much more besides, were not merely the slings and arrows of plebeian misfortune: they were the particular fate of all slaves. To cope, they all needed to adapt; to learn how best to cope with life's blows and insults. Every slave had to develop his or her own defence and resilience. This did not mean being cowed (though some clearly were), nor did it involve necessarily turning the other cheek (though that too was sometimes needed). What was required was an attitude, a way of looking at the world, that enabled them to persevere in the teeth of endless oppression. They also had to be resolute in safeguarding their own interests, and of those of their loved ones. Sometimes this required an angry reaction, sometimes a sullen withdrawal or a dawdler's approach to work. Sometimes, however, this involved something altogether more serious and dangerous.

Slave owners lived out a pretence that they exercised complete control over their slaves and that their slaves were totally subservient to them. This was an article of faith among slave owners and was frequently discussed, from classical Greece to the peak years of African slavery in the Americas. It was, however, an impossible ideal, which was in permanent conflict with the slaves' own will and their refusal to submit totally to their owners' powers. The simplest, but risky, solution for many slaves was to escape; to run away—to become a fugitive and seek freedom, or at least an escape from the tyranny of slavery. Slaves had escaped in Africa en route to the coast. They escaped from the slave ship (though that normally involved a suicidal dive overboard). And they ran away from their owners in all the American slave societies of which we know. Desperate slaves escaped from a brutal owner or master, sometimes returning after a few days. Often they headed to a loved one held on a distant property. Newspapers were dotted with advertisements for fugitive slaves, and often made clear that the owner had a good idea where the fugitive was heading: to a wife, husband, lover, parent.[1] For that, the runaway often needed help along the way; sanctuary on a distant property, food and drink from other slaves secretly helping them on their night-time travels. Striking out on their own posed enormous practical difficulties: of simple concealment, of nourishment, of knowing the directions and finding places of safety and security—especially when hunted by angry or vengeful owners or their agents, by slave catchers with dogs.

The Underground Railroad along which slaves from the US South were furtively moved to northern freedom became a highly complex, organised network that employed large numbers of helpers and sympathisers. But, as we shall see, even that could be disrupted, and the fugitive returned to southern bondage. Much more common, for slaves everywhere, were the personal, ad hoc and informal routes that enabled individuals to move away, on foot and by water, from their owners towards somewhere else— or someone else. They might hide in the bush, in inaccessible reaches of forests or mountains, in swamp lands and remote terrain, far from the reach of their owners and their agents. They might also try to pass themselves off as free people, claiming a false identity, background and skills. Fugitive advertisements carefully spelled out the runaways' personal details; the slaves' physique and features, their clothing, voice, human imperfections and their likely alibis. Runaways and their owners played out a game of bluff and counter-bluff, the one seeking freedom by flight, concealment and deception, the other simply trying to get their hands on their human property.

Brazilian slaves ran away in huge numbers. Police records and newspaper reports tell a similar tale of young Africans particularly prone to escape—not surprising perhaps. They were young and energetic, had known a different life, and had not yet been ground down by the slave system. Brazilian runaways fled for a variety of reasons; from fear and anger, in search of distant loved ones, even in search of work elsewhere, especially in the burgeoning cities. Some fled to join the military (in Brazil's frequent conflicts in the nineteenth century). Those living close to Brazil's borders fled for the security of freedom elsewhere (French Guiana, Uruguay or Argentina, for example) much as US slaves from the South, especially the border states, escaped to the free states of the North or to Canada.

Slaves escaped when they faced the threat of being sold—the ultimate risk and fear of slaves everywhere. Being wrenched from family, community, friends and loved ones, to be dispatched (often great distances), was to vanish. It had happened to Africans already; now, in the Americas, it was repeated whenever new economies sprang up and slave labour was required in distant locations. It happened in Brazil when slaves were moved huge distances from old industries to new ones, and it happened on a spectacular scale in the USA with the development of cotton in the South. Between 1790 and 1860, one US slave family in five was wrecked by enforced separation and sale. One child in three was forcibly parted from parents.[2] The shattering of slave families on such a scale was as brutal an emotional rupture as the original enslavement in Africa. Moreover, its threat continued to hang over every single slave in the Americas. Because they were property—material assets in an owner's portfolio—they went the way of any other item when the owner died, remarried, moved away, bequeathed or sold their assets. Slave owners passed on slaves to children, who might then move elsewhere with them. They bought and sold their land and businesses, trading the slaves just like another item on their list of possessions. Wise planters tried not to uproot slave families, sometimes even heeding a slave's request not to separate a spouse; some even brought them together by purchase. Slave owners knew that resentful and unhappy slaves were not good workers, and tried, if they could, not to disturb the local system. Often, however, they rode roughshod over such feelings: they were influenced not by sentiment, but by the numbers in their ledgers and business correspondence, and would shuffle their human assets to their best economic advantage. What made economic sense to a slave holder normally brought grief and anguish to their slaves. Many fled rather than face the consequences.

It is, then, little surprise that slaves escaped. Some fled by sea, some simply vanished into the anonymity of towns and cities, while others headed for the bush. They fled from remote plantations and from the homes of city-dwelling slave holders. Sometimes, they were encouraged to flee by others around them. They also beat a path to the isolation of distant, inaccessible communities that sprang up in a number of slave colonies. 'Maroon' societies became a feature of slavery in South America and the Caribbean—though less so in the USA. Much depended on geography, of course. On the small, flat islands of the eastern Caribbean, hideouts were virtually impossible, but the bigger, mountainous islands—Jamaica, Cuba and Puerto Rico—offered plenty of scope for slave runaways. Fugitive slaves developed communities of freed people, keen to preserve their independence, and able to use geography and guerrilla tactics to hold off armed efforts by planters and the military to bring them to heel. The British conducted the unsuccessful First Maroon War in Jamaica before finally agreeing a treaty (1739) that confirmed Maroon independence. The French faced similar difficulties in the rugged mountains of St-Domingue. The best-known Maroon community, Manicl, was—like the Jamaican version before it—finally recognised in 1785 when the French accepted the impossibility of bringing it to heel. When the British finally defeated the Maroons of Trelawny Town in the Second Maroon War in Jamaica, 1795, the duplicitous British governor broke his promise to the Maroons and had them deported to Nova Scotia. A comparable group (of 'Black Caribs') in St Vincent was also defeated, finally, in 1797: they too were shipped out, to Honduras.[3]

The immensity of Brazil offered great opportunities for runaway slaves to find freedom and possibly safety in numbers. Fugitive communities emerged in forested, swampy and mountainous regions, and even close to cities. Some even managed to trade independently in neighbouring cities, protected by local slaves and sustained by simple economic necessity: people wanted the goods they offered, brought from the distant interior. Communities of escaped slaves— *quilombos*—thrived on Brazil's political and military instability in the nineteenth century, and on slave owners' inability to maintain a firm grip over their slaves in times of confusion and disorder. Fugitives were also joined by criminals, by military deserters and by men keen to avoid being recruited for the wars. Sometimes *quilombos* themselves became aggressive and rebellious in light of specific injustices and outrages. Their intent was not the destruction of slavery, but making it more tolerable for its victims.[4]

Most slaves, however, did not run away (though in some places, considerable numbers did). Most of them simply remained where they were, coping, as best they could, with whatever difficulties and dangers life threw at them.

Though this might suggest a bland passivity, the reality was quite different. Slaves everywhere learned how to cope with life's daily torments via routines of veiled and even open defiance. At times, even their passivity had more to it than meets the eye. They were, after all, unwilling and stubborn recruits to the tasks they were given. Some, notably domestic slaves and others working close to their owners, chose to please them by a faux good nature and an apparent willingness to obey promptly. Such endeavours often flattered to deceive. Slaves knew that they might be rewarded, might win a master's approval and obtain benefits for themselves and loved ones. There was method and self-interest in their application and courtesy. Extra food, better clothing, the occasional treat, free time—preferential treatment for children and relatives—all and more might be secured from a master or mistress in return for good work and service. (It was no accident that, for all its particular risks, domestic work was a prized position among the slaves; better to work in the kitchen than in the fields.)

Slaves also took revenge for their various grievances. If a driver or master struck a slave, or assaulted him or her excessively, they ran the risk of physical retaliation: an angry blow or attack, even an assault with a weapon. Slaves, however, were all too conscious of where that might lead. Slave owners, and the legal apparatus that supported them, fell back on vicious reprisals and execution, often with body parts left rotting in the open where other slaves could see them. All this was a reprise of what had happened on the slave ships. We also know of slaves who retreated from life's miseries into a dark personal place. Africans fresh from the slave ships often seemed apathetic and even viewed their own mortality with indifference.[5] Some killed themselves. More common though was shuffling into some form of accommodation. Doing *just* enough to gain the boss's approval, while rarely taxing themselves to the limit. In any case, revenge beckoned in other directions. Damaging property and the owner's possessions (animals were a favourite target) or going through the motions of routine work without achieving very much. In the fields, however, this too was risky. Slave cultivation was a highly regulated and scrutinised business, and slave owners and their managers knew how much yield to expect from a gang; how much area of a field should be cleared in a given time, how much produce to be cut and bundled, plucked or picked. Back-sliding that threatened to fall below the expected pace could provoke a whipping. As in all things, slaves needed to learn the balance: between working at their own pace and not provoking anger from their superiors.

Much the same was true of face-to-face

dealings with white people. Slaves were hectored and yelled at, haughtily and often angrily ordered to do this and that. But they were expected to remain mute. Of course, there was often the problem of language. Africans from a variety of societies and language groups worked side by side with local-born slaves who spoke their own patois, part European, part African and part local hybrid—and not all would be understood by their masters. More significantly perhaps, how did the slaves understand the language of the men and women ordering them to do this or that? Not understanding an alien tongue, not grasping what was demanded, was often a simple fact of life. But so too was playing dumb. It was not always in a slave's interests to know exactly what was required of them: better to act ignorant or stupid, proceed at one's own pace and direction. Until, that is, the next blow fell or the next order was bellowed in their direction. Acting stupid was built into slave routines. Equally, part of the slave owner's creed was the belief that slaves were stupid, an idea that fed into the emergent racist view of Africans, which was itself a powerful buttress to the entire system. In any case, what benefit was it to the slave to be prompt and obedient, to work hard and be productive? What mattered, to them, was getting through the working day with the minimum of effort and without further trouble or harm. Being industrious and attentive were not qualities slaves sought to perfect—except when it was to their benefit or if it prevented trouble.

The threat of violence, as we have seen, was the lubricant of the entire slave system and became an inescapable feature of the slaves' working lives. Field slaves were marshalled at work by intimidating threats. The whip was everywhere. It was the slave drivers' distinguishing tool; brandished as he walked or rode among the labourers and used to searing effect when needed—or whenever he felt like it. Counting the frequency of whippings might seem, at one level, both prurient and obscene. Yet here was the slave system at work; a labouring environment that periodically echoed to the crack of a whip. It was no accident that slave owners recorded and tabulated punishments, listing how many blows—'stripes' to use the biblical phrase— were doled out to the slaves. They were lashed for any number of failings: for personal insults, for failing to keep up, for errors, back-sliding, or merely when the boss was angry and out of sorts. (In the sugar field, the driver using the whip was normally himself a slave.) Some men were infamous for their use of the whip, others used it sparingly. But few men working with slaves in the fields felt that they could manage the slaves without a whip.

On many sugar plantations, the onerous field-work was made worse by the nature of the physical environment and by the planters' failure to use animals for ploughing. All the heaviest work of digging, fertilising and planting was done by slave gangs, kept at work by drivers equipped with whips. The entire process was a highly regulated affair and it was the drivers' job to ensure that the field hands kept to the planters' timetable—encouraged by the whip. Sugar plantations evolved a code of conduct and punishment: who administered what kind of punishment—and to whom. Field slaves tended to be lashed on the spot for being tardy or unproductive. Punishments for more serious shortcomings (theft, for example) were ordered by senior plantation managers and were administered publicly. All this, of course, was in addition to unauthorised outbursts of personal antipathy and bad temper. Suspicious drivers, managers or owners often took out their suspicions on slaves: someone caught with sugar cane might easily be accused of theft—and lashed on the spot.[6]

In all the major slave industries—tobacco, sugar, cotton, coffee—slaves felt the lash on their back. The list of offences seems endless: accidents caused by inattention, disobedience, running away, going slow—indeed anything that seemed subversive or threatening—all could provoke some form of corporal punishment. Outsiders often recoiled when they saw and heard the violence and unpredictability of such punishments, especially when inflicted on female slaves. Yet such violence was an ingrained feature of slave societies everywhere. It was *so* ingrained that those who administered it tended not even to notice it: it was simply part and parcel of the way slaves were managed and controlled. More literate and reflective planters (the men who kept journals, who wrote long letters and accounts of their daily working lives) recorded the violence done to their slaves almost in passing. Just as they recorded the amount of sunshine or rainfall, they jotted down the number of lashes in a journal: mere facts of daily life in a slave society. Events that shock and startle the modern reader appear in the evidence as trivial and inconsequential incidents. A young pregnant woman—tired and resting in her cabin—dragged back to work shackled to a slave owner's horse; a gang of slaves 'whip'd day by day'; a diary note that a slave might be executed 'to terrify the rest'— these and more were the commonplace jottings of successful slave owners.[7] Such remarks about extreme acts of violence reflect a deeply ingrained and unquestioned acceptance of cruelty in the day-to-day handling of enslaved people. More startling still to modern eyes, such slave owners were often well-educated, sophisticated and God-fearing men who saw nothing wrong, unethical or unchristian in dispensing savage (and what we might today think of as unchristian) treatment to their enslaved labourers.

By the late eighteenth century, however, there was evidence that such punishments were frowned upon by increasing numbers of people. In the USA, the regular whipping of slaves was increasingly out of kilter with the morality of American society at large. Cruelty, formal or informal, was under attack on a wide front. An emergent feeling against cruelty (towards wives, children, criminals, animals) was evident in a number of Western societies. It was, for example, a major factor behind penal reform. Slavery itself came to be viewed as institutional cruelty and was denounced as such. Yet not only did US slavery thrive throughout the first half of the nineteenth century, but it continued to be lubricated by acts of cruelty that were themselves increasingly at odds with what was happening in the free states. Whipping had been a common form of legal and private punishment throughout North America until the early nineteenth century, but thereafter it found itself increasingly restricted to the slave states. What had once been unremarkable and acceptable was now unusual—except in slave societies. Now, it existed under the hostile gaze of outsiders. Visitors to the US slave South, to Brazil and to the Caribbean slave islands in the early nineteenth century were invariably offended and shocked by the sight and the sound of the lash on the slaves' backs. Yet the people who owned the slaves, and those who managed them at work, still regarded the whip—amply illustrated in any number of contemporary paintings and sketches of slave life—as an essential aspect of labour discipline. It was the natural penalty for wrongdoing and laziness, for disobedience and defiance, and was thought essential for extracting the necessary effort at work. The whip remained indispensable to the way slavery functioned.

The whip is the best-remembered act of violence done to the slaves. It had followed them on their long journey from Africa to the American plantations. It accompanied them on their daily tasks. Even when out of sight, it was rarely out of mind. It was the symbol of their servitude and suffering, and represented the mundane power of the people who claimed dominion over them. When it failed, when slave resistance threatened to disrupt the natural order, colonial militias, or informal armed gangs of neighbouring slave holders and friends, would impose their own violent control. If that failed, colonial and state authorities called upon the official military—all followed by a legal process that offered redress to no one but the slave holders.

The penal codes of slave societies were savage in the extreme and remained so long after Western legal systems began their slow, hesitant progress to reform. Brutal retribution for slave violence or slave plotting took the form of heads and body parts displayed in places where other slaves could see them. Rebellious slaves who were not cut down by bands of armed slave holders, by the militia or by the military, faced an even worse fate after conviction: hanged, beheaded, gibbetted. And slaves' testimony in court was not allowed in their own defence.

These were, of course, the extremes of slavery and they did not come close to the experience of most slaves. But *all* slaves were in no doubt about the nature of the power their owners held over them. This goes some way to explaining why slaves sought to channel their defiance in ways that might not bring the wrath of the system down on them. Though slave rebellions were part of the history of slavery, they were the exception rather than the rule. But once again, this, in turn, leaves an unanswered question in the minds of many modern students: why did slaves *not* overthrow their masters? This also perplexed contemporaries. It was a question that audiences asked the American abolitionist Frederick Douglass in the mid-nineteenth century whenever he lectured on the violent evil of slavery. After all, slaves formed a majority in most slave regions, sometimes a massive majority. In agricultural work they had access to a collection of tools and equipment that could readily be used as weapons against their oppressors. The question naturally arises: if the oppression of slaves was as bad, as cruel and as brutal as we claim, why did they not revolt? It is even possible to turn this issue on its head: the absence of revolt might suggest that slaves were more settled and content than historians generally claim. After all, large-scale slave upheavals against their owners in the Americas were unusual. Slave owners provide an answer: they could never relax or drop their guard. They knew that the threat of slave trouble was never far away. It was an ever-present concern and prospect. Why else did Dr Johnson raise a toast, in 1777, 'to the next insurrection of the negroes in the West Indies'?[8] Like everyone else, Johnson was aware that slave revolts had peppered that region—and knew that planters lived in fear of further eruptions.

Fear of slave rebellion had been acute on the slave ships. We have evidence for some 500 shipboard rebellions. In 1704, the Africans on board the English ship *Postillion*, anchored in the Gambia River, rose up, attacking the crew with staves: they were crushed when the crew fired into the crowd, following up with a cutlass attack. Thirty-three Africans died in the fighting or by drowning. Eighty died in a rebellion on the *Duke of Cambridge*, ten years later. Sometimes the losses were catastrophic—on both sides. In

1730, the Boston ship *William* was overwhelmed with the loss of the entire crew: 'murther'd by the Negro's they had brought on Board'.[9] Some of the rebellions on land in the Americas had very limited aims, but others were more sweeping and ambitious. Slave owners, however, feared the worst: they feared the risk of escalation and contagion. A small rebellious band driven to violent despair on one property might easily provide a spark, attract supporters elsewhere and coalesce into a large body of armed slaves posing a widespread danger. Hence they felt the need to nip slave revolt in the bud in the most savage and draconian fashion.

The massive slave upheavals we find in Brazil and the Caribbean were not repeated in North America, but revolts (and, more common, widespread fear of slave revolts) dotted North American slave history. Slave owners could not shake off the fear that unrest might get out of control. There was Bacon's rebellion of 1676 in Virginia (when slaves joined forces with indentured white workers), the Stono rebellion in South Carolina in 1739 (with Angolan slaves trying to reach the freedom of Spanish Florida), later the Gabriel rebellion in Virginia in 1800, a rising of some 200 slaves in Louisiana in 1811, and Denmark Vesey's revolt (1822) in Charleston. Most famous of all perhaps was Nat Turner's rebellion (in which about eighty rebels were involved and sixty whites killed) in Virginia in 1831. All these revolts led to ferocious retribution on the spot and, after subsequent one-sided trials, this was followed by a tightening of local slave laws. Turner's rebellion was to prove the last major slave revolt in US history, despite the fact that, at the time, slavery was expanding rapidly throughout the cotton belt.

However we look at North American slave revolts (the numbers of slaves involved, the levels of violence and the scale and intensity of retribution), they are markedly different from events in the Caribbean. In Antigua, the conspiracy of 1735–6, Tacky's revolt in Jamaica in 1760, Fédon's revolt in Grenada in 1795: all involved large numbers of slaves, and desperate and sometimes protracted fighting by colonial forces to suppress the upheavals. All were defeated and all were followed by bloody reprisals—in the field or after legal hearings (where accused slaves stood no realistic chance of receiving a fair hearing). Time and again, dozens of slaves were executed, often after protracted torture (being broken on the wheel, for example). And, again, severed heads and body parts were liberally distributed for other enslaved people to witness. The lucky slaves caught up in failed revolts were those transported to remote colonies and regions. The conclusion seemed clear: revolt could lead only to prolonged suffering and death.

Planters and colonial officials seemed to relish the barbaric rituals played out in the aftermath of a slave revolt, but, in fact, their reprisals were a reflection of their deep-seated fears about the slaves. They also suggest a paucity of ideas about how to cope with slave unrest.

Slaves' violent reactions were, then, the extreme element of slave defiance—and that defiance was an integral aspect of slave life in the Americas. Conceived in the violence done to millions of Africans during their enslavement and transportation, it was nurtured and shaped in the hardships of daily life across the Americas. The determination to cope with the injustices of bondage spawned a multitude of slave responses, from the simplest of personal insolence and truculence through to the extremes of collective violence. But it had to be tempered by the stark understanding of what happened to the slave who crossed the line; who reared up in anger—and failed.

This entire story—of slave defiance and the slave owners' fear of slave defiance—changed utterly in the last years of the eighteenth century. The French Revolution in 1789 and the upheavals in St-Domingue after 1791 transformed the enslaved Americas. Events in Haiti were the realisation of the slave owners' worst nightmares, and they haunted the subsequent history of slavery across the hemisphere. But

Haiti meant something quite different for those who continued to endure a life of bondage. Haiti and its revolutionary leaders, its myths and realities, became a potent and encouraging image for slaves everywhere. Their masters viewed it with dread; it was the inevitable outcome of not dealing firmly with slave defiance.

# 4

# The Slave Owners' Nightmare: Haiti

THE SIMMERING PROBLEM of slave defiance was utterly transformed by the French Revolution. In 1789 St-Domingue was the most valuable of all the slave colonies in the Caribbean. The colony's luxuriant plains and coastal stretches were ideal for sugar, while the fruitfulness of its higher altitude was perfect for coffee. Plantations had quickly transformed this tropical lushness into profitable tropical commodities. In little less than a century since its acquisition by France in 1697, the western part of Santo Domingo (the rest was Spanish) had outstripped France's other major slave islands of Guadeloupe and Martinique and even Britain's Caribbean jewel, Jamaica. Half of the world's sugar and coffee, along with an abundance of cotton and indigo, flowed from St-Domingue. On the eve of the Revolution, St-Domingue yielded more than the combined exports of Brazil and Mexico, and twice as much as the entire British Caribbean. France derived huge economic benefit from the colony, and it created employment for hundreds of thousands of French people.[1]

The entire system depended, of course, on African slave labour. By 1789 about 600,000 were at work in the colony: over the previous century some 800,000 Africans were landed there. In recent years, Africans had been arriving in huge numbers: almost a quarter of a million in the six years between 1784 and 1790. Sometimes 30,000 or 40,000 Africans disembarked in a single year. Large numbers of them were young men—and many had been prisoners of war in Africa, i.e. they had military experience. Slaves now greatly outnumbered the French troops based in the colony, and it was the European military, their offshore navies and their colonial garrisons, that formed the ultimate guarantee of security against dangers posed by the enslaved.[2]

What lay behind these remarkable figures was not simply the massive expansion of the economy, but the failure of the colony's slaves to reproduce. The traumas of enslavement and months on the slave ships clearly damaged the fertility of many African women. On coffee plantations, men greatly outnumbered women. In sugar, the excessive work and unhealthy locations had a similar lowering impact on fertility, and contemporaries regularly pointed to the extreme work regime, problems of diet and general social welfare. What made these conditions worse was the slaves' exposure to arbitrary and capricious violence and maltreatment. For all they knew, life's indignities were endless. Until, that is, events in Paris changed everything—for black and white.

The colony's slaves lived and worked alongside a white population of 30,000, and a similar number of people of mixed race (*gens de couleur*). This huge numerical imbalance was much sharper than we find in other slave societies in the Americas, and it revealed the vulnerability of the whites and the *gens de couleur.* Both these groups yearned for political and social stability, but they developed an oppressive culture, which left the slaves in no doubt what would happen to those who threatened the system—on the plantations, in the towns or in face-to-face encounters.

The colony's 7,000 or so plantations accounted for 40 per cent of France's foreign trade and, as French investment flowed in, the colony's ports—and especially Cap-Français (Le Cap, now Cap-Haitien)—became hives of expansive trade and social life. Le Cap was the centre of an astonishingly rich social and cultural life. The bigger planters and merchants were not to be outdone by other *arrivistes* in the Americas (nor even by their contemporaries in the homeland) and tried to create a life in exile that reflected, at a distance, the culture of eighteenth-century France. There were the latest Parisian fashions, theatres, newspapers and even a learned society.

The colony's capital, Port-au-Prince, may have been thought of by visitors as a rough, ill-built frontier town, especially when compared to Le Cap, but it still had bookshops, social clubs, a bath house and a theatre for 750 people. The colony's *grand blancs*, not unlike wealthy planters in Britain, held themselves in high social and cultural esteem, and also knew that France relied on the prosperity disgorged by the efforts of their slaves. They viewed themselves as 'fully fledged participants in Enlightenment culture'.[3]

For all that (and like most colonial slave owners), the elite did not regard St-Domingue as home. They lived an exiled tropical existence, which, if they survived, might yield a prosperous return to France. In the meantime, and despite the sophisticated society centred on Le Cap, planters spent most of their time in tedious isolation on remote rural properties. And it was there, deep in the country, that they relied on the company of female slaves, on the generally raw masculine companionship of plantation neighbours—and on the bottle. There too—at the very centre of the colony's wealth—the colony's whites found themselves greatly outnumbered and surrounded by Africans.

By 1789, one-third of St-Domingue's slave population had been born in the colony, had grown up speaking local creole, had developed family ties, and tended to occupy the skilled or domestic jobs. The field hands—the brute labour in sugar and coffee—were mainly Africans, from a variety of backgrounds: a plantation of 200 slaves might have people speaking a dozen different languages. Life was harshest in sugar, with its regime of arduous work by day in the fields and by night in the sugar works, and it was here that stories of regular brutality and violence were commonplace (and not solely in St-Domingue, of course). The men in charge—planters, managers, overseers—felt that only the most draconian control could keep the slaves at work and hold in check the violence that seemed to simmer just below the surface. Many properties, however, were in the hands of managers working for absentee planters, and it was in the managers' interests to maximise production, no matter how harsh the working regime. Conditions seem to have been most oppressive on the sugar plantations in the Northern Plain, and it was there, in 1791, that the slaves revolted. On the coffee plantations—housing an average of forty to fifty slaves—life was different: the work less onerous than in sugar and the management less aggressive.

One-third of St-Domingue's slaves were owned by the 30,000 *gens de couleur*, who ranged from freed African slaves to landowners. What made this group unusual was that many of them were prosperous planters, and some had been educated in France. They also held positions of authority (in the police or militia, for example). In a colony dominated by African slavery, the *gens de couleur* led an ambiguous life. Many had both slave and free white relatives and were often torn between an awareness of family links to the slave quarters and their status as people of property with a stake in the enslaved system. For all that, and despite their prosperity, the free coloured residents were discriminated against, notably by the law. Whatever their wealth, they could all recite a list of grievances about the way they were treated.[4] Not surprisingly then, there was a volatility at the very heart of life in St-Domingue, and even those who has escaped the formal bonds of slavery as *gens de couleur* harboured deep-seated grievances against their social and racial superiors. But *the* most persistent and inescapable threat to the colony came, of course, from the very people who made everything possible: the enslaved Africans.

Few slave owners worried more about slaves than whites living on remote sugar plantations where they faced hundreds of recalcitrant Africans kept at their arduous work by threats and by the lash. On the eve of the French Revolution, it was widely accepted in St-Domingue that 'the good master was regarded as an eccentric who could not interfere outside his own estate'. There is a chorus of agreement from contemporary writers, visitors and modern scholarship that severity was the daily lot of the enslaved. A harsh labouring culture was blended with brutal management and all spiced by random acts of capricious sadism. In the words of Justin Girod-Chantrans, a French scientist who served in the military in St-Domingue, 'After a certain time in the new world, the European becomes a different man.'[5]

For all that, the French slave system worked— for the time being. It yielded handsome returns, provided a substantial part of France's overseas trade and profits, employed huge numbers of Frenchmen, and enhanced the material wellbeing of a number of French port cities (Bordeaux and Nantes most notably). It also provided, along with Guadeloupe and Martinique, an important military base in the Americas. This French slave economy had by the 1780s outstripped British colonial production of sugar, coffee and indigo. Whatever the concerns of whites and *gens de couleur* about the delicacy of their position in St-Domingue, it was hard to deny that the colony was a source of great material wellbeing. Except, of course, for the slaves.

What made the slaves' lot all the more onerous was the nature of colonial administration in the colony. Anxious above all to maintain peace and tranquillity, French colonial officials inevitably sided with the slave owners, especially with the planters. This involved supporting racial ideas that targeted both slaves and people of mixed race, even those who were prosperous slave owners themselves, while the *gens de couleur* were keen to be distinguished from the ranks of black slaves toiling beneath them.

Colonial officials sided with the planters' repressive ways of running the system. Official reports to Paris regularly confirmed the widespread use of atrocities against slaves. There were, it is true, efforts at amelioration in the 1780s, and many planters came to accept that better treatment, rather than unrelenting brutality, made economic and social sense. But French legislation designed to help went largely unnoticed. Like other slave colonies, St-Domingue had experienced periodic alarms about slave defiance, though curiously—and unlike neighbouring Jamaica—it had few slave rebellions before 1791. Much more common was *marronage*: the escape of slaves from plantations into the wilderness or, where possible, over the porous mountainous border into Spanish Santo Domingo. There had been a mid-century panic about slaves poisoning their masters, and by the 1780s there were nervous complaints about the dangers of knots of slaves in towns refusing to make way for white people, while others retorted with insolence (and even blows) to commands barked at them by passing white people. Slave holders displayed a thin-skinned edginess whenever they faced slave defiance or whenever things went wrong. Sudden death and illness (both of them plentiful in the tropical climate), slaves assembling off the plantations or slaves meeting without slave owners' knowledge or consent—all and more worried slave owners.

Nothing concerned them more than clandestine slave gatherings for religious ceremonies. They called it voodoo, a name that has stuck in popular memory, with images of ceremonies and beliefs that were utterly unlike any form of Christianity. Slave owners were reluctant even to consider the slaves' beliefs and practices as religion: they were, at best, superstitious practices rooted in an African past. What we now call Haitian Vodou was a blend of African customs and others developed in the colony, and all mixed with traces of Christianity. In the years before 1791, Vodou played an important role in bringing together Africans of very different backgrounds and providing an opportunity for the emergence of slave leaders. It seems also to have reflected the growing Congolese influence in the slave population at large.[6]

Slaves had, of course, tried to flex their collective muscles long before 1791, sometimes withdrawing their labour in protest or as part of a bargaining for improvement, especially on the

Northern Plain. French colonial reforms of 1784 and 1786 allowed slaves to register complaints with government officials about abuses by their owners, but these measures were predictably denounced by slave owners as the cause and occasion of most of their subsequent troubles. Slaves in St-Domingue, like slaves everywhere, ran away from the plantations, mostly on their own, escaping from the harshness of life or, as likely, seeking a loved one held on a distant property. The colony's slaves also struggled against their bondage in less obvious, more humdrum (and sometimes unrecognised) ways. As mentioned, they went slow at work, they feigned ignorance and stupidity, they undermined the very work they undertook, they damaged property and animals. They also displayed a sullenness that slave owners everywhere complained about. It was, however, a dangerous game. All this (in effect, the story of slavery itself) was only as common in St-Domingue as it was in Jamaica or Barbados, but everything changed in 1789 and the revolutionary years that followed.

In the light of what followed, it is ironic that criticisms of slavery and the slave trade were more advanced and more widespread in Britain than in France before 1789. Though slavery had long been a target of French Enlightenment philosophers, their criticisms had little or no popular support. Voltaire, who mocked slave owners in *Candide* (1759), was only one of a number of French intellectuals who pointed to the ethical and economic irrationalities of the slave system. Yet even the *Société des Amis des Noirs*, founded in February 1788, remained an exclusive gathering of influential and propertied politicians and intellectuals. By then, in Britain, by contrast, abolition had developed a nationwide popular base. Yet it was French slavery that was to be undermined in the next year, suddenly and unexpectedly. The French Revolution was to destroy the *Ancien Régime*, of which colonial slavery was an integral feature.

The political turmoil in France after 1789 had profound consequences for the distant colonies. Serfdom in France itself was abolished in August 1789, but, more disruptive still, the National Assembly passed the Declaration of the Rights of Man that same month. Though passed 'without any thought for the colonies',[7] it was to resonate louder in the enslaved Caribbean than anywhere else. Deputies from St-Domingue were alarmed to see the Revolution begin to undermine the very basis of colonial slavery.

Although whites in the colony had long resented the role of royal government in the colony's affairs, the language of liberty had a natural appeal to colonial whites (as had the impact of the American breakaway from Britain in 1783). Now, however, they found themselves in a dilemma. Supporting the rights of man in a slave society created unpredictable and volatile difficulties. The *gens de couleur*, on the other hand, realised the significance of revolutionary ideals for their own claims to equal political representation. They formed their own political club in Paris, and petitioned for equality with whites. What most alarmed colonial whites, however, were the outbursts against slavery— as well as against racial discrimination—in the political turmoil after 1789. Some even considered independence from France. The whites' trump card was the value of the enslaved system to the French economy. Any change that jeopardised that arrangement could be rebuffed. When news arrived of a slave revolt in Martinique, the French National Assembly turned its back on demands from the free *gens de couleur*: their protests in St-Domingue itself were met with violence and intimidation. In this swirl of political and racial discussion, the *gens de couleur* 'had difficulty separating their cause from that of the enslaved'.[8]

Prominent among the free coloured representatives in Paris was Vincent Ogé, a wealthy merchant, who had openly advocated liberty and equality in Paris. Should liberty 'be given to all men?' he asked. 'I believe so.' But he also made a chilling prediction: 'If we sleep for an instant on the edge of the Abyss . . . Blood will flow, our property will be invaded, the fruits of our labor destroyed, and our homes burned.'

Frustrated by events in Paris, Ogé returned to St-Domingue in October 1790, determined to force matters in the colony. He gathered a rebellious band of 300 in the north in the hope of imposing the liberty and equality he had failed to secure in Paris. But Ogé had also predicted his own fate: 'If I risk my personal interest, my life itself is a sacrifice.'[9]

And so it proved to be. His rebellious band were defeated and fled to Santo Domingo, but were handed back by duplicitous Spanish authorities. Nineteen were hanged, and Ogé and another leader were executed by being broken on the wheel in Le Cap. When news of the revolt reached Paris, and under pressure from the *Amis des Noirs*, the Assembly (in a decree of May 1791) granted a restricted franchise to *gens de couleur.* This infuriated the colonial whites; Paris had breached the racial distinctions that were essential to the functioning of society in St-Domingue. Worse perhaps, the whites feared that this concession, however small scale and limited, was the first step towards the emancipation of the slaves. It could only stir the brew of racial trouble in the colony.[10] There was good cause to fear the consequences of Ogé's rebellion and its aftermath. Although that rebellion was not designed to end slavery (indeed, many of his followers were themselves slave owners), it was the first major armed attack to use the vernacular of the French Revolution against the colonial system of racial discrimination.

Frustrated by failures in the colony and Paris, in August 1791, free men of colour rebelled in the west and the south of the colony (where they were most numerous). At the same time, there was a massive slave rebellion across the Northern Plain. Though the two revolts were not connected, they obliged local whites to fight on two fronts. The much-feared slave revolt had happened.

Between 1789 and 1791, while Paris was convulsed by political and revolutionary change, the slaves in St-Domingue had remained relatively quiet. But that had been the case for many years. Whatever the cause, contemporaries agreed that, before 1789, African slaves proved the most loyal, and creolised slaves (i.e. local born) the most unreliable and dangerous, in the unfolding of the colony's troubles. The answer to this conundrum may be simple: creole slaves, often working close to white people (as domestics or skilled workers), were the ones most exposed to the news and the arguments flowing back from Paris. In towns, on docksides, in homes and taverns, in plantation houses and sugar factories, angry political disputes, careless gossip at the table—all and more caught the attention of slaves close by. News from Paris, gossip that the slaves had friends in Paris (and in Britain), the late-evening shouting of angry planters and merchants about the hazardous discussions taking place in both France and the colonies, all caught the attention and may have encouraged slaves in close attendance.

Even if the slaves had not grasped the significance of French debates about the rights of man, their owners had, and they protested long and loud in the colony and, via their representatives, in France. For years there had been regular warnings of potential slave trouble, and a variety of voices had predicted it (though this had been a mournful refrain in all slave colonies). But when slave trouble came to St-Domingue, it fell upon the slave owners with catastrophic force.

Between 1789 and 1791, slaves had been political bystanders to the growing friction between colonial whites and the free coloured. At the same time, the white population was itself divided. After the Ogé revolt, whites disarmed some of the free coloured (despite their importance in suppressing slave unrest) and they repudiated measures to secure racial equality. All this aggravated the deep-seated feeling among slaves that efforts to improve their lot were being thwarted by local men of property. Just as slave owners were susceptible to paranoid rumours about slave unrest, slaves themselves readily believed speculation that their slave owners and their friends were out to deny them any improvement. Rumours—often ill-founded, partial or simply untrue—became a critical element in what followed. Indeed, rumours were to become a stock-in-trade of Haitian politics for decades. There was no doubt that abolition was on the march in Europe, and the debates about abolition in London, Paris and St-Domingue were easily reduced in the minds of the enslaved into a conflict between their friends and their enemies. Then, in August 1791, Louis XVI fled Paris, was arrested and imprisoned.

As unlikely as it now seems, the king appeared to be the slaves' ally. Measures under the king seeking to ameliorate slave conditions had been rebuffed by colonial planters. In a world of transatlantic rumour and overheard gossip, Louis seemed like a distant friend in a sea of slave-owning enemies. On 21 August, slaves in St-Domingue rebelled, claiming they were seeking the freedom granted by the imprisoned monarch. Rebellions erupted in the Northern Plain, with authority there weakened by the removal of a mutinous regiment, and in the midst of rising friction between whites and the free coloured. The rebels planned to kill the politicians gathering at Le Cap for the Colonial Assembly, and launched an unprecedented wave of murder and mayhem. Led and organised by elite creole slaves, tens of thousands of rebel slaves spilled out from Le Cap across the Northern Plain and into the surrounding mountains. Their demands were confused (initially that whites leave the colony) and they made no claims for universal freedom for all the slaves. Colonists refused to negotiate, and rebel leaders were in no position to order a ceasefire. So, the rebellion continued. Planters contained its spread by the most brutal of reprisals, and France dispatched 12,000 extra troops (though these, like so many before them, quickly succumbed to tropical illness).

Adding to the complexity, free men of colour revolted in other parts of the colony and persuaded planters to make concessions—but resistance from Paris and among local poor whites prolonged the fighting, and unrelated rebellions erupted across the colony. Free men of colour rebelled in the west and south. In the north-west, the free coloured joined the whites in suppressing slave rebels. Elsewhere, free coloured landowners joined the slaves. It was a devil's brew of racial and sectional conflicts, of personal and communal antagonisms, of score-settling and local vendettas—often under the banner of ideals forged in France.

Everywhere, the conflict was a confusion of

changing alliances between the various groups (enslaved, free coloured, whites and the French military). Freemen, some of them black, fought alongside slaves. In places, small bands of slaves were given arms and used as mercenaries. In isolated mountainous regions, armed bands took on a life of their own and survived like guerrillas groups. But the worst—most destructive, widespread and uncontrollable—of slave upheavals was in the north. Whites fled in terror, seeking the relative security of the towns, leaving their properties at the mercy of the insurgents who torched and pillaged the plantations. Throughout, the fighting and its suppression were characterised by extreme brutality, torture and mutilations.

Violence flared in different parts of the colony, often at the same time. Viewed from Paris—itself in the middle of revolutionary upheavals—it seemed that the entire colony was being consumed by rebellion. No French government, whatever its political shade, could allow its most valuable colonial asset to be torn apart in this fashion, and even the most unreconstructed of planters recognised that they needed help—from freemen of colour and from the French. But France sometimes stoked the flames. France's decree of April 1792 banning racial discrimination, and the appointment of new, hardline French commissioners to impose the decree, led to the deportation of whites who resisted. Having purged the whites, the commissioners turned to rebellious slaves and were initially successful. But then, in 1793, events in France changed the entire story.

The execution of Louis XVI and the outbreak of war in Europe pitched St-Domingue into further chaos and confusion. The British in particular were keen to add the wealth of St-Domingue to their own lucrative portfolio of Caribbean possessions; so too Spain (poised just over the border in Santo Domingo). France herself was stymied: she needed troops in Europe, and colonial whites seized the opportunity to reverse the recent changes imposed by Paris. Spain, keen to grab the rest of the island, offered freedom and land to existing slave insurgents. In reply, and in a desperate move to try to save the colony for France, the twenty-eight-year-old commissioner, Léger-Félicité Sonthonax (acting with no authorisation except his own secret abolition sentiment—and hoping for the best), abolished slavery on 29 August 1793.

The French Convention, hoping to undermine British power in the Caribbean, followed Sonthonax's emancipation of slaves in St-Domingue by freeing slaves throughout French colonies—and giving them the rights of citizens. It was, as David Geggus reminds us, 'one of the most radical acts of the French Revolution'.[11]

There was resistance in some colonies, but the outcome was freedom for 600,000 people. It was a stunning turn of events: a transatlantic blend of French revolutionary fervour and colonial mayhem, which inspired and horrified in equal measure. It offered hope to slaves elsewhere in the Americas, while petrifying slave holders everywhere.

This first slave emancipation in the Americas was a stunning bolt from the blue, as unexpected as it was bewildering: its consequences—despite all the subsequent reverses, violence and obstacles—were to be felt clean round the Atlantic. Black freedom had suddenly emerged (albeit temporarily) in the midst of a devastating revolution and massive slave insurgency. The slaves had rattled their cage, and it had apparently fallen to pieces.

Even before that act of emancipation, the shockwaves from the turmoil in St-Domingue had sent thousands of people fleeing from the colony. Slave violence and the threat of further insurgency turned thousands of people into refugees. Planters and free people of colour scurried to neighbouring islands—Jamaica was only a day's sailing away—many taking their slaves with them. Others fled to North America, especially to New Orleans (where their expertise helped the subsequent Louisiana sugar industry), Charleston and Philadelphia. To this day, the graveyards of Catholic churches in those cities provide ample testimony to this Haitian refugee presence.

Wherever they landed, these émigrés were understandably objects of deep suspicion. In the heady mix that was politics in St-Domingue, who could tell an insurgent from a loyalist, a Jacobin from a Royalist? Nonetheless, their gruesome accounts of events in the colony chilled people to the marrow, not least because slave holders across the Americas were primed to fear the worst, and were always ready to believe the most lurid of tales about slave rebels. The refugees had no need to exaggerate: the simple truth, agreed by all sides, was enough to terrify any slave holder. As if to underline those fears, slaves everywhere picked up the news, the hard evidence and the gossip, about what their fellow slaves had done in St-Domingue. Slaves everywhere seemed naturally jubilant about the news of emancipation.

Within months of the first revolutionary tremors in St-Domingue, enslaved people throughout the hemisphere responded—and white observers were alarmed by their reactions. In the Jamaican capital, Spanish Town, 'a body of negroes' calling themselves 'the Cat Club' met in 1791 and secretly toasted the health of 'King Wilberforce', drinking from a cat's skull in honour of the leader of the British anti-slavery movement. The island's Assembly blamed such troubles on the rise of British abolition—but their fears were made much worse and more immediate by the arrival of refugees from St-Domingue. By the end of 1791, an anonymous colonist in Jamaica feared that 'the Ideas of Liberty have sunk so deep in the minds of all Negroes that whenever the greatest precautions are not taken they will rise'.[12] Not surprisingly then, officials and planters throughout the region feared the arrival of refugees—but especially their slaves—from St-Domingue. The prospect, for example, of the arrival of slaves who had witnessed the fighting or, worse still, of black troops (ex-slaves recruited to fight for Spain or France in St-Domingue) terrified officials in Cuba and Puerto Rico.

As David Geggus records: 'Wretched slaves yesterday, they are today the heroes of a revolution, triumphant, wealthy and decorated. Such things should not be seen by a population composed primarily of people of color oppressed by a small number of whites.'[13]

War came to St-Domingue not merely in the wake of the slave revolt but as one corner of the complex conflict that centred on revolutionary France. France had been at war against Prussia and Austria from April 1792: Spain and Britain joined the conflict in February 1793, and both sent armies to St-Domingue hoping to acquire that fruitful colony. It was to prove an ill-fated invasion; though the military losses were never close to those in warfare in Europe, they were heavy. Most were caused by tropical disease rather than combat.

The consequences of French emancipation were soon felt elsewhere. The French tried to use the example of black freedom to turn the slaves against their colonial masters in the British islands. In St-Domingue, it served to rally insurgents—some fighting for the Spanish—to the French Republic and to confront the British invaders. From this political and racial confusion there emerged a military force of ex-slaves, headed by black military leadership, that was to forge an independent black republic. The most famous leader was Toussaint L'Ouverture.

Born to African parents, Toussaint became a free man who owned land and slaves of his own. Involved in the rebellion of 1791, he fought on before siding with the Spanish; he took the name L'Ouverture in 1793—but refused to side with the French. On the emancipation of the colony's slaves in 1794, Toussaint changed sides and helped drive the Spanish from lands they had conquered. Spain, defeated in Europe and St-Domingue, signed a peace treaty with France. The British hung on in the west and south of St-Domingue, though they were crippled by tropical disease, and were forced to use slaves to fight for them. The real military power was now Toussaint's army, which consisted mainly of Africans led largely by creole officers. Conflicts flared across the colony, each with its own leader, rank and file, and allegiances, but gradually, by force of personality, shrewd military intervention and clever gathering of political loyalties, Toussaint rose to colony-wide prominence. He became commander-in-chief of the colonial army, negotiated the withdrawal of the British and oversaw the freeing of the colony's surviving slaves. It was an astonishing story, which established Toussaint's name as one of the great leaders of the enslaved (despite the fact that he had been a slave owner himself). In 1798, however, he was faced by the need to salvage some material wellbeing for St-Domingue from the ravages of the past decade.

Toussaint now acted as the head of state of an independent nation, making peace with Britain and the USA, and pursuing whatever course seemed to be in the country's best interests (even warning Jamaica of a threatened slave revolt there). Although slaves were now freed workers, they were employed as forced labour—with pay. Toussaint persuaded absentees to return to their lands, while ex-soldiers took over abandoned estates, all with the aim of reviving the economy. In the process, a new black landowning class emerged. Bitter fighting continued between followers of Toussaint and of his rival, André Rigaud (another free man of colour), both sides using former slaves, and both sides using terror and mass killings to impose their will in the contested region of the south. Helped by the military victories of his commander, Jean-Jacques Dessalines (a former slave born in St-Domingue), by the summer of 1800 Toussaint had effectively conquered the entire colony. A year later he was named governor for life, annexing Santo Domingo and declared 'slave emancipation inviolable'.[14] Yet beneath the surface of these grand achievements there simmered a very different story: of military leaders skimming off the profits while ordinary, unpaid soldiers pillaged the countryside for their sustenance and pay. Toussaint had also permitted the purchase of fresh slaves to replenish the labour force. His foes regarded him as an unprincipled, self-serving hypocrite: his admirers viewed him as a pioneer forging freedom and independence from the wreckage of slavery and French colonial control.

This new post-slavery nation was in a fragile state, dangerously weakened by racial divides and antagonism, and prone to outbursts of violence, notably between workers and colonists. Toussaint had no hesitation in suppressing such troubles with brutality. Once again, how-ever, events in France determined affairs in

St-Domingue. Napoleon's rise to power in 1799 and his ambition to revive French colonial authority faced a unique—and highly volatile—problem in St-Domingue. Napoleon decided both to remove Toussaint and to reintroduce slavery.

European armies traditionally fared badly when dispatched to the Caribbean but, this time, the French did better. For a start, there was a period of peace and the major maritime powers were generally agreed that firm colonial control was better than government by ex-slaves. An experienced army under Charles Leclerc sailed for St-Domingue with British and American approval, and with Dutch and Spanish help. They took with them many who had fled the colony and were now seeking lost lands—and revenge. Three months of yet more savage fighting led to the surrender of Toussaint and Dessalines in May 1802. The French now promised that slavery would *not* be restored, and Toussaint was shipped to France—where he died in prison in April 1803. Disease intervened, decimating the French army, and the country once again slid into open rebellion, primarily to maintain racial equality and to resist Napoleon's desire—contrary to his earlier promises—to reimpose slavery.

This was now a war for independence, and it proved, even by local standards, especially brutal. When Dessalines inaugurated the new state of Haiti on 1 January 1804 (the name derived from the island's traditional Indian name), it shook off its colonial past and created a new American identity for a population consisting overwhelmingly of people of African descent. Political independence was promptly followed by the mass slaughter of many remaining colonists: all political and human traces of France were effectively purged. In the words of David Geggus, 'Haiti's independence was achieved among apocalyptic destruction.'[15]

The upheavals of the past thirteen years had left Haiti in a parlous condition. The population had fallen by a third—a decrease of 180,000 people—in addition to the deaths of 70,000 European troops and untold numbers of sailors. The economy was in ruins, plantations destroyed, the workforce decimated, and the educated classes exiled to Europe and North America. A mere generation earlier, the colony had been the Caribbean's major producer and exporter of tropical produce, and had been the source of much of France's trading prosperity. Now, at independence in 1804, Haiti was fast becoming a poor nation of peasant smallholders. Yet for all the suffering, and despite the death and destruction on an epic scale, Haiti was the first nation in the Americas to both overthrow slavery and abolish racial discrimination. It was the first independent black republic outside the continent of Africa.

It was many years before other nations fully recognised Haiti's nationhood. France, determined to make its former colony pay dearly for its independence, waited until 1825—and only then at the cost of enormous reparations paid to France. Those reparations shackled the new nation to crippling debt repayments, which lasted into the twentieth century and became a major cause of Haiti's chronic and persistent indebtedness and poverty.

Slave defiance—ubiquitous across the Americas—had taken on a new threat and significance (for both slaves and masters) after 1789. What had happened in Haiti provided, by turns, inspiration and alarm: inspiration for the slaves, alarm for the slave owners. As long as Africans continued to spill from the slave ships (to Brazil and Cuba) that defiance would find an African expression and energy that directed itself at local grievances.

Black freedom in Haiti had been won at a terrible human cost for all the sides involved in the prolonged and complex conflict. For slaves, and freed slaves, the complexities were easily distilled into a simple issue. Black freedom had been achieved by the defeat of a colonial system and its imperial armies. Whatever the cost, and however flawed the leaders who emerged from the conflict, Haiti offered an example: a beacon of hope and inspiration for millions of others across the Americas who continued to yearn for freedom. But it also stood as a cautionary tale for slave holders everywhere. Whatever its cruelties and brutality, slavery was a volatile force; tamper with it at your peril. The subsequent suppression of slave unrest by slave owners, from Brazil to the USA, was profoundly influenced by the memories of Haiti. The determination not to make concessions and to curb slave defiance with an iron fist was the pre-eminent lesson that slave owners derived from the story of Haiti. It proved to be a nightmare from which they never really escaped.

# 5

## The Friends of Black Freedom

THE DEVELOPMENT OF African slavery in the Americas had few critics at first. Although both Spain and Portugal had complex theological discussions about the enslavement of Indians, they paid little attention to African enslavement and it was to be a supreme irony that Bartholomé de las Casas (Bishop of Chiapas) supported the enslavement of Africans as a way of protecting local Indians.[1]

The Catholic Church sanctioned both the early Atlantic slave trade and the use of African slaves in the Americas. When the nations of northern Europe also embarked on their own slaving empires, they too felt unrestrained by moral or religious doubts about slavery. They faced few major institutional or individual objections to the enslavement of Africans. Early French slavers were expected to convert enslaved Africans to Catholicism, while Flemish, Dutch and English slaving ventures generally went untroubled by the questions, rehearsed at home, about the freedom (or otherwise) of Africans landing in European ports. Thus, as the various European settlements in the Americas evolved, neither church nor state thought to prevent or restrain the emergence of African slavery in the colonies. Nor did they seek to stop the growth of the maritime trade in African slaves. All soon accepted that the raw conditions of colonial settlement required enslaved labour; and equally, that such labour could only be adequately supplied by a long-distance oceanic trade in Africans, first to Brazil, then to the Caribbean and North America. By the mid-eighteenth century the Atlantic slave trade and plantation slavery were securely embedded as pillars not only of colonial development, but of Western wellbeing and power. Both were central to the wider Atlantic economy, and both had blossomed with barely a squeak of opposition. Who could dispute the raw economic facts of empire—even when it was anchored in slavery?

When critics did emerge, and when Africans finally began to have friends speaking up for them, such voices grounded their objections in the brutal evidence that, along with the profits, began to spill forth from the slave ships and the plantations. Long before the political blossoming of abolition (after 1787 in Britain), critics had begun to collect and publicise the chilling human evidence that emerged from accounts of Atlantic slavery. Portuguese and Spanish (often clerical) observers had travelled much the same route two centuries earlier, but the rapid development of the world of print in the eighteenth century made available a growing body of data about maritime and colonial life, which revealed the brutal realities of slavery to an expanding readership. As that century advanced, authors from various political and religious positions began to criticise slavery, denouncing its inhumanity, claiming it to be contrary to Christianity and even arguing that slavery involved a denial of the African's right to liberty.[2]

Above all, it was the shocking accounts from the slave ships and plantations that provided ammunition for the early attacks on slavery. The range of literature involved was astonishing and embraced travel accounts, narratives of trade and empire, theological discussion, and political and economic debate. A mounting curiosity about the wider world was stimulated by newspapers, journals, broadsheets, pamphlets, magazines and books. Slavery was a dominant theme, mentioned time and again, and it was the eye-watering accounts from men who had seen it on the slave ships and plantations that brought home its brute realities. Such accounts prompted moral qualms about slavery among both writers and readers, but in the colonies opposition was easily bypassed by crude economic realities: profits from slavery simply swamped any moral concerns. Nonetheless, scenes from the enslaved Americas made a deep impression on readers, and their feelings of outrage began to spread.

The early British eyewitness accounts of slavery were authentic and visceral, though they did not offer a philosophical or even an economic critique of slavery. Bondage on such a widespread and brutal scale was unknown in Britain itself, notwithstanding naval press gangs and enslaved Scottish miners, and such accounts provoked indignation; comparisons with ancient villeinage and serfdom simply failed to convince. American chattel slavery, passing from mother to child in perpetuity, with no legal remedy and characterised from childhood to old age by a brute violence was, quite simply, utterly different from anything in British memory or historical experience.[3]

The irony was that colonial slavery developed at the very time the British began to think of themselves as a people uniquely blessed by their freedoms. The parliamentary victories of the seventeenth century and the rise of common law as the safeguard of every citizen—as enshrined in the Habeas Corpus Act of 1679—helped to mould a sense of nationhood that was rooted in legally guaranteed personal and political liberties. When they looked to their European neighbours, the British considered themselves distinctly privileged—with liberty. Yet at the same time, the British were shipping ever more Africans into perpetual bondage and were benefiting hugely from that enslaved labour.

Though this irony was later used to great political advantage by abolitionists. Who, say in 1750, so much as paused to consider the irony when they enjoyed the abundant pleasures and benefits of slavery? Who was troubled by the legal or political inconsistencies when they lit their pipe of slave-grown tobacco, sweetened their tea with Caribbean sugar or dined at a mahogany table made from timber felled by gangs of African slaves?

One small group who did worry about the inconsistency, and who had direct dealings with slavery, were North American Quakers—even though many of them, by the mid-eighteenth century, were direct beneficiaries of enslaved labour. Soon after the creation of the Society of Friends, in the wake of the British Civil War, a group of Quakers settled in the relatively new colony of Barbados. By the time George Fox visited the island in 1671, they had formed the largest Quaker community outside the British Isles. When Quakers began their settlements in New Jersey and Pennsylvania, there were at least fourteen Quakers in Barbados who owned plantations worked by sixty or more slaves.

Slaves quickly followed Quakers and other Europeans to their new settlements in North America. In 1671 George Fox urged Friends to treat their slaves well 'and deal kindly and gently with them'.[4] He did not, though, demand freedom for the slaves, nor did Quakers living close to slavery in North America. There was, however, a growing unease among North American Quakers about the spread of slavery (and of the involvement of Quaker businesses with slavery). Quaker meetings and individuals expressed disapproval, but it took the influence and writings of two remarkable men, John Woolman and Anthony Benezet, along with the Philadelphia Quakers, to push the Society towards supporting formal abolition in the 1750s. In 1758, the London Yearly Meeting urged Friends to avoid the slave trade; to 'keep their hands clear of this unrighteous gain of oppression'. That same year, the Philadelphia Yearly Meeting formally condemned slave holding. Three years later, the London Yearly Meeting followed suit.

The problem for American Quakers who were already commercially successful in a variety of fields was that some of them owned slaves. Slavery had crept into all corners of American life, from domestic service in towns through to the better-known field labour in major agri-cultural industries. Quakers who prospered from slavery were initially reluctant to heed the Society's call on behalf of the slaves, and even the early Quaker abolitionists felt that slaves could only be weaned gradually from slavery towards full freedom. Despite such complications, the criticism of slavery by the Society of Friends proved a seminal force in the emergence of a more broadly based attachment to abolition in the late eighteenth century. No single person proved more influential than Anthony Benezet.

Born Antoine Bénézet to a French Huguenot family who migrated first to England then, in 1731, to Philadelphia, Benezet rejected the commercial life of his father for the more scholarly life of teaching and preaching. He married into and joined the Society of Friends, became an energetic teacher, educating local blacks in his home before founding what became the hugely influential African Free School. Benezet was now on his chosen path: of educating blacks in the expectation of ultimate emancipation.

Benezet loathed the pursuit of wealth and of luxury, and he came to see the Atlantic slave trade as the very worst example of both. He also anchored his intellectual opposition in a range of secular literature, making use of Friends' private libraries and the Library Company of Philadelphia. Though biblical sources liberally peppered his writings, he made great use of legal and philosophical sources. He found support, for instance, in Baron de Montesquieu's *L'Esprit des Lois* (1748): 'The state of slavery is in its own nature bad. It is neither useful to the master, nor to the slave.' Benezet also turned to the writers of the Scottish Enlightenment, with Francis Hutcheson's *System of Moral Philosophy* (1755) proving a rich source for his ideas: 'no endowments natural or acquired, can give perfect rights to assume power over others, without their consent'.

Benezet—a Quaker wedded to non-violence—parted company with Hutcheson in his belief that slaves had a right to use violence to secure their freedom. Benezet was also influenced by the Scottish jurist George Wallace: 'Men and their liberty are not "*in commercia*"; they are not either saleable or purchasable.' Wallace argued that 'liberty is the right of every human creature . . . And no human law can deprive him of the right, which he derives from the law of nature.'[5]

Via extensive reading in all the appropriate literature—in English, French and Dutch—Benezet gradually developed an argument against slavery. He delved into travel literature: accounts from mariners on the slave ships and adventurers on the coast of Africa. The result was a series of publications between 1759 and 1771 that not only had a major impact on contemporary attitudes to slaves and slavery, but left a corpus of literature, which historians have been feasting on ever since. His was a studious and sympathetic appreciation of Africa and its myriad societies and was totally at variance with prevailing views, which consigned Africa and Africans to a realm of barbarity (thus serving to justify Europeans in their rapacious dealings with the continent). But Benezet also went further. His research into shipping records in English newspapers enabled him to make estimates of the numbers of Africans annually transported on board the slave ships. He made similar forays into the evidence about the treatment of slaves in the Americas. In effect, Benezet made himself the master of the contemporary data of the British slave trade—at all three points of the Atlantic system: Britain, Africa and the Americas. It was a remarkable, innovative feat, and testimony to his industry and single-minded commitment. It also pointed the direction in which the slave trade has been studied by scholars ever since. Benezet located the essential sources, extracted the statistical evidence and drafted a persuasive argument—against the slave trade.

Both Benjamin Franklin and Benjamin Rush were greatly influenced by Benezet. So too was the Virginia House of Burgesses (which petitioned George III in 1772 for an end to the slave trade). Not satisfied simply with publications, however, Benezet wrote countless letters to politicians and preachers on both sides of the Atlantic. Like Dr Johnson in London, during the drift to American independence in 1776 Benezet was alert to the striking contradiction that the language of liberty was proclaimed loudest by men who were themselves slave owners. Nor was Benezet's abolitionist work merely literary or by correspondence. He agitated for the freedom of slaves passing through Philadelphia, and demanded the same rights for black people that American revolutionaries were claiming for themselves. He was out of step on one major issue, however; as a pacifist he continued to refuse to concede the colonists' right to a violent break from the British.

Benezet's initial target was North American slave traders and owners, but in the late 1760s he began a correspondence with sympathisers in England. In the years before the outbreak of the American War in 1776, English Quakers responded to Benezet's ideas by quietly agitating against the slave trade. In the long term, these transatlantic links were crucial in disseminating abolitionist ideas on both sides of the Atlantic, and in encouraging English Friends to publish and circulate cheap (or free) literature against the slave trade. English Quakers had an effective national headquarters (in the form of the London Yearly Meetings), and also had a network that spanned the entire country, stretching from Plymouth to Newcastle. Crucially, too, they had a committed publisher, and prosperous Quaker backers happy to finance any Quaker campaign. This nationwide network was organised and run in an efficient and prudent fashion by men whose business acumen had propelled them to commercial success in a string of businesses. Even before 1776, Quakers were well placed for abolitionist agitation: as well as their formal network, they had powerful individual spokesmen writing and preaching against the slave trade, and had strong transatlantic links that ensured the flow of abolitionist ideas back and forth. What seems at first glance to be a relatively small voice in the wilderness—a sect of perhaps no more than 20,000 Quakers in England and Wales—was poised to become *the* major catalyst for a full-scale onslaught on the relatively unchallenged slave trade. The entire problem of slavery was transformed by the British defeat in North America.

English Quakers also faced difficulties about slavery. Like their American counterparts, some had a direct or indirect stake in the slave system. Between 50 and 75 per cent of British metal manufacture was in Quaker hands, and how could the ironmasters avoid entanglement with the Royal Navy or the slave ships (both requiring huge volumes of ironware for armaments and ships fittings)? And should Quaker pharmacists refuse to dispatch medicines to the sugar planters to treat their slaves? Even the apparently innocent production of metal pots and pans by Quaker manufacturers raised problems, because huge volumes were shipped to Africa to be exchanged for African slaves. The enormously wealthy Quaker, John Hanbury, made his fortune from the tobacco trade to the Chesapeake—and that tobacco was cultivated by slaves. The simple truth was that slavery had so infiltrated British economic and social life by the mid-eighteenth century that even its Quaker opponents found themselves enmeshed.

The Quakers' abolitionist ideas began to spread. Benezet's publications were to prove especially important for the work of the man who became the indefatigable foot-soldier for British abolition— Thomas Clarkson. William Wilberforce also quoted Benezet at length in trying to persuade Parliament to end the slave trade. And Benezet also had a lively correspondence with sympathisers in France, notably with the leaders of the *Société des Amis des Noirs*, and with a range of men drawn into the upheavals in France after 1789. His influence extended much further than formal political links, notably to Africans living in London. All were former slaves or born of slave parents, and for them the slave trade was not merely an abstract, moral issue. Benezet's account of Africa gave them a context for their own writing about their enslaved experiences.

Though it is hard to exaggerate the influence of this one simple Quaker, today his importance is rarely fully recognised, even though the key abolitionist pioneers openly admitted their debt to Anthony Benezet. In addition to the rich corpus of literature, Benezet effectively established *the* central principle of the campaign that followed. Although he ranged far and wide in his study of Atlantic slavery, his concentration and his point of attack was on the slave trade itself. Slavery was at its most violent in the belly of the slave ships, and those ships were effectively the umbilical cord for slavery in the Americas. With a few exceptions (most notably in North America), slave societies continued to depend on the regular arrival of new supplies of Africans from the slave ships. Benezet established a method of confirming the pivotal fact that, if slave owners were denied the Atlantic slave trade, slavery itself might wither and die. Benezet was among the first to realise that this reliance on the slave ships was the slave holders' Achilles' heel. They were highly vulnerable—if only the slave trade could be stopped. Abolishing the slave trade was, however, the most daunting of prospects. The first step was to raise public awareness of the problem.

With that in mind, Benezet petitioned the British royals (as early as 1783) against the slave trade. He pointed out to Queen Charlotte that the slave traders had taken Africans and 'forced them into your ships, like a herd of swine'.[6] He urged slave captains and their commercial backers to desist, and to have nothing more to do with the slave trade. He attacked the planters who bought Africans from the slave traders, accusing them of being 'the spring that puts all the rest in motion'. Benezet denounced everyone involved; from the initial slave kidnappers through to the merchants whose commercial machinations orchestrated the entire system. Aware of the planters' claims that their industries—especially sugar and tobacco—would simply collapse without slave labour, Benezet argued (optimistically) that there was plenty of free, white labour available. He also warned slave owners of the dangers they faced; unless they altered their ways, slaves would surely seek their revenge. If the slave trade continued, an 'impending catastrophe' would inevitably follow. The slaves would revolt and lay waste to the slave colonies.

This was an astonishingly prophetic observation. Although Benezet was not the only one to predict a cataclysmic end to slavery (planters had nightmares about it), his warning came a mere decade before the slave upheavals totally destroyed slavery in St-Domingue. Everything Benezet had warned against happened: it was the grimmest realisation of a bleak prediction. He did not live to see his warning come true, however: he died in Philadelphia in 1784. The people who indeed fully grasped his importance and his value—a large crowd of mourners

155

weeping for the passing of their greatest and most influential friend—followed his coffin to the grave: 'hundreds of Negroes testifying by their attendance, and by their tears, the grateful sense they entertained of his pious efforts on their behalf'.[7]

By the time of Benezet's death, Quakers had become the most vociferous opponents of the slave trade and had converted abolition into a political movement in North America and Britain. Until 1787, British abolition was in effect still a Quaker campaign. What had begun in and around Philadelphia had now taken on a British complexion. Its ambition was to whip up a national feeling of antipathy, channel it at Parliament, and then oblige the legislature to act against the slave trade. They petitioned the House of Commons, and formed anti-slavery societies across Britain and in Philadelphia. They also published cheap abolitionist tracts—a trickle that later became an astonishing flood. At the heart of that literature lay the writings of Anthony Benezet, whose words became the texts used by a swelling band of new abolitionists, and the bulk of the literature flew off the London presses of the Quaker printer James Phillips.

The Quakers' abolition campaign did not abate after the death of Benezet. In fact, the mid- to late 1780s saw British Quakers more obviously break with their own tradition of quietism stretching back to their founding fathers. They had steadfastly resisted the temptation to join in public politics, except in defence of their own interests. They were inward-looking, withdrawn and deeply cautious about the world of public politics (they had, after all, emerged from the fire and brimstone of English Civil War and were scarred by their postwar sufferings). Quakers had secured a special place for themselves in Britain; and were tolerated—unlike other dissenting groups—in return for a quietism and a dogged refusal to agitate or speak out politically. All that changed after 1783 and the *Zong* trial, and henceforth the Quakers not only became a highly politicised organisation, but they emerged as an exceptionally influential group. In the brief interval between the end of the American War and the outbreak of the French Revolution, British Quakers exercised a political influence that swayed unprecedented numbers of people (and not merely Quakers). They obliged Parliament to pay attention, and forced ministers to rethink their attachment to the slave trade. In the process, the Society of Friends in effect created a campaigning blueprint that was to be followed by many other reforming groups in the nineteenth century (including parliamentary reformers, Chartists, women's campaigners and Catholic emancipists).

The British defeat in the American war had

not only exposed British imperial frailties, but had raised the question of moral culpability. The North Atlantic's major slaving power had been humbled, and many of the devout took this as evidence of the Lord punishing the unjust for their sins. What greater sin could there be, in Quaker eyes, than slavery itself? In addition to this religious support for abolition, the Quakers' push for abolition was aided by the American Revolution itself. Colonial complaints against Britain had developed into a full-blown declaration of rights, which were to echo down the years as basic human and social principles. Denunciations of the imperial system inevitably involved condemnation of slavery. After all, slavery was at the heart of Britain's imperial standing and prosperity. Opposing the British, and demanding colonial freedom, involved at least a tacit criticism of slavery. In addition, the vernacular of the revolution—denouncing the King and his ministers, insisting on American rights—provided a ready-made vocabulary for a parallel criticism of slavery.

The obvious and glaring problem remained: many of the leading American revolutionaries and patriots were themselves slave owners. This created a political and moral tension that was to be built into the very fabric of the American republic, and that has troubled the USA from that day to this.

British Quakers were nudged towards more overt political activity by the British policies in America. Any number of Quaker businesses conducted lively trade with America, and the various British taxes imposed on the colonies before 1776 alarmed British Quakers as much as Americans. Prominent British Quaker businessmen lobbied ministers both to avert economic damage to Quaker interests, and to preserve the peace.[8] They failed, of course, but their activities (many of them hidden and behind the scenes) began to break the traditional Quaker mould of political independence and quietism.

The war itself made open criticism of the British government difficult and, despite their economic security, Quakers continued to worry about their marginal status, and remained conscious of the need to tread carefully in public. Peace in 1783, however, swept away many of those concerns, and it was then that nascent Quaker abolition took on a new, public and more aggressive life. The Quakers quickly emerged as *the* most important activists behind demands for an end to the slave trade. The hope was that the slave trade would succumb to the irresistible pressure of the rising public clamour against it. But that clamour needed to find its strength from the slaves themselves. The Quakers were joined by a small band of ex-slaves living in Britain. It was their stories—their sufferings—that became the critical element in the arguments. Those accounts were to be told most persuasively by a small band of Africans in London, who blended Benezet's work with their own personal experience to produce an irrefutable account of the horrors of slavery.[9] It was a black community and voice that exercised an importance far beyond their numbers, and their words and activities were to have ramifications at the highest level of legal disputes, and in the emergence of public outrage against slavery.

For years, England had had its own eccentric critic of slavery. Granville Sharp, a member of a large family of music-loving Anglicans, was a self-taught man of prodigious energy. From the 1760s, Sharp became *the* major defender of slaves and freed slaves living in England: people who found themselves caught in the legal complexities of slavery in England itself. In 1765 he cared for an injured black youth, Jonathan Strong, who had been badly beaten by his owner, David Lisle, in London. Two years later, Lisle attempted to seize Strong and take him back to slavery in Jamaica. When Sharp—outraged by the incident—consulted lawyers, he was alarmed to learn that slave owners were legally entitled to remove slaves, against their wishes, back to the slave colonies. Sharp promptly immersed himself in legal texts, refashioning himself both as a legal expert on slavery and a draughtsman of a string of important and persuasive pamphlets on slavery and related issues. He became a serious thorn in the side of slave owners, and of Lord Chief Justice Mansfield, who presided over a number of the subsequent legal cases.

Sharp was convinced that slavery in England was illegal, and set out to prove it in English courts. It was an important issue, not only for the growing ranks of black people living in late eighteenth-century London, but for the broader question of slavery at large. The critical case— Lord Chief Justice Mansfield's judgement relating to the slave James Somerset in 1772— was that blacks could *not* be removed from England against their wishes (as guaranteed by the Habeas Corpus Act of 1679). Mansfield's decision, much discussed then and since, left open the bigger issue: was slavery legal in England? Though it was widely believed that the Somerset case abolished slavery in England, Mansfield's carefully chosen words show that this was not the case and the legal status of slavery in England remained unclear. Mansfield died in 1793, and his will ensured that his black servant and the child of his nephew, Dido Elizabeth Belle, was legally free: 'I confirm to Dido Elizabeth Belle her freedom.'

Why would Mansfield make this provision if his judgement of 1772 had freed all slaves in England? In fact, we know of other people brought to Britain as slaves long after 1772.[10] Fugitive slaves escaping from owners in England periodically came before the courts in search of freedom, years after the Somerset case. Though their numbers were small, the social and legal issues at stake were enormous.

Granville Sharp had, then, established his name as the most dogged and prominent defender of black people in England long before the American War. His research into the law and slavery, and his encounters with aggrieved blacks in London, not only revealed individual cases of black suffering, but exposed the multiple outrages of the slave system. Sharp's reputation spread, especially among fugitive slaves in England, who learned that Sharp was the man to turn to for help. The problem went much deeper than the woes of individuals—however grievous their sufferings. The most outrageous— scarcely believable—illustration came to Sharp's attention in 1783 when Olaudah Equiano (to become the most famous of England's ex-slaves) knocked on Sharp's door with a horrifying tale about the murder of 132 Africans. They had been thrown overboard from the *Zong*, a Liverpool ship heading to Jamaica, in the hope of claiming compensation for their deaths as an insurance loss. Even by the wretched standards of the Atlantic slave trade, the *Zong* killings took the story to a new level of horror.

When Granville Sharp heard of the *Zong* massacre from Equiano, he flew into a furious rage of activity and publicity, bombarding his associates, clerics, ministers, law officials, Admiralty officers—indeed anyone who might carry weight—with news of the *Zong* murders. What compounded the horror of that event was the determination of the Liverpool ship owners to seek compensation for the murdered Africans. (Indeed, it is unlikely we would have learned about the case had the ship owners *not* brought their demand for compensation to court.) Those who learned of the *Zong*—especially London's black community—were outraged, though many people realised that this was only an extreme example of what happened on slave ships on a regular basis. Resistant, rebellious Africans were often killed on slave ships, and English maritime law (of which Lord Mansfield was the master) accepted that such deaths, along with African deaths in shipwrecks, would be compensated by the insurers.

The insurance claim for the murdered Africans on the *Zong* was contested by the insurers, and in May 1783 the terrible details of the *Zong* story were paraded before Lord Mansfield's court in Westminster Hall. This was the murderous background to the post-war revival of interest in the slave trade, and it generated a sense of outrage for abolitionists to draw on. Granville Sharp, with twenty years of agitating about slavery behind him, dashed off lengthy missives to his extensive network of old and new contacts. He pressed high-ranking clerics, Oxford academics, admirals and any number of reformers.

Sharp's correspondence fizzed with anger about the *Zong*, and about the apparent impunity of the guilty men on that ship. His letters to the Prime Minister and others, to newspapers, his copies of the shorthand version of the *Zong* trial itself—all insisted on 'the absolute necessity to abolish the Slave Trade and West-India slavery'. Yet, for all this post-*Zong* anger, the British slave trade continued to boom. The voracious appetite of the Caribbean islands for Africans slaves was unabated. Between 1780 and 1810, the British ships delivered more than 900,000 Africans to the Americas.[11] There was little sign that slave trading was about to succumb to its outraged opponents. It was as profitable as ever, and slave labour in the sugar islands remained vital to the old plantocratic order.

The African Olaudah Equiano, from whom Sharp had first learned of the *Zong* murders, is today the best-remembered black activist from the early days of British abolition. There had been others before him, notably Ignatius Sancho, who had cultivated a correspondence with friends in high places in the 1760s and 1770s. Sancho's

*Letters* had returned time and again to the plight of Africans, but he was not formally abolitionist—though his letters were an eloquent posthumous denunciation of slavery. Twenty years later, the dramatically changed circumstances of the 1780s galvanised Equiano. The plight of Africans became ever clearer and more public, thanks to the grim evidence in the *Zong* case, the arrival in London of large numbers of poor black loyalist refugees from the American war—and the efforts of Granville Sharp and the Quakers. Equiano and a small coterie of other ex-slaves turned writers and activists now added an African voice to the abolitionist cause. It was to make a profound difference to abolition. Equiano's autobiography, published in 1789 (and today viewed as an iconic testament to the enslaved experience), instantly became part of the campaign against the slave trade. His industry and self-promotion were channelled largely through abolitionist (primarily Quaker) networks, enabling him to convert his self-published book into a profitable enterprise. Equiano's was a distinctive black voice which spoke to the major issues of slavery and the slave trade. Like others, he had used Benezet's early work when drafting his autobiography.[12]

Equiano's experiences of slavery, on both sides of the Atlantic, were now directed into political activism. In 1785 he led a delegation of London blacks to thank the Society of Friends for their work against the slave trade. He also wrote pieces in the London press to support the abolitionist petitions arriving at Parliament. Even before he published his memoir in 1789, Equiano had established his name as a critical black figure in London. But he was not alone: his work was paralleled by another African, Ottobah Cugoano, whose *Thoughts and Sentiments* . . . , published in 1787, adopted a much more root-and-branch critique of British slavery. Cugoano denounced the British, from the Crown downwards, for their complicity in slavery. He also went further than Equiano was to do, demanding an end to slavery itself and insisting that the Royal Navy be employed to prevent the Atlantic slave trade. These were militant proposals that went far beyond anything British abolitionists discussed in the 1780s.

What Cugoano and Equiano wrote in the late 1780s was worlds removed from the *Letters* of Sancho drafted only twenty years earlier. The most prominent black men in London in the 1780s were writing with a political assertiveness that was new to abolition. More important still, they brought an African dimension to the discussions about slavery. The experience of exiled Africans added incalculable value and weight to the abolitionist demands and broadened the platform.

Thomas Clarkson, a brilliant mathematics

student, was to prove one of the most transformative figures in the entire history of the campaign against the slave trade and slavery. What became his full-time career as abolitionism activist was launched as an intellectual exercise: a scholarly essay, in Latin, by a young man who previously had not given a moment's thought to the slave trade. News of the *Zong* killings had persuaded the Vice-Chancellor of Cambridge University to set a prize essay on the topic: 'Is it lawful to make slaves of others against their will?', which Clarkson won in 1785.

Clarkson found the evidence he needed for his Cambridge essay on the slave trade in Benezet's publications. He was amazed, soon after, to discover, in London, a band of Quakers and sympathisers who were *already* busy and active on the same mission. In 1786 they agreed to publish his revised essay as a tract (*Essay on the Slavery and Commerce of the Human Species, Particularly the African*), which was distributed through Quaker meetings across the country. Clarkson had joined a small group of committed people, mainly Quakers, who were to become the basis of the Clapham Sect and who were to form the heart of British anti-slavery sentiment and agitation. Clarkson took to the road to promote abolition, covering tens of thousands of miles on horseback, criss-crossing the country with his anti-slavery message. By 1794 he had travelled an astonishing 35,000 miles in the cause. He attracted ever-growing crowds to his lectures and distributed anti-slavery tracts that came spitting off Quaker presses. He also helped to drum up abolitionist petitions, signed by as many people as possible. This was to prove one of the most potent expressions of popular feeling and one of the most persuasive means of winning Parliament backing for abolition.

The campaign against the slave trade quickly got into its political stride after the formation of the Society for Effecting the Abolition of the Slave Trade (SEAST) in May 1787. (It was essentially a Quaker organisation, with the addition of a few other sympathisers.) They faced an uphill struggle. The owners of the *Zong*, for example, continued to trade profitably in African slaves: between 1785 and 1788 they fitted out two more slave ships, and, year after year, British ships continued to deliver ever more Africans to the colonies. Critics confronting this industry in 1787 must have felt like David tackling Goliath.

Thomas Clarkson's essay set the pattern; crisp missives, printed in their tens of thousands, distributed mainly via Quaker networks, aimed at an eager popular readership. All this was bolstered by hundreds of public meetings and lectures, spearheaded by the indefatigable Clarkson. The aim was to win over parliamentary support, by exerting public pressure, to change the law by outlawing the slave trade. The campaign was lucky to recruit William Wilberforce as their parliamentary leader and spokesman. To this day, Wilberforce personifies the campaign against the slave trade, and it is true that he undertook the lion's share of the work inside Parliament. But his efforts were directed primarily at fellow MPs, peers and ministers (notably his old friend, the Prime Minister William Pitt the Younger). What Wilberforce needed—and what Clarkson generated in abundance—was the power of popular feeling, expressed through the flurry of petitions that periodically descended on Westminster. By the end of 1787, demands for the abolition of the slave trade were regularly heard in the Commons and the Lords (where they faced a much more resolute opposition) and were forcefully expressed at large, crowded public meetings across the country, and in the subsequent petitions which made their way to Parliament. The focus of all this popular antipathy was the conditions endured by the African slaves.

The abolitionists regaled the British public with the factual details of the slave ships. The *Zong* was, of course, the most graphic and horrifying example of the inhumanities that haunted those ships, but the campaign concentrated on the *exact* details of the Africans' sufferings. The facts were clear and undeniable. Clarkson's own research, among sailors and in the evidence from the slave ships, created a rich body of abolitionist evidence. Although the campaign presented an emotional appeal, it was anchored in hard, factual data. Clarkson not only provided data about the slave trade—the numbers of deaths and levels of sickness—but he displayed, almost like a travelling conjurer, a box of tricks: a chest that accompanied him containing a host of African products and commodities (woods, peppers, leathers, seeds). Here were items that could form the basis for profitable trade with Africa—if only Britain would trade in commodities rather than humanity. Equiano, too, picked up on the potential for normal trade to Africa; why not develop a commerce in Africa's multitude of products rather than the insatiable demand for African humanity?[13]

Abolitionist publications flew off the presses in astonishing numbers: an estimated 51,432 pamphlets and 26,525 reports and papers in 1788 alone, in addition to pieces in newspapers and magazines around the country. What had begun as a London movement quickly spread across the country. Even more surprising—certainly to Clarkson—was the size of the crowds turning up to hear abolitionist lectures. Clarkson sometimes had to elbow his way to the front of the crowd to speak to the assembled throng. The huge number of people signing abolitionist petitions was equally unexpected: 103 petitions descended on Parliament in the first wave of 1787–8. From the Prime Minister down, contemporaries were astonished by the power of public feeling about the slave trade, among all sorts and conditions of people. The campaign had hit a popular nerve and the slave lobby was alarmed, recognising, by the summer of 1788, 'The stream of popularity runs against us.' Abolition sentiment popped up everywhere. In the words of Lord Carlisle, 'the question of the Slave Trade has engrossed the attention of every part of the kingdom'.[14]

The early abolitionist petitions were planned to arrive at Parliament to coincide with the first parliamentary scrutiny of the slave trade. Prompted by Wilberforce, a Committee of the Privy Council spent a year scrutinising the details of that trade, poring over the data provided by Clarkson and others, and interrogating witnesses (many of them sailors with first-hand experience of the slave trade). The slave traders lobbied furiously in their own defence, but they were, from the first, on the back foot, and permanently defending a beleaguered position. Their major problem was that the evidence Clarkson and friends had marshalled for the hearings was incontestable. The statistics about life, death and sickness on the slave ships (among Africans *and* the crew) were irrefutable. What Clarkson had perfected in his initial work, and which was now extended for parliamentary scrutiny, was a new *methodology;* the gathering and analysis of statistics to provide the shank of political argument. What emerged, from this abundance of evidence, both within the parliamentary analysis and in the country at large, was a deep-rooted sense that the Atlantic slave trade was *wrong*— an abomination—and a national outrage. Yet, for all that, it continued to be a very profitable trade.

In the wake of the *Zong* trial Granville Sharp had set out, in a fury, to tell as many people as possible about the horrors that had unfolded on a Liverpool slave ship. He hoped that 'hundreds can come and say that they heard the melancholy evidence with tears'. A mere four years later, 60,000 people signed petitions against the slave trade. It seemed barely credible that the issue should have surged to such popularity, so soon after the American War, and so soon after the infamous *Zong* trial. It even appeared, in 1788, that the abolition campaign was on the cusp of success. It enjoyed an unprecedented level of popular backing in the country at large, it had taken root in the House of Commons (though not in the resistant Lords) and it had won over key figures in government. Popular abolition was surging ahead, dragging parliamentary opinion in its wake. By 1792 seven times the number of people signed abolition petitions than in 1788.[15] The trade in African humanity was under serious threat. Yet it was to be another twenty years before the trade was ended.

British abolition was in the ascendancy just when revolutionary turmoil swept first across France and then across its slave colonies. The seismic slave upheavals in St-Domingue/Haiti after 1791, the success of French revolutionary armies threatening to export revolution clean across the face of Europe, and the emergence of Britain as the pivotal nation in the European-wide battle against France (not fully ended until the final defeat of Napoleon in 1815), put paid to abolitionism's immediate prospects. Year after year, Wilberforce's motion for the abolition of the slave trade had gained support in the Commons, but support began to drain away in the face of revolutionary turmoil in Europe and the Caribbean. Time and again, its opponents pointed to Haiti as proof of the dangers of tampering with the slave system. Word from other Caribbean colonies suggested that news of the Haitian revolt had 'sunk so deep in the minds of all Negroes, that wherever the greatest precautions are not taken they will rise'.[16] A new reactionary mood settled on the British nation, and moderate reformers took shelter. Reforming organisations were harassed and banned, their leaders jailed and dispatched to

Australia. Popular politics halted and fell silent, its spokesmen denounced as agents of a bloody Jacobin disease contracted from France. Even the godly Wilberforce was condemned as a Jacobin.

The buoyancy and optimism of the initial attack on the slave trade peaked in 1791. It had been sustained by outrage and sympathy: by a growing public feeling that the slave ships were the cause and occasion of unspeakable outrages. When the Africans rose in defiance, they were brutally cut down. Some were even discarded, like flotsam and jetsam, when a slave ship was in danger. Moreover, this was not a distant form of trade, but a slave system that was sustained and strengthened by British politics and law. The sufferings of the Africans could even be seen in London itself, in the form of the plight of fugitive slaves from North America. And it surfaced regularly in law courts and in legal arguments about the status of black people in Britain and on British ships.

Africans in England asked some simple questions. Were they really *things:* mere items of trade? Were those black faces—so common as servants and domestic helpers in eighteenth-century family portraits—simply images of an object with a commercial value? Or were they, as Equiano argued (echoing Sancho's earlier claims), to be recognised as people possessed of the rights of any other? Equiano died in 1797 and did not live to see the slave trade abolished, though it came soon afterwards, thanks largely to the change in political and international climate. Napoleon *restored* French colonial slavery in 1802 and war broke out again between France and Britain. Following a change of British government, British abolition revived and was greatly helped by a new government that was sympathetic to abolition. When the British trade was abolished in 1807 (the Commons voted 175 for, 17 against)—there was much self-congratulation and moral breast-beating in Parliament. Abolitionists applauded and turned to the figure of William Wilberforce, weeping silently in his seat in the chamber. A year later the USA also abolished its own slave trade (though by then North America had little need of new Africans: its slave communities were expanding by natural growth).

The British slave *trade* had gone, but slavery itself was not outlawed. British colonial slavery lived on for another generation and continued to provide profitable business for the colonies and Britain. We need also to remind ourselves that some three million Africans crossed the Atlantic on slave ships in the sixty years *after* the British and Americans banned the trade. Nonetheless, the abolition of 1807 was an extraordinary volte-face by Britain and forms a major turning point in modern Western history. It was as if the

English-speaking world had turned its back on its own history of the past two centuries. Thereafter, Europe's most powerful and bellicose nation—Britain—and the emergent power of the USA were formally wedded to ending the slave trade. Both began to gird up their naval and diplomatic loins for what must have seemed an impossible task—to stop others shipping Africans to the Americas. The heart of the problem lay in Cuba and Brazil, where demand for Africans continued to thrive. Persuading other European slave-trading nations of the importance and justice of abolition was, as we shall see, to prove a difficult and protracted affair.

In 2007, the British took immense pride in commemorating the bicentenary of the events of 1807, prompting many critics to point to an obvious puzzle: the North Atlantic's great slave trader of the late eighteenth century had become the world's aggressive abolitionist of the nineteenth century. How do we explain the slaving poacher turned abolitionist gamekeeper? This immensely complex issue was often simplified by distilling the story into an account of virtue triumphing over evil. Casting aside such simplicities, however, is not to deny the remarkable upheaval that abolition involved: an upheaval not merely in the practical issues of maritime trade and investment, but in deep-seated cultural attitudes

176

and values. The British ended the slave trade not because it had become a loss-making venture (the slave traders fought to the end to maintain their trade in humanity) but because slave trading had come to be seen, by huge bodies of people, as a moral and religious outrage.

What is less obvious—but critical—is that they had come to that opinion thanks to the lives and the words of the slaves themselves. Opinion turned against the slave trade when people learned about African sufferings on the slave ships. It was helped by African accounts of the slave experience: African voices began to matter. Most important of all, but much less obvious, was evidence about Africans from beyond the grave: the anonymous lives and deaths of huge numbers of Africans cast overboard—mere figures in the records—by a rapacious slave system. Not long before, they had gone unnoticed and unremarked. Now they were memorialised in the publicity of the abolition campaign: still anonymous— but remembered. The evidence from the slave ships—collected, tabulated and presented in irrefutable detail—might seem at first sight to be mere statistics: the simple data of life and death on the slave ships. What that data revealed was the extent of the African sufferings. It was as if the data breathed life into the lost Africans, giving them a presence and an incalculable influence.

Here, then, was the most damning and persuasive African influence on the emergence of abolition sentiment before 1807. The Africans—the living and the dead—had begun to test the fabric of British slavery. Though the miseries of their lives seem hidden beneath the welter of detail presented to Parliament and the public, they came to form a critical mass that swung opinion against the slave trade. It was the start of a protracted process: of slave lives and experiences laying down the foundations of damning evidence against slavery. This was the background against which slave defiance morphed into something more disruptive in the nineteenth century, when slaves in all corners of the Americas began to challenge their own miserable bondage.

# 6

## Freeing Britain's Slaves

BRITISH CARIBBEAN PLANTERS and their friends felt sure that the abolition of the slave trade was meant to harm them by undermining their essential supplies of African slaves. For their part, abolitionists hoped that the ending of the trade would force planters to treat their slaves better: starved of new supplies, they now had to rely on the slaves already in the islands. The planters were determined to hang on to slavery: abolitionists were keen to bring it down—eventually. In the event, it was a further generation before British slavery finally fell— under pressure from forces neither planters nor abolitionists had imagined (though planters came closest to guessing what might happen). The final push that brought it down came from the very people who had demanded freedom since time out of mind—the slaves. What happened in the slave communities created an irresistible force that brought down the entire system. But, for years, it must have seemed it would never happen.

From the earliest days, British abolitionists had been in favour of gradual emancipation. After

1807 they concentrated on improving conditions for the slaves in the Caribbean while pressing for the total abolition of the entire Atlantic slave trade. Like many others, Wilberforce felt that the slaves needed to be prepared for freedom and that immediate freedom would be a mistake. This 'gradualism' characterised British anti-slavery for twenty years. But how could anyone *know* precisely what was happening in the slave islands? Were Africans being smuggled in illegally and had the end of the slave trade actually improved the lot of the slaves already there? The only certain way of knowing was to have a slave census—what became known as 'Slave Registration'—a government measure supported by abolitionist leaders. Devised by James Stephen, a lawyer at the Colonial Office, in 1812, it emerged from the growing interests in demographic data (the English had their own first census in 1801). Not surprisingly, colonial authorities—and the sugar lobby—disliked the idea. It seemed yet another step towards freeing the slaves. After a prototype was tested in Trinidad in 1813, the Slave Registration scheme was introduced throughout the islands in 1820—and undertaken at three-year intervals thereafter.[1]

When British abolitionism was revived after 1823, it was largely thanks to the work of a Liverpool abolitionist, James Cropper—yet another Quaker activist. The new Anti-Slavery Society, like its predecessor forty years earlier, was formed by Quaker backers. And, just like the campaign against the slave trade, it had in Thomas Powell Buxton a powerful leader in Parliament, and enjoyed the support of influential backers in the country at large. Once again, the Quaker business model was put in place: a national network, which enjoyed people's trust and which had sound finances making possible the flow of free abolitionist literature and the convening of multiple mass meetings. And once again, the campaign quickly established itself as a *popular* movement, which caught a national mood and expressed that mood forcefully to Parliament. This time, however, the aim was an end to slavery itself.

From 1823 onwards, the debate was about the nature of black freedom. Should it be immediate or gradual? And should there be earlier or intermediate forms of freedom—for children, for example? The British government eventually opted for gradual emancipation, with different possible solutions for different islands. Throughout, it was accepted that slave owners' views had to be accommodated in any final settlement of the slave question. The obvious question—who should represent the three-quarters of a million slaves?—seems not to have entered the debate and its outcome. Even so, slaves had their own way of affecting the debate, though their methods were not always to other people's satisfaction. The two sides were poles apart: planters determined to resist slave emancipation, the slaves anxious to promote it—as best they could. The entire debate was changed when a new weapon, quite unlike anything before, came into the hands of the slaves—and it was to prove decisive in bringing slavery down.

Defenders of slavery had always believed as an article of faith that, because slaves had been plucked from non-Christian societies, enslavement provided an opportunity to win them over to Christianity. In fact, it was mainly Catholic colonies that seemed interested in converting slaves—even if in the most rudimentary fashion. British slave colonies were notorious for *resisting* efforts to convert the enslaved. Bishops and local clerics kept slavery at arm's length, and by and large seemed happy to leave the slaves to the tender care of their owners. The end result was that, in the late eighteenth century, as for the past century and a half, the British slave populations remained attached to the beliefs and practices they had carried with them from Africa, though often modified by the peculiarities of life in the islands. Ending the slave trade, and the subsequent question of 'slave amelioration', brought the issue of slave baptism and conversion to the fore. Many came to believe that converting slaves would be a good way both of improving their lives and of preparing them for freedom. The planters, of course, saw this and they fought it to the last.

Planters directed much of their ire (and their physical assaults) at the missionaries, active on the islands, especially the Methodists and Baptists who were making considerable inroads among the slaves in all the slave colonies (Moravians had been the initial pioneers). Although their work had begun in the 1780s, it only began to bear fruit in the 1820s. Throughout, it was carried along by the dramatic rise of non-conformity in Britain itself. The proliferation of chapels, the emergence of powerful Baptist and Methodist central organisations, and the growing concern about the plight of the slaves produced a heady brew that no amount of plantocratic resistance could withstand. When slave rebellions erupted in the years between 1816 and 1831, it was easy for planters to make the link between slave unrest and the emergence of enslaved Christianity. They blamed the missionaries.

By 1830, missionaries had permeated the slave colonies. In the British West Indies there were sixty-three Moravian missionaries, fifty-eight Methodist, seventeen Baptist and about a dozen others. There were an estimated 47,000 communicant members of island chapels, and perhaps 96,000 attenders at local congregations (from a slave population of 776,000). The efforts of the evangelicals in Britain to persuade the Anglican Church to pay attention to the slaves via the London Missionary Society now meant that about a hundred ministers were at work in the islands, and upwards of 200,000 slaves attended Anglican churches. There was, however, hostility between Anglican and dissenting missionaries, largely about the question of supporting the local social order. What few of the missionaries recognised (whatever their theological stripe) was that slaves had their own reasons for turning to the chapels and churches. Whatever the aims of the missionaries, slaves had their own agendas.

The new black churches revolutionised slave life. Congregations, chapels and public gatherings for worship provided a place for slaves to meet, away from their plantation homes. In effect, the churches lured them away from the close scrutiny of their owners. In addition, they had a new kind of leader in the preachers, who spoke to them in a language and with an imagery that addressed their earthly condition—but with the added spice of offering better things to come. They offered a promise of salvation. Much of that message was extracted from the Bible, and the story of the Gospels began to disseminate a vision and the prospect of a different and better world—one utterly untouched by slavery. Missionaries were dispatched from their British organisations to take a hopeful message to the enslaved, though the missionaries were instructed not to tamper with the slave system, and to urge slaves to render unto Caesar what was Caesar's: 'not a word must escape you in public or in private,' the Revd John Smith was told in 1816, 'which might render the slaves displeased with their masters or dissatisfied with their station'.[2] Inevitably, and just as the planters feared, their work proved disruptive. The chapel, the preacher and the Bible—together and individually—created a hazardous mix, which both planters and colonial government found impossible to handle.

Most disruptive of all (and most worrying for the authorities) was the rapid emergence of slave preachers. A charismatic black preacher, steeped in biblical language and imagery, able to captivate an enslaved congregation with promises of salvation and a better life to come . . . this was exactly what planters feared and what they sought to prevent. Yet this is just what transformed British slavery, and the entire politics of emancipation, by 1831.

The slaves' newfound Christianity provided a stout defence against the slavery that oppressed them. It created a community of friends away from the plantation or other enslaved workplace. Slaves now met and mingled with people from other properties and locations, and there they could speak and behave relatively freely. It also provided hope—the prospect of better things. Churches with black preachers were even more attractive to slave congregations—for a host of obvious reasons. Black preachers spliced the voice of outraged experience with biblical support and were, from the first, a troublesome presence. Their activities and services developed a social momentum, which slave holders disliked and which they sought to prevent or contain. Consciously or not, slave preachers were leading their enslaved congregations in the direction of freedom.

All this took place in Caribbean colonies at the very time slave emancipation was becoming a major political issue in Britain itself. Missionaries departed for the slave colonies armed with the latest news of that debate. Throughout, planters and their allies in the colonies fulminated about the news from Britain, usually in the presence of their domestic slaves—who promptly relayed the gossip to relatives and friends in the slave quarters. Thus did the question of freedom flow quickly and easily, back and forth between Britain and the slave colonies—and thence into the slaves' quarters. Slaves knew that they had friends in distant Britain and, much closer to hand, in the persons of the missionaries. But they also realised that their traditional enemies remained unbowed: intransigent planters with their terrifying denunciations of black freedom, ever willing to pronounce on the violence and bloodshed that was likely to follow emancipation. As proof, they continued to point in the direction of Haiti. Who, asked the planters, was going to compensate them for the potential loss of their valuable enslaved property?

This world of emergent black Christianity in the slave colonies was shaken by major slave revolts. Rebellions were built into the fabric of slave history, but what happened after 1815 was different. For a start, Africans were no longer arriving on slave ships, and the slave populations were, slowly but steadily, become increasingly local born. Previous revolts had tended to be Africa-inspired or African-led (as indeed they continued to be in Brazil and Cuba). Against the backcloth of heightened missionary activity, and intense debate in Britain about slave emancipation, major slave revolts severely shook the British colonies. Most perplexing of all, to slave owners, it started in Barbados.

For some time that island had experienced a growing slave population. It also had the largest proportion of whites in the British islands and seemed the most peaceable and settled of all Britain's slave possessions. But at Easter 1816, news reached the slaves of Wilberforce's bill to register slaves. This was promptly interpreted as freedom being thwarted by local planters. A major slave uprising, led by Bussa, an African-born slave, and featuring around four hundred mostly creole slaves-turned-freedom-fighters, quickly destroyed seventy plantations and their crops. Revenge was prompt and ruthless, with widespread executions and displays of body parts to intimidate survivors. The revolt shook the confidence of those who believed that Barbados was proof of slavery's value and stability, and that slavery was weathering the storm of hostility gathering in Britain. Much worse was to follow, in 1823, in the recently acquired South American colony of Demerara.

The slaves in Demerara were overwhelmingly African, and subject to an extremely brutal labouring system on raw frontier lands. They, too, were soon alert to the discussion taking place in London about their future, and they were also aware that local officials and planters were blocking measures aimed at local amelioration. In August 1823 they revolted. Upwards of 12,000 slaves were involved and a handful of whites were killed—but about 250 slaves were killed in the fighting or following trials. The savagery of this repression (and the death from tuberculosis in jail of the missionary, the Revd Smith—accused of fomenting the revolt) was massively counter-productive to the planters' aims. When news reached Britain of mutilated slave bodies rotting in the tropical sun, the public was horrified. Compounding the shock was the knowledge that, in many cases, the dead slaves were their co-religionists. Slaves from the missionaries' churches were being put to death for asking for freedom: the very thing being promoted by British abolitionists. What possible justification could be offered for savagery on such a scale? Was cheap sugar a sufficient reason? This seemed especially troubling when it was becoming obvious that sugar—cultivated by free labour—could be acquired more cheaply from other regions of the world.[3]

Planters took a very different view. Events in Barbados and now in Demerara confirmed their worst predictions. Careless talk about slave registration, amelioration, education and conversion merely encouraged slaves to revolt. It had happened in Haiti only thirty years before, and the same sequence of events was now unfolding in the British slave colonies. After a fashion, of course, the planters were right. But the tide was running against them—especially in Britain.

The violence in Demerara caused a political scandal in Britain, and pushed the question of black freedom centre-stage. By then, Thomas Clarkson was already—fifty years after his first epic abolitionist treks—once again stomping the country on the slaves' behalf. He was a marked man, vilified and denounced by planters and their friends wherever he spoke. But news of the Demerara repression came to his rescue and rallied support to the slave cause. The news was more alarming because it told of physical attacks on missionaries and their churches. The Revd Smith died of consumption in prison, a martyr (to many British eyes) and his enslaved followers were being persecuted. To the huge numbers of British dissenters, this smacked not merely of racial oppression, but of religious persecution. By the mid-1820s, huge numbers of British people had added their voice to the outcry against the Demerara outrages—and against slavery in general. Before 1823, planters and colonial officials had usually got away with their repressive violence against rebellious slaves with little outrage in Britain. Now, a much-changed Britain was enraged by their violence. British Christians were appalled to hear of the fate of enslaved Christians in the colonies.

There followed a massive campaign, led by dissenting churches, demanding an end to slavery. In the election of 1826, slavery was a major electoral issue. The question of slavery was re-established as a pressing matter for Parliament. And, like abolition sixty years before, emancipation was hugely popular. Petitioning took on a life of its own, shaped and directed by local chapels, churches and their crowded congregations, drumming up tens of thousands of signatures from all corners of the country and from men and women of all social groups. In the six months following the Revd Smith's death, 600 petitions were garnered—all of them bearing many thousands of names. Throughout, women were the key players in their locality, writing and distributing emancipist literature and, in what was a highly effective innovation, leading an influential boycott of sugar and slave-grown products.[4]

In seeking to generate sympathy for the slaves, some British commentators—notably evangelical Anglicans—portrayed the Demerara revolt as if it were a labour dispute: a clash between disgruntled labourers and harsh employers. The reality was altogether bleaker and most savage. The analogy, however, was to surface again, a decade later, when early critics of British factory conditions talked about 'factory slavery'. What was happening in the 1820s and 1830s was a crossover—a transfer of experiences: slave resistance was supported by many because it seemed a reasonable reaction of exploited labour. And, later, the exploitation of British factory labour (especially child labour) was denounced because it carried the shadows of slavery.

Here, then, is stark evidence of the degree to which the problem of slavery had come to permeate British life by the second quarter of the nineteenth century. Not long before, slavery had been a distant issue, which yielded bountiful wellbeing to the metropolis. Now it was an issue of widespread domestic moral and political concern and indignation. It was also a matter of pressing political concern, regularly discussed in both the Commons and Lords. It had become the stuff of popular politics and was an electoral question whenever general elections took place. Parliamentary candidates were forced to declare their position: for or against slavery? And almost invariably, those who defended slavery lost. The popular voice had become the voice of emancipation, but it had also become a voice demanding reform on a wide front. These were the years that echoed with demands for Catholic emancipation, an extension of the franchise and the reform of Parliament. Thus, from the mid-1820s onwards, freeing the slaves became part of the warp and weft of British reforming politics. What made this unusual was that the ebb and flow of domestic British politics was shaped, to a degree, by events 5,000 miles away in the Caribbean. This was underlined in 1831 when slaves once again took matters in their own hands.

The revived push for the reform of Parliament between 1830 and 1831 was paralleled by an unprecedented 5,000 emancipation petitions cascading onto Parliament in the same timeframe. Then, over the Christmas period of 1831–2, in the space of a month, slaves in Jamaica's western parishes revolted. Jamaica's slaves, like those in Demerara, were aware that their fate was under discussion in Britain and their actions were clearly inspired, to some degree, by events there. Something like 60,000 slaves joined the uprising.[5] What became known as the Baptist War was the most massive and destructive slave revolt in the history of British slavery, prompting memories, among older folks, of what had happened fifty years before in neighbouring Haiti. Once again, and like at Demerara, local churches were at the heart of the trouble.

The influence of Baptist chapels and their preachers had spread widely across Jamaica, especially in the west. They had powerful, charismatic black preachers: men who preached wherever slaves gathered. Like dissenting preachers in Britain in the eighteenth century, they did not require formal chapels or churches, speaking instead—normally with dramatic effect—wherever knots and gangs of slaves gathered together to listen to them. The most prominent was Sam Sharpe (today, a member of the Order of National Hero in Jamaica, with a statue in Montego Bay), whose aim was the protection of slaves' labouring interests. The anger of the insurgents quickly spilled over into widespread destruction and killings. Fourteen whites were killed, and plantation properties were torched across the west of the island. For a while, the planters and colonial authorities lost control. But when the governor applied both martial law and the unrestrained power of the local militia and the military, a savage repression imposed a resentful peace. Planters destroyed the missionaries' chapels and sent the terrified preachers packing, back to Britain. More savage still was the onslaught on the rebels. Some two hundred slaves died by the sword and perhaps three hundred more were executed following hasty trials. It was a reprise, on an even more brutal scale, of what had happened in Demerara almost a decade earlier. It was also the latest spasm of a recurring theme in the history of British slavery: slave unrest followed by massive and savage reprisals. When news reached Britain, the emancipation movement turned the planters' frequent assertion against them: where did savagery reside in the slave colonies? Among the slaves or in the planters' great houses?

Missionaries, fresh from the Jamaican rebellion, criss-crossed Britain explaining what they had seen. It was an uncanny repeat of what happened in the build-up to the abolition of the slave trade. The fate of the slaves, their efforts to secure freedom and their continuing oppression by slave owners became the stuff of British popular politics. Large crowds listened to missionaries describing the violence of slaves' daily life and the brutality of the planters' repression. All this was confirmed in evidence submitted to Parliament. It was as if the anti-slavery lobby had caught the slave system in a pincer movement.

Jamaican planters had feared that the Baptist War would be their Haitian moment: violence would bring the entire slave edifice crashing down around them. In the event, the revolt was suppressed (though at the time it seemed a close-run thing). Even so, the Baptist War revealed slaves loosening their own shackles. More than that, their rebellious actions, and the violence of their owners and colonial officials, proved the final straw in Britain itself. An agitated and vociferous British people, and an increasingly sympathetic Parliament, came together, after 1832, to usher emancipation through Parliament. The Reform Act in 1832 sealed the matter. Under pressure from the Anti-Slavery Society, the general election (obligatory after the Reform Act) saw the return of some 200 MPs who were sworn to emancipation. That was immediately followed by yet another massive flood of petitions—this time containing 1.3 million signatures demanding an end to slavery. After the reform of Parliament, under the shadow of Jamaica's slave rebellion and amid an unprecedented public clamour for black freedom, slave emancipation was now inevitable. Yet it was to come at a price. A staggeringly high price, paid in compensation to the slave owners.

From its inception, the Atlantic slave system had been based on the idea that the slave was an item of property. At every point of the slavery system, slaves were treated, in practice and in law, as chattels; items to be bought, sold and exchanged. Each one had a price on his/her head (hence the need to insure African slaves on board the Atlantic slave ships). For British slave owners, emancipation meant surrendering or losing a valuable commodity. The value of slaves was an ingrained, unchallenged feature of the entire slave system. (Why else did abolitionists need to assert their contrary mantra: 'Am I not a Man and a Brother/Sister?') Not surprisingly then, when abolitionists and politicians began to discuss freeing the slaves, slave owners asked some obvious economic questions. Who would compensate them for the loss of such valuable property? How much would they receive? And who should calculate how much their slaves were worth? In the protracted public and parliamentary discussion in the 1820s and 1830s about emancipation, spokesmen for the slave owners insisted that freedom for the slaves involved a tampering with the principle of property. At its bluntest, freeing the slaves meant removing the slave owners' property, and what right did Parliament—or anyone else for that matter—have to trample on the principle of property ownership?

There were many contentious issues at play in the general election of 1832, but slave emancipation loomed large, not least because the prospects of further slave revolt continued to cast a long shadow. Abolitionists were determined not to lose the political momentum by allowing the issue to become bogged down in political and procedural infighting, in Parliament and in government. On the other hand, the West India lobby (that enormously powerful body of planters and merchants which had, for more than a century, exercised such decisive influence over British Caribbean policy) was not about to relinquish slavery without a fight. There was a prolonged debate about the exact form emancipation might take, with all sides negotiating the principles and practicalities. One central concern lay at the heart of the argument: how could freedom be achieved without harming the planters' economic interests, and without removing their source of labour for the plantation? Britain's leading statesmen were themselves major property owners, and they were not about to violate the principle of the property rights of the planters.

The resulting Emancipation Bill, put before Parliament in May 1833, created a system of 'Apprenticeship': it freed all slaves aged under six: adults would become 'apprentices' for a number of years before being accorded full freedom. A large team of new magistrates would supervise the entire system—and a loan of £15 million would cushion the planters from any subsequent labour losses. Not surprisingly, Apprenticeship outraged many: it seemed like slavery under another guise—even if only for a few more years. Planters, on the other hand, were equally outraged by the idea of a repayable loan for the loss of their enslaved property. Negotiations finally persuaded the government to change the loan of £15 million into an outright grant of £20 million compensation. Apprenticeship was to last for six years, with ex-slaves working forty to forty-five hours a week unpaid for their former owners.[6]

A month after the death of Wilberforce, the Act enshrining these conditions passed through both Houses of Parliament. Slavery ended at midnight on 31 July 1834. But the fight was promptly renewed, to bring Apprenticeship itself to an end. It lasted until 1838, with some places conceding freedom earlier. The slave lobby—once perhaps the most powerful pressure group in London— had been defeated, and slaves were freed.

For all the gnashing of planters' teeth, it is hard to feel sorry for their plight. In return for emancipation, British slave owners found themselves amply rewarded from the massive government grant of £20 million (with the money to be derived from sugar duties), in a deal brokered by the Rothschilds. Slave owners could claim for their loss of human property to special commissioners, who computed their awards on the basis of 40 per cent of the market values of the slaves.

Recent analysis of the slave compensation papers has proved astonishingly revealing, not only about the nature of slave ownership in Britain itself as well as in the slave colonies, but also about what happened to the compensation paid to the former slave owners. Slave ownership was much more widely diffused throughout British society than previously thought. Slaves were owned not merely by major Caribbean interests, but by a range of people, many of them resident in Britain. They had acquired slaves via marriage, death and inheritance, many without having stepped foot in a slave colony. Indeed, more than half of the compensation was paid to people living in Britain. Compensation was an indispensable element in bringing British slavery to an end and it seems unlikely that slavery could have ended—peacefully—without the financial arrangements it entailed.

What then happened to that money is another, equally revealing, aspect of this complex story. Huge chunks of compensation subsequently found their way into investments in a wide range of public and private properties: in industries, housing, schools, universities, public facilities and in landed property. It thus became part of the physical fabric of modern Britain.

Twenty million pounds was the price paid by the British people, and accepted by slave owners as a fair sum for ending British slavery. It was an act of emancipation that was later to inspire others. Both the French and the Dutch compensated their slave holders for emancipation. Danish slave owners petitioned for the same, but only Venezuela of all American slave societies paid slave owners for freeing locally embedded slaves.[7] Throughout the prolonged debates about what form emancipation should take, there was no serious suggestion that the slaves themselves should be compensated for their bondage. This was to nurture a grievance that festered until the present day. If compensation was to be paid—why not to the slaves? And if not at the point of emancipation, why not later— why not now? Here was the seedbed of recent and continuing demands for reparations.

What lies at the heart of the entire debate is the property-status of the slave. The millions of Africans and their descendants scattered across the Americas had been imported as items of trade. They were listed in ships' logs and plantation ledgers alongside the beast of the field, each with an economic function and each with a value. It was a peculiarity of the British emancipation process that they were finally freed *still with a price on their heads*. British emancipation was that country's final—and titanic—act of slave trading. The British *bought* the freedom of almost 800,000 people by levying duties on popular consumption.

Would freedom have come without compensation? Perhaps not—not then. More pertinent—and yet generally marginalised in the entire discussion—would freedom have been achieved without the slaves' own efforts? The persistent defiance that had always been an ingrained feature of slave life was transformed in the early nineteenth century into something much more potent and decisive in the British colonies. The voice of enslaved Christians demanding freedom became a mighty force in destabilising colonial slavery. What ultimately brought down the entire system, however, was the regularity and severity of slave revolt—and the grotesque brutality of suppression. At the simplest level, slavery was ended by a piece of parliamentary legislation. But that legislation was itself made possible by the major social changes both in Britain and in her Caribbean colonies. Abolition became an immensely popular political force in Britain—but that popularity was shaped and guided by events in the slave quarters, thousands of miles away.

The freedom which finally settled on the islands after 1838 was flawed, and left the former slaves struggling to make their way, but freedom is what slaves had struggled for since time out of mind. For the time being, it seemed enough. Elsewhere in the Americas there were armies of slaves (many more, indeed, than the British freed) who continued to be locked in miserable slavery, and their struggles for freedom were to continue for many years.

# 7

## The Fall of US Slavery

WHEN THE BRITISH emancipated their slaves, the USA was home to more than two million slaves. But had not the republic been founded with resounding exclamations about human rights? American independence appeared to have been an ideal moment to bring slavery to an end. Thomas Jefferson's ringing phrase 'that all men are created equal; that they are endowed by their Creator with inherent and inalienable rights; that among them are life, liberty, and the pursuit of happiness' seemed at first glance to sound the death knell for slavery. These lofty ideals, however, were drafted by a Virginian slave owner. At their height, Jefferson's slave holdings stood at about three hundred people, many on his magnificent property at Monticello. To modern eyes, Jefferson and George Washington were in a curiously contradictory position: proclaiming freedom, denouncing British tyranny, yet securing their own wellbeing through the enslaved labours of Africans and their descendants. Those two American heroes personified a political tension that was to characterise American society and politics for the next eighty years.

The American republic came into being arguing about slavery. The Constitutional Convention had frequent discussions about slavery and the slave trade, but finally left matters relating to slavery to individual states—and that laid the foundations for the divide between North and South. The political decision to define the enslaved as three-fifths of a person enhanced the power of the southern states, while the Northwest Ordinance of 1787 (prohibiting the expansion of slavery into the West) meant that slavery would be permanently rooted in the South. What shaped the story of slavery in the early years of the republic, however, was not so much political discussion but rather the revolutionary impact of cotton.[1]

Slaves had already been basic to the economic development of both Virginia (tobacco) and Carolina (rice), and although slaves were scattered throughout the former American colonies, northerners possessed only a small percentage of the nation's slaves, and gradually shed their attachment to slavery. It was abolished by Vermont in 1777, and thereafter in New Hampshire, Massachusetts, Pennsylvania, Rhode Island, Connecticut, New York and New Jersey—though with various conditions attached to local emancipations. Three-quarters of the new republic's enslaved people lived in the 'Upper South', but that changed rapidly in the early nineteenth century. In 1790 the USA was home to 697,897 slaves, but on the eve of the Civil War that had increased to almost 4 million, almost 2.5 million of whom lived in the Deep South. Most slaves now resided in the rapidly expanding states strung out along the vast Mississippi. And there, they worked in cotton.[2]

More slaves lived in the USA in 1850 than in all other contemporary slave societies combined, and unlike earlier slave communities in the Americas, the North American slave population was now growing solely by natural increase. The voracious southern demand for slave labour was satisfied by a major internal US slave trade. Almost one million slaves were uprooted from their families and communities in the Old South and marched, or sailed, south and west towards the cotton plantations of the New South. Twice as many slaves were taken to the cotton frontier than had originally crossed the Atlantic to North America. Like its oceanic forebear, this domestic trade involved a massive destruction of slave families, and left deep personal and social scars on survivors (at both ends of the trade). One slave marriage in five was wrecked, and one slave child in three was parted from parents. Like their ancestors sailing away from Africa, slaves who were moved to the South effectively vanished. The emotional distress and human misery spawned by this internal US slave trade is impossible to quantify, but the heartache was to remain a refrain in African-American life from that day to this. For decades after the end of slavery, it echoed in heart-breaking advertisements—some well into the twentieth century—placed by parents and children, searching for their loved one, lost to the slave traders before 1860. Lev Hall wrote to a Greensboro newspaper in April 1902: 'I am a colored man and was sold away from your county in 1839 . . . I left a mother, two brothers and two sisters.' Ann Waley was 101 when she wrote to the Mayor of Baltimore in 1911 asking for help finding 'some of "her people", white or black, before she died'.[3]

Slave ownership spread widely among southern whites and, by 1850, more than a third of a million Americans owned slaves, though most owned only a handful. By 1860 the great majority of them were employed in cotton. Slaves had been cultivating cotton for many years in the Caribbean and Brazil. The Bahamas and Barbados, for example, were especially important for the British cotton industry before 1800, yielding 8 million pounds of cotton by the late eighteenth century. All this was swept aside by the new US industry, launched by the adoption of Eli Whitney's cotton gin (1793), which encouraged the widespread cultivation of short-staple cotton. The cotton industry of

Lancashire (then of Massachusetts and Germany) began to devour cotton from the US South in ever-increasing volumes.

In 1790 the US produced 1.5 million pounds of cotton: by 1825 that had grown to 167.5 million pounds. At mid-century, it was producing 2.5 million bales of cotton—each weighing 181 kg. At the outbreak of the Civil War, cotton exports were worth more than all other US exports combined. These figures for US cotton production paralleled the imports of cotton into Liverpool, and the export of cotton goods from the mills of Lancashire. Not long before, Liverpool had been the centre of Britain's Atlantic slave trade; now it was the entrepôt for slave-grown cotton and manufactured cotton goods. Eventually, the US slave South provided between 70 and 80 per cent of the British demand for cotton.

The expansion of the US cotton industry was astonishing. Between 1786 and 1810 the US provided only 0.16 per cent of the world's cotton: that increased to 50 per cent between 1806 and 1810, rising to 80 per cent between 1836 and 1860. Had the South been a separate nation in 1860, its prosperity would have ranked it above France, Germany and Denmark, and it would have been surpassed only by England.[4] The South was especially successful and modern in the way it managed its slave labour force. In both cotton and the thriving new sugar industry in Louisiana, planters introduced innovative ways of producing and packaging their products, *and* in managing their enslaved labour force. In the cotton fields of the US South, slave labour was marshalled by a discipline that would have been envied by the factory owners of Lowell, Massachusetts, and Lancashire. Moreover, cotton and sugar were not the only US industries worked by slaves. They continued to work in tobacco in the Chesapeake region and in rice in South Carolina and Georgia.

The wealthiest planters advertised their success in a manner similar to many other barons of the railway age: lavish mansions, extensive and elaborate gardens and parklands, eye-catching personal and domestic consumption, and a social life that captured the attention (and envy) of outsiders. While the lifestyle of the cotton barons could stand comparison with their northern industrial peers, the most striking contrast was with the wretchedness of their enslaved labourers, and the threadbare fabric of both rural and urban life in the South. For all the success of cotton and sugar, the southern economy lagged well behind the North—and was falling further away, fast, by mid-century. Unlike the rapidly urbanising North, the South remained an overwhelmingly rural society—and that was due largely to the South's dependence on slavery.

In Cuba, Brazil and the USA, the attacks on

slavery did *not* originate in a belief that slavery had had its day, or that the system no longer yielded profit for those involved (excepting the slaves, of course). The South may have been lagging behind the North in terms of heavy industry, but, at mid-century, American slavery was as robust, profitable and successful as ever. Of course, it was only one element in the remarkable growth of the wider US economy. Canals, railways, river transport (especially steamboats for the cotton industry) plus improvements in oceanic transport all encouraged the large-scale and quicker movement of people and goods. The growth of banking (with occasional blips) was also critical. These changes affected all corners of US business, and the slave South was a beneficiary of this modernising economy. Northern banks, for example, were happy to finance slavery, and there was no clear division between the slave South and the non-slave North. The economies of both regions were intimately connected. Despite the northern states having turned their back on slavery within their own borders, they continued to do good business with the slave South. Put crudely, slavery was economically profitable, whatever the mounting ethical and religious doubts contemporaries might have about it.[5] At mid-century, cotton dominated the nation's major export market, and slave labourers formed a large (and growing) corner of the US labour market, while the financial and commercial networks spawned by slavery spread far beyond the Mason–Dixon line. In 1850, slavery was more important, more pervasive and more fundamental to the American economy than ever before.

Trade, finance, banking and slave-grown commodities held both South and North together in a complex web of economic interdependence.[6] Yet despite these economic ties, slavery remained a deeply divisive political and social issue, not least because of the increasingly strident American abolition movement, rooted in the towns and cities of the North. In the 1850s, abolition sentiment spread like a bush fire across the North. There were conflicting forces at work within the USA—a buoyant slave economy and rising abolitionism—which were eventually to tear the Union apart.

Understandably, the North had its own divisions. For a start, there was white racial hostility, which periodically erupted in northern cities. New immigrants from Europe, many working in new heavy industries as day labourers, did not take kindly to the arrival of freed slaves from the South. Nor did they warm to existing black communities, which were attacked by white mobs in a number of cities in the 1820s. Black survivors were traumatised and some considered migrating to Canada. Such events temporarily stifled abolition, but all that changed after 1831 with the rapid expansion of a new kind of idealistic abolition movement.

The real obstacle facing abolition was the entrenched power and hostility of the South. The economic links between North and South could not disguise the fact that the South was *different,* and southerners were developing a growing resentment about the challenges from outsiders. The beating heart of that southern difference was slavery.

Slavery was much more than the economic foundation of the South: it shaped and directed southern culture at all levels. Southern politics became an expression of slave interests, while the religion of southern whites became the scriptural voice of slavery. In effect, slavery defined the South and shaped its inhabitants (both free and enslaved). Southern culture also held the North in its gravitational pull: opposite and different. The South, of course, had its own regional and occupational fissures and divides. In places, there were even doubts about slavery itself. But such divisions disappeared when southerners confronted the North. The central issue was clear. The South was slavery, the North was anti-slavery.

The South was emboldened by its citizens' own widespread commitment to slavery. Even non-slave-owning whites (poorer by a degree than slave owners) were themselves wedded to slavery, and most aspired to become slave owners. Moreover, as far as we can tell, most of them feared the rise of black equality and political power. While the USA as a whole experienced the rise of widespread democracy, whites in the South regarded black freedom as a threat, fearing that it would not only bring economic ruin but also destroy the very culture of the South. As the voice of northern abolitionists became more strident, the South became more resistant, isolationist—and racist. A laager-like mentality developed: at ease and at one in the company of fellow southerners (even those of vastly superior wealth) but doggedly opposed and hostile to the siren calls for black freedom that echoed from the North.[7]

The outlook from the slave quarters was utterly different and depressing. For all they knew, their bondage might never end, for them and for their offspring. What alternatives did life offer? Escape—to a hostile wilderness? The risks of fleeing to the North, Canada or Mexico? Rebellion—and likely suffer the well-known agonies of vicious revenge? For all that, there were some glimmers of hope, and slaves continued to challenge the system as best they could. Slaves in the USA—like slaves everywhere—did not meekly bend their backs to the demands made of them. Slave resistance, in all its forms, taxed slave owners everywhere.

Conspiracies and plots, for example, abounded, though it is true that slave masters were far too ready to fear the worst. Theirs was a fevered world outlook, distorted by worries and exaggerated by their suspicions about their enslaved labour force. Unusual slave gatherings, overheard whispers, rumours passed on by other slaves, all blended into a disquieting vision: of slave owners fearing slave plots where none existed. Sometimes, however, their fears were real enough. Slaves ran away, reacted violently and frequently posed threats. Violent outbursts litter the records; on Long Island in 1708, in New York in 1712 and 1741, and two years earlier in South Carolina. Each outburst was answered with extreme vengeance. Even conspiracies that were nipped in the bud were often followed by the killing of suspects, and by the tightening of local slave laws. Louisiana was especially troubled in the wake of the Haitian revolt. The Pointe Coupée slave conspiracy in 1795 ended with the execution of twenty-three slaves, their heads staked along the Mississippi road to Pointe Coupée.[8] The slave Gabriel Prosser ('The American Toussaint') attempted to organise an insurrection in Virginia in 1800 but was betrayed, and this was followed by an all-too-familiar mass execution, this time of twenty-seven slaves. One of his men escaped and planned another uprising in 1802, but that too was uncovered, the leaders executed and others mutilated.[9]

The pattern was repeated from one place to another. A revolt in Louisiana in 1811 attracted an estimated 250 insurgents: about 100 of them died and their heads were displayed along the road to New Orleans. In 1816, slaves being shipped from Virginia to the South turned to shipboard violence—with large numbers of casualties. More serious still perhaps was the revolt in South Carolina, in 1822, when Denmark Vesey, a literate and devout ex-slave, used his command of the Bible to rally slave support for an ambitious plan to seize control of Charleston and its ships (though recent suggestions are of exaggerated alarm and fears on the part of the authorities). It too was betrayed, and Vesey and thirty-four others were hanged, and others deported. The South Carolina legislature then sought to ban the teaching of literacy to slaves and to outlaw slaves from worshipping independently. However real or overblown, the Vesey plot underlined the slave owners' deep-seated concerns.[10]

In August 1831 the most serious of North American slave revolts broke out in Virginia. Led by Nat Turner, the two-day insurgency led to the deaths of fifty-seven white people (including whole families), the levels of violence spreading alarm among the slave holders. Nat Turner was a black preacher, regarded as a prophet by his followers, who believed he was on a divine mission. When captured, he asked, 'Was not Christ crucified?' The outcome of the insurgency was predictable. It prompted a white backlash that took numerous black lives. The repression was out of all proportion to the initial violence, with slaves (many of them unconnected to the revolt) killed on the spot, executed or murdered by vengeful mobs. The final indignity was left to the doctors, who anatomised Turner's body. Almost as if to confirm the slave owners' deepest concerns about the threat posed by slaves, shortly afterwards Jamaican slaves rose in the latest rebellion. There, 344 slaves were executed, and hundreds killed in the fighting.[11] When news of the Jamaican revolt reached North America, it must have seemed that there was a contagion of slave unrest.

Two major successful slave revolts at sea had a major impact on US slavery. The rebellions on the *Amistad* (1839) and the *Creole* (1841) became the subject of fierce legal and political argument: about the right to compensation for lost slaves, and the central question of black freedom in an Atlantic world deeply divided by delicate diplomatic issues about slave trading. Beyond the specific legal and diplomatic issues, however, both cases, played out in US courtrooms, caused outrage among US abolitionists and strengthened their resolve to press on for black freedom at home.[12] All this—news from Jamaica and slave rebellions at sea—fed into the rising tide of American abolition in the North and helped to persuade growing numbers of people of the intractably wicked nature of slavery itself. What justification could there possibly be for such periodic violations of enslaved people?

In the thirty years before the Civil War, life in the South was periodically rife with rumours about slave unrest. Anything unexplained or suspicious, rumours of plots, random acts of violence—all were reported as signs of slave insubordination and unrest, and all prompted the familiar reaction by the forces of law and order. Slaves were killed, sometimes after legal hearings or, as likely as not, on the spot, and many more were whipped and punished. Plots were uncovered in Louisiana (1835 and 1837), in the District of Columbia (1838 and 1840) and in Arkansas (1856). In Texas, Kentucky and Tennessee, gangs of slaves attacked property, telegraph lines and jails. In 1860, Texas suffered a six-week-long wave of slave unrest, with slave attacks on towns. The rebels were, of course, executed.[13]

Slave violence was the slave masters' greatest fear, but the most common form of slave resistance was escape: running away. Some tried to make a mass escape: 400 slaves from a single parish in Louisiana planned to get to Mexico in 1840. In 1853, 2,500 were involved in a plot to escape from New Orleans. More desperate still, in 1849 a group in Georgia planned to seize a ship and sail to the Caribbean.[14] Most runaways, however, fled on their own.

No escape route from slavery was easy or without enormous risks for the fugitives, and often for their loved ones. The free states of the North beckoned, but getting there (even with the help of experienced sympathisers) was 'a task of almost herculean proportions'.[15] Frederick Douglass famously borrowed false papers from a free sailor, then took a train and boat, to northern freedom. More spectacular still, Henry Box Brown shipped himself in a crate from Richmond to Philadelphia. Many slaves simply walked, others stole a horse or travelled by river, some used fake papers—or a combination of all these methods. Fugitives needed friends and allies to help them: people denounced by southerners as 'slave stealers'. Some, however, proved to be false friends, keen to make money by betraying and selling fugitives back to southern slavery.[16]

The most famous and organised assistance came from the men and women who organised the Underground Railroad. The term does not literally refer to a single railroad, but was used to describe a complex network of land and sea routes, helpers and safe houses used by those seeking freedom in the North and Canada. Harriet Tubman used the Railroad to free first herself in 1849, then relatives and friends, in an epic tale of astonishing bravery and persistence, but there was a multitude of dramatic and heroic escapes. Large numbers of slaves were hidden on board ships plying their trade from southern to northern ports. They were helped on their way by black dockside workers and crew. Ships from Norfolk, Virginia, regularly carried fugitives. In 1855, the black cook on one ship hid a mother and her child on the journey from Norfolk to New York. Law officers tried to stop these 'negro-loving captains of Yankee vessels', but the flow never stopped. Most escaping slaves, however, went by land, aided by prominent abolitionists and prosperous supporters.[17]

Though the numbers remain unclear, the most persuasive estimate is that, between 1830 and 1860, 150,000 slaves ran away. If we include slaves who ran away for a brief period before returning, the number is much higher. Fugitives posed a persistent worry for southern slave owners.[18] The foundations of the Railroad were laid by the slaves themselves—individuals finding a route north—but it quickly attracted help and support from white friends and activists—often Quakers—with free blacks in the North opening their homes to the fugitive. A quarter of a million free blacks lived in the North on the eve of the war, though their freedom had its limitations. They faced what has been called 'cradle-to-grave discrimination'. For all that, they enjoyed opportunities that were unimaginable to southern slaves. They could secure education, worship as they wished, organise among themselves, write in newspapers, acquire trades and even open businesses. They also had free black leaders and abolitionist friends who rallied support for black people—enslaved and free—throughout the USA. The free black community understandably lured fugitives north from southern slavery.

The Underground Railroad expanded greatly in the 1830s and 1840s when the increase of new cotton lands created an ever-greater demand for slaves—in its turn prompting fugitives to flee in growing numbers. As abolitionist sentiment grew in the North, the Underground Railroad expanded to incorporate the real railway systems. Ohio—separated by the Ohio River from the slave state of Kentucky, and with links via Lake Erie to the freedom of Canada—was the most active region for the Underground Railroad.

A host of southern laws and patrols with tracker dogs and 'slave catchers' were put in place to stop the flow northwards, and rewards encouraged hunters to seek out and capture fugitives. None of this stopped the flow of fugitives, driven on by hope and fear, while their helpers were emboldened by a resolute commitment to justice. The entire business created added friction between North and South, and by 1850, there was a hardening of hearts on both sides of the line.

Fugitive slaves were never safe, not even in American courtrooms. The contradictions and confusions between the laws of different states (and the federal government) often meant that they found their newly won freedom denied by the courts, compelling them to return to the place from where they had fled. When courts upheld the concept that the slave belonged to a claimant (i.e. recognising the slave *as a thing*), they sometimes felt obliged to return a fugitive to a southern owner or their agent. One slave case after another was played out in court, each involving the fate (and conducted in the presence) of apprehensive and worried fugitive slaves, but more profound issues were at stake than the future of one individual. These were, in effect, recurring conflicts between slave and free states and were legal reflections of an acute social and political cleavage. The slave South and the free North were like tectonic plates, in growing tension with each other along the legal borders between the two regions. Fugitive slaves were cause and occasion of a tension that heightened and became more troublesome as the century wore on, as King Cotton continued to demand ever more slaves for the plantations, with growing numbers of cotton's enslaved victims seeking sanctuary in the North. A fundamental question hovered over everything: could the Union survive half free, half slave?

Whatever the risks, fugitives continued to head north, many along the increasingly sophisticated Underground Railroad, but often they escaped alone and unaided. By mid-century, more than a thousand a year, mostly men from the border states, were arriving in the North. Many more failed to make it, and were returned, defeated and punished, to the house of bondage. Others simply fled to the wilderness or into the anonymity of towns and cities, but perhaps the largest number were 'truants'—slaves who needed to break away, visit a loved one or friends, or merely hide for a while. Slave owners reluctantly came to accept that slaves escaping was one of the many irritants of life: a vexatious reality they had to keep to a minimum. But southern slave owners were united in their refusal to tolerate the flight of slaves to the North. Their powerful representatives in Congress made sure that their interests were safeguarded by law.

Tired of the constant haemorrhage of fugitive slaves, the South persuaded Congress to pass the Fugitive Slave Act of 1850. It was reviled by abolitionists and hated by free blacks. Harsher and more intrusive than earlier laws, it authorised federal law officers to enforce its terms in free states. It enabled aggrieved slave holders to pursue slaves into other states, and imposed heavy penalties on people harbouring fugitives. The law thus greatly increased the risks of recapture and being shipped back to southern slavery. It also terrified free blacks living in the North (with many fleeing to Canada from fear of its consequences). At a stroke, it also emasculated local courts and forced them to accept federal authority in returning slaves. It was a slave owners' law that seemed designed to antagonise the North. But it also meant that northern officials and private individuals who defended fugitives were defying the law. Designed to satisfy the South, the 1850 law was bad legislation because it brought the law of the land into disrepute. Abolitionists viewed it as an invitation to disobedience, and many made public declarations of their moral obligations to disobey the new law, and to continue to help fugitive slaves. There was a flurry of public disturbances, with crowds fighting to free slaves from the authorities, and armed police enforcing the law, with death and injuries on both sides. Such skirmishes were small-scale, local snapshots of the wider problem: turbulent clashes about particular slaves. They were troubling symbols of the massive conflict to come.

The implementation of the Fugitive Slave Law in the 1850s was not only a cause of friction, it was also counter-productive. An estimated 900 slaves were returned to bondage in a ten-year period, but something like ten times that number made successful escapes. The law, clearly, did not safeguard the interests of the slave owners, yet it strengthened the resolve of the fugitives and their helpers. Worst of all perhaps, the law, and the physical and moral conflicts it caused, served to widen the gulf between the North and the South. Each side was gradually boxing itself into a corner, allowing little room for manoeuvre or change. The tectonic plates were shifting, with much of the pressure being exerted by the slaves' refusal to submit, and by their unending flight.

From the first, the American abolitionist movement faced a massive and apparently intractable problem. Not only was slavery a hugely important element in the wider economy, but untold numbers of American citizens owed their livelihoods, directly or indirectly, to slave labour. Slavery inevitably lay at the heart of US politics: five of the first seven presidents were slave owners, and Congressional politics were often in the hands of slave-holding members or interests. The South was united in its opposition to northern abolition. Northern abolition faced a wall of resistant hostility, from the state governments to local churches and newspapers, right down to the grassroots of southern life.

Any anti-slavery sentiment that had existed in the South in the early years of the republic had simply drained away, and demands from the North for abolition were viewed as a threat to an entire way of life. There had been, for example, some early support for colonisation schemes (of returning slaves to Africa), but they floundered and withered in the face of the practical difficulties and failures. Though the South experienced the religious revivalism enjoyed by the North after 1830, it did not join in the northern surge for wider reform. Reform in the South meant the unthinkable—tampering with slavery. While the North experienced periodic campaigns of social and political reform (for women, socialism, temperance, organised labour), southerners seemed happy to rest on their enslaving laurels and even mocked what they regarded as the passing political fashions and fads of their northern neighbours. Southern critics denounced abolition as the subversive heir to revolutionary ideas, and from 1830 onwards, largely in response to the rising voice of abolition in the North, that defence took on a sharper and more belligerent tone.

From 1830, the growing opposition in the North to slavery was driven forward by the transformation of religious sentiment, which started in New England. Proliferating congregations of Presbyterians, Congregationalists and Unitarians spawned a 'New Divinity', which became the bedrock of a new, powerful anti-slavery movement. It paralleled a massive increase in following for the Methodist and Baptist churches: by 1850, for example, there were 1.25 million Methodists in the USA. They formed an army of followers who believed that they could achieve salvation by faith and appropriate behaviour on earth. And what better way was available to them than by attacking the national sin and wickedness of slavery itself?[19]

The Baptist Church had its origins in the late seventeenth century, but over the next century, missionaries and their revivalist meetings had spread the faith across the American north-east and westward along the path of migration and settlement. There were upwards of 750,000 Baptists by the mid-nineteenth century.[20] Alongside Congregationalists and Presbyterians, Baptist missionaries created a remarkable religious phenomenon that swept across the USA in the years after 1830. Inspired by some charismatic preachers, a wave of Christian revivalism transformed life in all corners of the Republic.

It was as if the USA was convulsed by a sense of personal and communal sin—and there was a religious crusade afoot to change the nation's ways. It was a campaign that aimed both to renounce personal sin, and to overcome the corruption and sin that had gripped American life in general.

Although 'The Awakening' in the North had spread the belief that slavery was a sin, in the South, theologians and preachers went in the opposite direction, teasing out biblical justifications for slavery and supporting it from their pulpits. Some even argued that to challenge slavery was to challenge God's word. Both sides, *pro* and *con* slavery, dug deep into their faith to sustain their cause. Christian vernacular and imagery, biblical scrutiny, sermons, prayers and hymns—all and more were marshalled to the task of both attacking and defending slavery. At its starkest, both slaves and slave owners found strength and justification for their cause in their faith. In the end, both sides were to go to war convinced that God was on their side.

'The Awakening' had a major impact upon the slaves. Black churches were already well established (most notably in Philadelphia), but the Methodist and Baptist initiative of taking their message directly to the slaves set in train that most powerful of American movements: the emergence of a dissenting voice among armies of black Americans. In the Caribbean, as we have seen, Methodists and Baptists had been the first to bring the transforming qualities of their faith to the slaves. What emerged in the USA was that potent mix already evident in the Caribbean:

black preachers, the Bible (and the slaves' own interpretation of its message), and a physical place where slaves could worship and meet beyond the reach and control of their masters. Above all, here was a message that promised a better life, in this world and the next. In the thirty years before the American Civil War, the voice of enslaved Christians was to prove one of the most galvanising and inspirational elements in the rising denunciation of US slavery.

For their part, slave owners feared slave literacy and warned about slave Christianity: reading, writing, the Bible, gathering to worship, preaching or being preached to— all had an unsettling impact on slaves. They learned, they discussed, they organised and planned, in and around their churches. Enslaved Christianity became not merely a crucible for private and communal worship, but a means to assemble independently of their owners. Black churches, black preachers, black faith and black congregations, all converged to form a potent and critical force in the way the enslaved coped with the world around them. The church also offered hope—hope of a better life both here and in the hereafter—and it enabled slaves to cope with the harsh realities of slave life.

The abolitionists' aim after 1830 was to win support for their belief that slavery was wrong and sinful. Slavery was 'a sin—always, everywhere, and only a sin'. On 1 January 1831, William Lloyd Garrison launched his abolitionist paper the *Liberator*, helping to prompt an evangelical religious revival that was fired by the belief 'that slavery was the most God-defying sin of all'.[21] The *Liberator* quickly attracted a large readership, notably among blacks. Garrison, along with the wealthy abolitionist and social reformer Gerrit Smith and supported by a number of churches, was intent on 'immediate abolition'. The American Anti-Slavery Society (AASS), formed in 1833, was also backed by north-eastern philanthropists and reform sympathisers. All this evolved under the long shadow cast by the slave upheavals in Jamaica and the subsequent move to end slavery in the British colonies. The Jamaican slave revolt—the Baptist War of 1831–2— seriously alarmed Southern slave owners: they looked at Jamaica and concluded that here, once again, was proof—if more were needed after Haiti—that you tampered with slavery at your peril. Jamaica helped to stiffen their resolve to resist the siren calls for black freedom.

The slave owners and planters also felt that economic sense was on their side in the defence against reform. The abolitionist attack on slavery that blossomed in the fertile soil of North American faith could offer little by way of an economic critique of slavery. How could it? How could abolitionists point to the astonishing economic success that was cotton and argue that slavery had had its day, and ought to make way for free labour? Those most closely involved with slavery saw no economic reason to seek an alternative to slave labour, and although southern slave owners found themselves under increased attack after 1830, it was not because slavery was uneconomic.

But the abolitionists had other weapons at their disposal. Now that slavery had been elevated from being a secular and constitutional issue and thrust securely into the heart of American faith, the anti-slavery argument was strengthened and given a new political edge through the personal testimony that emerged in the writings of black abolitionists.[22]

Forty years earlier, British abolition had been greatly enhanced by the voice and writings of a small band of Africans offering personal testimony about slavery. American abolition, on the other hand, had a much more extensive list of former slaves to call on. There were plenty of African-Americans whose experience of slavery added a searing personal quality to abolition gatherings and writings. Frederick Douglass became perhaps the most charismatic presence following his escape from slavery in 1838. An orator of formidable power and presence, Douglass attracted huge crowds, on both sides of the Atlantic, and his restless energy drove forward the slaves' cause throughout the USA (and Britain). Others added their own experiences to the mix: William Wells Brown, Ellen Craft, Henry Bibb, Harriet A. Jacobs, Sojourner Truth and Solomon Northrup. They are only the best-known of a host of black abolitionists. Their writing, speeches and activities formed a rebuke and refutation of many old myths and prejudices about black life. These black voices overturned the slave owners' hackneyed arguments about attainment and achievement, and—just as important—they destroyed the much-advertised ideal of the contented slave. The chorus of black abolition formed a denunciation of everything the slave South represented; a refutation of the very culture of the South itself.

In alliance with the tireless energy of black workers in the Underground Railroad, the irrepressible urge of the slaves to flee served to undermine and contradict old shibboleths of the slave South. Black abolitionists offered a blunt denial of widespread racism throughout the USA. By 1840 US abolition had grown by leaps and bounds, at least in the North, with the formation of hundreds of abolition societies and millions of pieces of abolitionist literature spilling from US presses. Yet this abolitionist clamour seemed to be getting nowhere. Despite numerous crowded abolitionist meetings, the tons of print, the packed abolitionist lectures and the wider public outcry against slavery, and despite the continuing flight of refugee slaves, there was little sign, by the 1840s, that slavery had been weakened or was ready to capitulate.

The slave economy remained strong, the South continued to hold great political sway, and throughout the 1830s and 1840s abolition (despite its northern strength) remained a weak political force in the South. For all its religious strength, it faced opposition in the North, too. There was widespread racism among whites, who were fearful of the economic threat posed by free black workers migrating north; northern mobs regularly threatened abolitionist meetings.[23] There was, moreover, an unwritten agreement among political parties 'that all discussion of slavery must be repressed'. The South embargoed abolitionist literature (as did the Post Office) and for a while Congress refused to accept abolitionist petitions. But one basic question remains puzzling. Why, asks David Brion Davis, was the South so obviously *frightened* of abolition?

Antagonism between North and South was worsened as the US expanded westward in the 1850s, raising the prospect of slavery seeping into new territories. There was rising tension, too, about the threat posed by the fugitive laws to free blacks in the North. And there was periodic outrage at the violent and costly (but entirely legal) dragooning of fugitives from northern states back to slavery in the South, despite the efforts of aggressive crowds trying to prevent it.[24]

In the midst of this mounting social and political turmoil, Harriet Beecher Stowe published *Uncle Tom's Cabin* in 1852. It was a book that had a seismic impact on opinion in both North America and Britain in adding to the religious crusade and in rallying support for black freedom. Within a year, it had sold 300,000 copies in the USA, almost one million in Britain. By 1860 it had sold four million copies, and Stowe had become 'the most famous writer in the world'. The book was, in effect, a sermon against slavery (the author came from an evangelical family) and was sprinkled with biblical references. It proved enormously influential in persuading readers that slavery was sinful and should be abolished. But it was hated and reviled in the South.[25] Slave owners continued to be defiant, and it seemed that nothing short of force could spring the locks that bound the slaves to the land and to their owners.

Many American politicians recognised the need to compromise on the politics of slavery, and accepted that slavery and its political contradictions remained at the heart of American life. Slavery was a political minefield, and politicians trod carefully for fear of triggering an explosion.

This stand-off between the two sides was interrupted by periodic clashes in Congress, with points of friction, disputes, threats of secession and even of war from southern politicians aggrieved by what they deemed to be threats to the slave system.

Through all this, the British remained an issue in the dispute about slavery. Ever since 1776 there had been a residual hostility to Britain. In their turn, British visitors and writers made no bones about their contempt for America's inconsistency about slavery: proclaiming the high principles of 1787, yet enjoying the fruits of a slave economy. Americans felt insulted by British disdain, and their dislike was compounded by massive immigration of Irish people into the USA, carrying with them their own hostility towards the British. It was hardly surprising, then, when the British preached to Americans about abolition, that many Americans tended to see it simply as a disguise for British self-interest. It was just the latest version of British humbug masquerading as high principle. The Americans had other reasons to dislike the British, who refused to pay compensation for fugitive slaves who managed to reach Canada. They also freed slaves who landed on British islands from American ships in distress. When southerners looked at the mounting crises of the sugar industry and the diminishing prosperity of the British Caribbean, they felt justified in their belief that if you tamper with slavery, economic and social gloom will follow. As if to compound southern antipathy, there was mounting evidence that British statesmen were actively promoting an end to slavery the world over. The old deep-seated anti-British feeling in North America was thus revitalised. Perfidious Albion was up to her old tricks and southerners had no trouble denouncing American abolitionists (on their successful visits to Britain) as treasonable agents of the British. For years, it proved difficult for American abolitionism to shake off the accusation that it was a stooge for Britain's devious interests.

The South exercised great influence in Washington, and its power in the Senate would be strengthened if new states were allowed to be slave states. Thus the issue of western expansion became central both to slavery itself and to political power in Washington. Furthermore, the rising population of slaves in border states, notably in Virginia, prompted the encouragement of western migration of slavery—if only to prevent slaves outnumbering whites in older states. Such was the basis of the 'Missouri crisis' of 1820–1: should settlement west of the Mississippi be free or slave? The outcome was notable for hardening divisions between the slave South and the free North. The Missouri Compromise of 1820, which allowed for one new slave state (Missouri) and one new free state (Maine), came at a time of feverish reaction to Denmark Vesey's slave revolt in Charleston and helped to convince the South that slave unrest (supported by free blacks in Washington and elsewhere) was being played upon by northern politicians. Whatever their political differences, southerners had shuffled themselves into a ragged unity against the North, and against any public debate about slavery. Once again, they had reacted much like their contemporaries in the British Caribbean: slave owners of diverse views and standing found unity in stark opposition to abolitionist opponents and to any discussion about slavery and freedom.

Debates in Washington were increasingly bitter and divisive. But it was the Dred Scott decision of the Supreme Court in 1857 that thrust slavery centre-stage of American politics. Dred Scott and his wife Harriet were slaves from Missouri, but living in Illinois; they sued for their freedom in a complex case that reached back to the 1840s. The Supreme Court ruled, by seven to two, that slaves were property, not citizens, and had no right to sue for freedom in a court of law. In the words of Chief Justice Roger B. Taney, slaves had 'no rights a white man need respect'. The judgment also confirmed that Congress had no power to exclude slavery from new territories. In effect, the court ruled the Missouri Compromise of 1820 to be unconstitutional.

The Dred Scott decision was that people of African descent were 'regarded as beings of an inferior order, and altogether unfit to associate with the white race'. It was a legal judgment of the deepest racist hue and it electrified abolitionists and slaves alike. In the words of one abolitionist, the decision was 'the moral assassination of a race'. Slave holders were now free to take their slaves anywhere in the USA and settle.

Abraham Lincoln was only one of many who denounced the decision: 'All the powers of earth seem rapidly combining against him[the slave]. Mammon is after him, ambition follows, and philosophy follows, and the Theology of the day is fast joining the cry. They have him in the prison house.' It was around these issues that Lincoln began to stake out a national political career in the 1850s, placing the question of slavery at the heart of his public politics. When he stood for election, as a Republican Senator for Illinois in 1850, he stressed the centrality of slavery. 'A house divided against itself cannot stand. I believe this government cannot endure, permanently half slave and half free.'[26]

This was *the* great turning point in American history. Lincoln's electoral battle to the Senate faced fierce opposition from an opponent who used the race card mercilessly against him, tapping into popular racism to ridicule Lincoln's views on slavery. In fact, Lincoln was not an abolitionist at this point, and he did not believe in black equality. But he *did* believe that blacks should have equal access to the rights offered by the Declaration of Independence. Although Lincoln was not elected to the Senate, he had become a national figure.

By 1859, North and South were locked in fierce opposition to each other: the South, disturbed by the shadow of slave emancipation elsewhere, the North committed to helping fugitive slaves, and refusing to countenance the consequences of Dred Scott in allowing the expansion of slavery westwards as the US grew. In this increasingly febrile atmosphere, in October of that year John Brown (a volatile abolitionist who had come to regard insurgency as the only way of ending slavery) launched his raid on the federal arsenal at Harpers Ferry. He hoped his attack would ignite a slave revolt. It failed, and Brown was hanged—but he went to the gallows proclaiming biblical justification for his actions. Southerners were deeply shocked when they learned of the widespread northern sympathy and support for Brown. In the subsequent political disputes about slavery, the Democratic Party split, and Lincoln secured the presidential nomination for the Republicans. The presidential election of 1860 was rowdy and divisive, and the result was a nightmare for the South. Newly elected President Lincoln and his party were committed to the principle that slavery was a moral outrage, but now they had the power of federal authority to confront the slave-owning South.

South Carolina was the first state to take the step that many southerners had been threatening for years: they withdrew from the Union. Six others followed to form the Confederate States of America. On 12 April 1861, when forces fired on Fort Sumter, a Union position controlling Charleston harbour, the Civil War had started.

Within a single lifetime, this astonishing country had emerged from a loose collection of colonies into a thriving nation, with an expansive economy and a booming population. As it looked westward to the boundless land of the frontier, the future of the USA seemed bountiful beyond imagination. Yet here it was, at war with itself. North and South viewed each other with deep distaste: each thought the other to be the denial of all they admired and held dear. And each was preparing to fight a war, at the heart of which lay the question of slavery. Lincoln's fervent hope was to hold the Union together, but the war that followed tore it apart.

• • •

Recent scholars have taken to writing of the Civil War as an 'abolition war'. Yet on the eve of the war, in 1860, US slavery was more valuable and important than ever, and not solely to the South. The slaves' total value—calculated at $3.5 billion—made them forty-eight times more valuable than the entire spending of the federal government. Five years later, when they emerged from the Civil War as free people, they had lost their monetary value. US slave owners found their most prized possessions rendered worthless.

The Civil War proved to be the first 'total war' in modern times, inflicting death and destruction on a catastrophic scale and affecting all corners of American life. The human cost was appalling. The Union army of 2.1 million suffered 360,000 deaths, the Confederate army 260,000. One-fifth of the 200,000 African-Americans in the Union forces died. On both sides, disease killed as many men as combat. The conflict was marked by a litany of acts of savagery on both sides, culminating (and decided by) the scorched-earth march from Atlanta to Savannah in 1864, led by the Union general William T. Sherman. Long after the war had ended, reminders of the war's profound and long-lasting damage lived on in the huge armies of wounded and disabled survivors.

Americans who had, before 1860, inveighed against slavery as a national sin, viewed the wartime sufferings as the Lord's way of cleansing a sinful nation. Even Lincoln hinted as much: 'Surely he intends some great good to follow this mighty convulsion.'[27] The most striking impact of the Civil War was its enormous destructiveness—and the most important destruction of all was the ending of slavery. It dawned on many in the North that emancipation must become a key war aim for the Union: only freedom could undermine the South's wellbeing based on slavery.

In his public life in the 1850s, Abraham Lincoln had recognised slavery as a great injustice, but he had not supported emancipation. Struggling to keep the Union together during the war— he hesitated (he even considered colonisation a solution). Yet on 1 January 1863, while the war had still two years left to run, this same man issued the Emancipation Proclamation. He had finally accepted that black freedom was vital to the cause, and more than three million people were freed, at least on paper, by the proclamation. It became clear, however, that only military victory could secure both the survival of the Union—and the freedom of those slaves.

There can be no doubt about the slaves' attitude towards the war. They voted with their feet, leaving the plantations in droves while the war continued. They travelled in families and in groups; they took to boats to carry them to northern ports; others loaded their meagre possessions onto carts and wagons and headed for freedom. The streams of fugitive slaves continued to pass through border towns on their way north. The old Underground Railroad was effectively bypassed and rendered superfluous by the wave of assistance that carried along refugee slaves, leaving slavery behind them. Slaves no longer had to worry about the dangers of flight—they travelled in the open, during daylight hours. Anyone trying to apprehend a fugitive 'would be a fool'. Where possible, the slaves crossed to the Union lines. (More slaves fled across than had escaped in the previous thirty years.) Most were simply seeking freedom and refuge beyond the conflict. The slaves' flight was deeply distrusted by the Confederacy because the fugitives often took with them invaluable logistical and military information, which they passed on to the Union army. In places, the arrival of Union troops gave slaves the opportunity to wreak vengeance on their owners' property.

At first the Union army found the refugee slaves a problem; black volunteers were not allowed to join their ranks and some were even returned to the owners, but, soon, the fugitives became military 'contraband'. Eventually, with Lincoln's encouragement, black volunteers were accepted as auxiliary workers (cooks and the like) before being allowed to enrol as soldiers. Fifteen black soldiers and eight black sailors won the highest military award, the Congressional Medal of Honor, and black regiments secured lasting fame for their exceptional gallantry. One-half of the black 54th Massachusetts Regiment died in the attack on Fort Wagner in 1863. Black military valour and assistance clearly helped to undermine slavery itself, as 150,000 joined the Union army as willing combatants, and 70,000 died in warfare and from disease. The Confederacy, by contrast, put slaves to work as labourers—but more and more of them simply melted away, intent on ending their own bondage. The Confederate army only agreed to accept black troops in 1865—far too late to affect the outcome of the war. Slavery simply crumbled in the course of the conflict.

Yet the military outcome remained uncertain until Sherman's breakthrough in November to December 1864. Even then, Congress continued to struggle with the question of slavery before finally passing the Thirteenth Amendment on 31 January 1865. On 14 April, in his second Inaugural Address, Lincoln was unsparing about the role of slavery in the country's history— and in the unfolding of the Civil War. It was a remarkable acknowledgement of the debt owed by the USA to its enslaved people, referring to 'all the wealth piled by the bondsman's two hundred and fifty years of unrequited toil'.[28] These words proved to be Lincoln's own memorial. He was assassinated three weeks later. Lincoln's address was as perceptive and poignant an account as any by subsequent historians of the centrality of slavery in the making of the USA.

Full, formal freedom granted to the slaves by the Thirteenth Amendment in 1865 was legal recognition of what they had been struggling towards since time out of mind. The defeated South, however, had lost everything it had fought for. The British had given their slave holders £20 million compensation for the loss of their slaves: American slave owners received nothing.

Southerners gradually drifted into a strange mood of cultural amnesia, coming to regard their defeat as a result of the North's numerical and industrial power. In time, the South looked back to its pre-war Golden Age, but in doing so it forgot the centrality of slavery in the entire story. A popular southern culture evolved— ultimately secured and propagated in movies of the twentieth century (and even shored up by a number of eminent historians)—which effectively erased slavery from the historical narrative of the coming of the Civil War. Today, it is difficult to grasp how this happened, but, bit by bit, slavery was marginalised in the southern understanding of the origins of the Civil War. The historical disputes continue, of course, but today slavery and emancipation are accepted as the essential elements in provoking and resolving the Civil War. Equally—and no less important—without that war, slavery in the USA would likely have continued to provide the economic rewards that had inspired its initial establishment in North America two centuries earlier.

The slaves had been basic to the remarkable success of the USA in the first half of the nineteenth century, but they were also the country's most obvious victims. Yet they had struggled against their bondage throughout, subverting it as best they could, denouncing it from first to last, campaigning against it and abandoning it whenever possible. Finally, during the conflict itself, they fled from the plantations in their thousands. Their mass flight helped to undermine the vital prosperity the South required to fight the war. Slaves' defiance was corroding slavery itself: the system that had been built on their own sweat over the past two centuries. Four million former slaves were now free people—but their freedom was to be beset by a multitude of problems, and the shadow of slavery was to lie heavy on the subsequent history of the USA. In 1865, however, freedom itself seemed enough. Here at last was something to celebrate.

# 8

## The End of Slavery
## in the Spanish Empire

SPAIN HAD BEEN the first European country to introduce Africans into the Americas, and Spanish colonies clung to slavery longer and more tenaciously than all others lands apart from the former Portuguese colony of Brazil. Like all European colonial powers in the Americas, imperial Spain made great use of African slaves, although, unlike others, it did not become a major Atlantic slave trader. Instead Spain relied on other nations' trading and maritime expertise for its supply of Africans.

Spain conquered, or claimed, vast areas of South America and the Caribbean islands. 'New Spain' embraced Puerto Rico, Cuba, Jamaica, Mexico and Central America, and Spanish Peru consisted of the entirety of South America with the exception of Brazil. Slavery spread unevenly across so huge a landscape. Spain's mainland American colonies absorbed slightly more than a quarter of a million Africans. At the most southerly tip, Río de la Plata, only 67,000 Africans arrived as slaves. In the Caribbean, 26,700 Africans went to Puerto Rico, but by far the largest number—more than three-quarters of a million—were taken to Cuba, most of them during that island's boom years in the nineteenth century. Compared to the millions poured into Brazil, these numbers seem small, but this does not diminish the importance of slavery to Spanish colonisation in its American empire.

Unlike Portugal and Britain, Spain developed only a marginal role both on the continent of Africa and in the Atlantic slave trade. Partly as a result, it was widely thought both that slavery was peripheral to Spanish history, and that the Spanish version was also more benign than other slave systems. (This was a view sustained by twentieth-century Spanish politics.) It is now broadly accepted that this analysis was wrong and, on the contrary, African slaves were basic both to the establishment and to the development of Spanish America. Equally, Spanish slavery was no less harsh than slavery elsewhere. Older arguments that imperial law and church practices served to temper Spanish slavery have been replaced by the awareness that slavery was propelled by the dictates of plantation labour. And that involved the harsh exploitation of African slaves, especially in Spain's sugar and coffee industries. Spain's initial slave system in the Caribbean faded as Spain turned its attention away from the islands and towards the rich potential of Mexico, Central America and the wealth of the Andes, but it revived in the nineteenth century.

Although the numbers of Africans taken to Mexico and Central America were small compared to other regions of the Americas, the impact of slave labour was vital across the region. The background was the disaster that befell indigenous Indian populations in the wake of the European invasions. The impact of alien diseases imported by Europeans was catastrophic, with native peoples suffering massive population losses: in places, upwards of three-quarters of their pre-conquest levels. Indeed population collapse seems 'to have been the rule across Spanish America in the aftermath of conquest'.[1] From the first, Spanish settlers had needed labour, but Indian people fled, fell ill or died.

Long before the European invasions, forms of slavery had existed among indigenous people of the Americas, and the Spanish conquerors used Indian slaves on an enormous scale across Mexico and Central America, developing its own important slave trade in Indian people. Hernán Cortés, who led the Spanish colonisation of Mexico in the early sixteenth century, himself owned more than five hundred slaves in his mines and for sugar cultivation. This enforced movement of Indian slaves had its own dire consequences. The trade from Honduras and

Nicaragua, for example, was a major factor in the massive drop in the local population there. Wherever Spain used Indian slaves, it was characterised by a savage brutality. Indeed, the excesses of this system caught the attention of Bartholomé de las Casas, the Bishop of Chiapas, who later bore the official title 'Protector of the Indians'. Partly because of his efforts, a new law of 1542 outlawed the enslavement of Indians, which, although it was widely ignored (especially in frontier regions), hastened the drive to seek alternative labour—and that meant African slaves. But who was to deliver the Africans?

Spain had initially acquired African slaves from Portuguese traders through *Asiento de negro* agreements—in which the Crown gave the traders a monopoly on the supply of African slaves to its territories—following the unification of Spain and Portugal in 1580 and the development of the Portuguese Atlantic slave trade. Portugal shipped Africans to Spanish America, mainly to Veracruz, from Portugal's main African slave-trading base at Luanda in Angola. By the time that agreement ended in 1640, 70,000 African slaves had been transported. Aftcr 1640, the Atlantic trade opened up to other European trading nations, and increasing numbers of Africans arrived in Spanish America via other slave-trading entrepôts. The British, for example, transhipped large numbers of Africans to Spanish

America via Jamaica. The changes *within* the slave population of Spanish America changed the slave trade. A rough balance emerged between enslaved men and women, with the result that the slave populations of Spanish America increased by natural growth, rather than via the importation of yet more Africans. Long before slave societies in the Caribbean and North America began to increase naturally, Spain's mainland slave system could survive without the Atlantic slave trade.

In the hundred years following the Spanish conquests in the first half of the sixteenth century, almost one-half of all the Africans landed in Spanish America were transported to Mexico. There they were used in every conceivable enterprise. They worked at a huge range of jobs in the urban areas that quickly evolved in Spain's empire. Slaves worked in domestic service, as street vendors, as porters and in all forms of urban tasks. They also worked in the sugar fields and sugar mills, though sugar in Mexico and Central America was a small-scale industry, primarily for the local market. Slaves also worked alongside free labourers on cattle ranches and in crop cultivation, and formed an important labouring presence in Mexico's textile workshops. More brutally, they were used in Mexico's important mining industries (notably in silver). But wherever they lived and worked, the enslaved had to devise means of coping with life as slaves. That involved the development of complex forms of resistance.

African slaves were very rarely a dominant presence. By the late seventeenth century, local-born (creole) slaves outnumbered Africans; a century later, most slaves in mainland Spanish America were not only mixed race (rather than African), but were now hugely outnumbered by the massive expansion of free people of mixed race.

Part of the reason for the number of freed slaves and their mixed-race descendants was that manumission in Spanish America was more commonplace than in the slave colonies of other European powers. In addition, by marrying free women (of colour, or Indian women) many slaves married out of slavery—a process which led to a rapid 'lightening' of the overall population. These were fundamental demographic changes, which made slavery become a much less striking, less visible feature of life across Mexico and Central America by the late eighteenth century.

The massive expansion of the local population created large numbers of free labourers, so more and more masters rid themselves of their slaves. Many slaves simply took matters into their own hands—and fled. The end result was that slavery was simply withering away and by 1810 there were perhaps only 10,000 slaves in Mexico, and only half that number throughout Central

America. Where it lingered on, slaves sought to escape (many in the north of the country headed for the USA), while others joined the fight for Mexican independence. Indeed, throughout Spain's colonies in the early nineteenth century, there were important links between the fight for independence from Spain and the campaign against slavery. How could a conflict that turned on questions of colonial liberty, freedom and rights *not* have consequences for slavery? In Mexico, independence in 1821 was the death knell for slavery, which was finally abolished in 1824, though by then it had effectively vanished, and its people had blended into the population at large.[2]

As Spanish conquistadors had moved south, along the Pacific coast, fighting and settling as they destroyed the Incas, they were accompanied by African slaves. Here again, in the wake of Spanish settlement, the decline of the indigenous populations created a need for an alternative labour force. To work the mines and the newly established plantations, and to safeguard the much-diminished Indian peoples, Spain encouraged the importation of African slaves. After all, Spain was already using African slaves (on a small scale) in the Caribbean. A regular traffic developed, with Africans landing in Cartagena and thence onto Lima. From there, Africans fanned out across the enormity of Spanish settlements. When, by the late eighteenth century, the British and French had come to dominate the North Atlantic slave trade, Africans were being shipped to Spanish America via Caribbean islands. It was along these immense sea routes, followed by protracted and exhausting overland journeys across South America, that Africans were settled in what became Argentina, Chile, Peru, Colombia, Bolivia, Paraguay, Venezuela and Ecuador. It was an astonishing enforced diaspora of African people.

African slaves worked and lived alongside indigenous peoples, and the mixed-race descendants of Indians, Europeans—and Africans. And though they did not dominate the local labour force, wherever they settled African slaves were regarded as essential: in mining and in various branches of agriculture. The largest single slave owner in Spanish America was the Catholic Church: Jesuits were notable for the huge numbers employed on their extensive properties.[3] Spain faced the persistent problem of how to control their slaves in South America. This became a particular problem when significant numbers settled in urban areas, many living away from their owners. One regular ploy was to tempt slaves with the prospects of emancipation, hoping to secure loyalty and hard work by the promise of freedom. The Catholic

Church also played its part in maintaining slave stability via the social organisations they formed for slaves, and by specific instruction at worship, all aimed at maintaining the delicate balance between master and man across Spanish America. When all failed, when slaves rebelled or flared up, Spanish slave owners resorted to the universal armoury of slave holders across the Americas: informal and legally sanctioned repression and violence. Whippings, banishment, executions— the full array of slave society's punishments were available when slaves in Spanish America stepped out of line.

One recurring fear of Spanish authorities was that slaves and local Indians might join forces against them. In practice that rarely happened. In fact, slaves were frequently used to suppress troubles and uprisings among Indians, while for their part, Indians seldom went out of their way to help the slaves. Both sides seemed to exist in mutual distrust of each other and saw no reason to unite to confront their common oppressors. Things were different at a social level. African and Indian peoples mingled, settled down with and married each other, adopted each other's languages and customs, and produced a variety of creole cultures that were a complex blend of Indian, African and European.

Like other European slave empires, Spain's imperial capital dictated important features of colonial slavery. When the Bourbons determined to restore Spain's fading power in the mid-eighteenth century, they tried to revitalise the colonial economies. An obvious target was the Jesuits, whose colonial wealth (including their slaves) was absorbed by the Crown. This was accompanied by a major renewal of importations of African slaves by the opening up of the Atlantic trade to outsiders. With a more open slave-trading market, substantial numbers of Africans began to arrive—notably in the Caribbean, in Cuba, Santo Domingo and Puerto Rico. This was to become important after the collapse of the Haitian sugar economy and the expansion of Spanish sugar production in the early nineteenth century. These reforms by the Spanish Crown effectively extended and revitalised colonial slavery, with major repercussions throughout Spanish America. But the Crown also began to sell off its own slaves, who were often moved huge distances to new owners and workplaces in far-flung regions. This, mirroring the experience of other slave societies in the Americas, involved the widespread break-up of slave families. The much-hated and destructive internal dispersal of slaves was accompanied by the arrival of Africans, fresh from the Atlantic slave ships, all with their own agonies of enslavement and prolonged upheaval. Spain's colonies thus became home to deeply disaffected slaves: many torn from families in distant parts of the colony, and Africans wrenched from their various African homelands. It was a recipe for trouble.

Not surprisingly, slave trouble flared across Spanish America, with uprisings, resistance and general slave belligerence taxing Spanish colonial life throughout the late eighteenth century. The Spanish Crown hoped to stabilise the situation by imposing the *Código Negro* (Black Code) in 1789. Unlike earlier codes, this was an attempt to reform African slavery throughout the Spanish Empire, stipulating that masters should provide adequate food and clothing, and imposing working regulations—which allowed days off. Masters were now expected to have slaves instructed in the Catholic faith. New restrictions were placed on masters; they could only punish a slave with a maximum of twenty-five lashes, for instance.

The slave owners tended to view the new code as yet another attempt to impose Bourbon absolutism on the colonies. Slaves, of course, viewed it differently. From what they gleaned via angry gossip among their owners, it seemed clear to them that efforts were being made, in distant European palaces, to safeguard slaves' interests against the resistant wishes of slave owners.[4] The idea took root in the slaves' minds that monarchy was on their side.

Some of the problems facing the Spanish

Empire in the late eighteenth century had their origins in British imperial issues. The American War of Independence and the loss of Britain's North American colonies created a volatile problem across the enslaved Americas. For slave owners everywhere that conflict was all the more worrying because both sides, American and British, had used slaves and ex-slaves to bolster their military strength (a pattern repeated in South America in the 1820s). The USA confirmed its commitment to slavery in 1787, and especially after 1800 and the rise of King Cotton.[5] These initial concerns about slavery were as nothing compared to the tumultuous events that followed the French Revolution of 1789. In common with all other slave colonies, the Spanish Empire was shaken to the core by the revolutionary tremors and ideals flowing first from Paris and then from Haiti. The language of freedom, already promoted and advocated by Enlightenment writers before 1789, was quickly translated into Spanish.

Slaves in Spanish America, like their contemporaries elsewhere, were soon alert to the revolution in St-Domingue (especially those in neighbouring Santo Domingo). It was news that exacerbated local frictions and proved to be the start of prolonged slave troubles for Spain. It also formed the origins of the campaign for colonial independence. Napoleon's invasion of the Iberian peninsula in 1807 threw both Spain and Portugal into turmoil. The Portuguese court fled to exile in Brazil—escorted by the Royal Navy—where they stayed until 1822, and where they presided over a booming slave economy. The Spanish monarchs, Charles IV and his heir, Ferdinand VII, were less fortunate and were imprisoned by Napoleon. The French occupation of Spain unleashed a savage war for liberation, which lasted from 1807 to 1814 (and is best recalled perhaps in Francisco Goya's series of prints, *The Disasters of War*). To resist the French occupation and to devise a new system of government in the absence of the King, the Spanish Cortes were convened, first in Seville, then in Cadiz. With deputies from the Spanish colonies in attendance, the Cortes opened up a wider debate about the links between Spain and her colonies. The absence of the monarch also raised the fundamental question of political legitimacy. In Caracas, Buenos Aires and Cartagena local elites declared that political power had, in the absence of the monarch, devolved to them. This marked the start of the struggle for independence, and the break-up of the massive Spanish Empire in the Americas, which in its turn was to lead to the end of slavery.

The anti-colonial wars, inspired by the revolutions first of 1776 and then of 1789, pointed the way towards black freedom. Slaves in North America had fled their bondage to join the

British, in anticipation of freedom. (In the event, it proved a bitter-sweet decision, with thousands shipped onwards—free but impoverished—to Nova Scotia, to London and some to Sierra Leone.) But the Haitian revolution had put an end to slavery there, and thereafter, across the Americas, slaves and slave owners were left in no doubt that attacking European colonialism was to attack slavery.

We need to note, however, that Spanish slavery was relatively small-scale. In 1820, there were about 250,000 slaves across Spain's American empire; the most condensed area was Venezuela, where the number of slaves totalled 87,000. By comparison, the slave population of the Caribbean was 1.3 million, with 1.5 million in the US South and 1.2 million in Brazil. Attacking Spanish slavery was an easier, more manageable target than the massive slave populations elsewhere in the Americas. What undermined Spanish slavery were the wars for colonial independence in the 1810s and 1820s.[6] In Caracas, Simón Bolívar led the charge to independence from 1810, banning the slave trade (partly to keep the abolitionist British on their side) but accepting the existence of slavery itself. The restoration of the Spanish monarch, Ferdinand VII, in 1814 after the defeat of the French, led, however, to an imperial counter-attack and a war against colonial independence. Spain had some temporary success in its military efforts against colonial rebels in Chile, Peru, Gran Colombia (consisting primarily of present-day Colombia and Panama) and Venezuela. But as the wars dragged on, both sides needed to find manpower. Just as in Haiti earlier, both royalists and patriots turned to slaves to bolster their military ranks.

In the subsequent wars of independence, both sides promised freedom to the slaves involved in return for military service. Recruiting slaves to fight for an ideal—colonial independence—was clearly fraught with dangers. A fight for freedom was no mere abstraction for enslaved soldiers— as Simón Bolívar himself recognised: 'It seems to me madness that a revolution for freedom expects to maintain slavery.'[7] Though other forces were also at work edging Spain's slaves towards freedom, warfare and colonial independence proved corrosive of Spanish colonial slavery.

The fierce arguments about slavery and the slave trade taking place in Spain were soon reported in the colonies. Slaves inevitably learned that their fate was being discussed, but in what was, by then, a common pattern, what they heard was garbled and inaccurate—but always tempting. Many simply believed that Spain had freed them, but that freedom was being withheld by colonial officials and planters. Officials in Puerto Rico and Cuba, for instance, reported numerous examples of local slaves openly discussing—and even celebrating—their freedom. The truth was painfully different.

The new Spanish Constitution of Cadiz in 1812 had confirmed the importance of colonial slavery. Under pressure from Cuban planters, all criticism of slavery and the slave trade was suppressed. (Cuba was on the cusp of a massive expansion of slave-cultivated sugar.) The Constitution specifically excluded Africans and their descendants from citizenship, and strengthened Spanish control and power over the slave colonies. Large sections of the population—touched by African heritage—were excluded from a raft of political and social rights. Spain was building a rod for its own imperial back by driving alienated colonial classes into the company of the slaves. Both sides could see no future in continuing colonial Spanish rule. The independence movement across Spanish America now appealed to a majority of local people— slaves and people of colour.[8]

In the years after independence, the new South American republics legislated against slavery. In Chile and Mexico, where it had already declined substantially, it was ended immediately. Where it remained important (Venezuela, Colombia, Peru and parts of what became Argentina), slavery lingered on into the 1850s. In places, slavery remained resistant, and some independent governments even reneged on their promises of slave freedom. Even slave trading continued in some areas, with Africans infiltrated over the borders from Brazil. Some Spanish American slave owners managed to resist emancipation; often they proved too strong, too politically powerful, too tenacious in their control of slaves to relinquish and concede black freedom. For many slaves, full freedom had to wait a full generation after the wars of independence. But wherever we look, there we find slaves taking matters into their own hands. Ex-soldiers and their families demanded their freedom. Others simply fled. Some rose up and some were even able to purchase their own freedom. In Colombia, sympathetic friends provided money for slaves to buy themselves out of slavery. Where land was abundant, ex-slaves simply squatted and made it their own, while the anonymity of growing towns naturally attracted slaves anxious to escape; they simply walked away from bondage and blended into the wider labouring community.[9]

Warfare was the *coup de grâce* for slavery in Latin America. The independence wars against Spain, and later the conflicts *between* Latin American nations, unleashed violence which loosened the bonds between masters and slaves, and enabled slaves to shake themselves free. Most disruptive of all, slaves joined the fighting as an escape route from slavery. (It is surely revealing that so many risked the dangers of combat rather than remain as slaves.) People who had been combatants, especially for the cause of colonial freedom, were unwilling to return to the world of slavery when the fighting stopped. What had happened in South America in the early nineteenth century was a reprise, across the immensity of Spanish America, of the pattern that had unfolded in Haiti. What had emerged was a potent social and political mix: of anti-slavery ideals (derived originally from the revolutionary turmoil in France and her colonies) and the urge towards independence from Spain.

Throughout this entire story in Spanish America there lurked the presence and influence of the British, lending support to local abolitionists, applying diplomatic muscle to new and inexperienced states, and making commercial and naval threats when necessary. The British approach to the new South American republics was simple, often brutal and sometimes illegal, but it worked—and helped to destabilise slavery in South America. It sapped the will of slave owners to cling to a declining system. The last Spanish country on the mainland to abandon slavery was Paraguay—forced to do so by Brazil in the war in 1869.[10]

A fear that haunted slave owners everywhere from their very first settlements in the Americas was the danger posed by armed and resistant slaves. Yet the South American conflicts found both sides recruiting slaves to their cause. For slave holders and those seeking to maintain slavery, arming slaves involved much more than simply bolstering their military ranks. It was a step fraught with dangers. Armed slaves, their defiance more focused and disciplined by the rigours of military command, posed very great risks. Who knows what organised and disciplined armed slaves might do? Yet in the revolutions that eventually destroyed Spain's American empire, both sides (Spain and the revolutionary independence movements) had turned to slaves for military manpower, despite both sides knowing that the slaves would recognise the significance for their own condition. For the slaves, freedom from a colonial power was little different from escaping from an oppressive slave owner.

Many South American slave holders dug in, hoping to cling to their source of labour. But they faced growing resistance from the slaves themselves, who fled, notably to the relative safety of generally welcoming cities. Some cities even held lotteries that slaves might enter and win their freedom; others set up special funds for slaves to use to buy freedom. Throughout the new South American republics, abolition established itself as a major political issue; the more liberal a local party, the more likely it was to advocate slave freedom. The wars against Spain had spawned a broad ideology of freedom: freedom from Spain, freedom from the traditional world of social privilege, and freedom from the old tyranny of racial hierarchies. A sense of 'racial harmony' had been at the heart of the independence conflicts and, as Bolivar had intimated, in the wake of South American independence it proved increasingly difficult to justify slavery.[11]

Travellers in the Americas were struck by the sharp contrast between the South American republics and the US South. While cotton strengthened the growing power of US slave holders, the South American republics were travelling in a different direction. Having set out to be independent, freed from the shackles of imperial Spain, they were anxious to establish freedom for all their people. Local slave owners were fighting a rear-guard (and a losing) action. Slavery everywhere was being undermined by the politics and conflicts of independence, by the ending of the Atlantic slave trade and, crucially, by the actions of the slaves themselves—by their recalcitrance, their flight and their open defiance.

The South American republics were also distinguished from North America by their growing attachment to racial equality. Although the pattern was uneven, the republics emerged from the wars generally anxious to cleanse themselves of the stains of the old regime. That meant an affirmation of racial equality. With some notable exceptions, the language of fraternity entered the political vernacular of the hemisphere. The major exceptions were Spain's colonies in the Caribbean.

In Cuba and Puerto Rico, slavery and racial inequality not only survived, but, thanks to a massive revival of sugar and tobacco plantations, thrived as never before. Cuban sugar (and slavery) were sustained by major US investments, and the slave-grown Cuban produce flowed into the expanding consumer market of North America. It was a matter of great concern to Spanish and British abolitionists that, despite their best efforts, slavery flourished in those islands.

This new Cuban slave system was also a modernised industry. The first Cuban railway lines, for example, were built in 1837 to link Havana to the nearby sugar plantations. These new transport systems encouraged a major expansion of sugar cultivation, linking plantations to large central factories for sugar production, thence to the ports for export. Yet in this same period of modernisation, Cuban slave owners worked their slave labour force harder than ever, augmenting their gangs by bringing in enormous numbers of slaves via internal and coastal slave routes, where conditions often replicated the miseries of the Atlantic crossings. Sugar plantations in Puerto Rico were on nothing like the scale of Cuba's (or Brazil's), and when the Atlantic trade ended, planters there were able to force an impoverished local peasantry onto sugar estates in conditions that looked unnervingly like slavery. The centre of slavery in Spanish America was now Cuba. And it was increasingly dominated by Africans.

Cuban slavery had already developed its own distinct features. There was, for example, an important tradition in the island of slaves buying their own freedom, and they had the right to register their price with an official and make a down payment, becoming *coartados*: slaves en route to freedom. They could even demand the right to change owners. Cuban slaves had their own long-established political, religious and military organisations, which were often based on African and ethnic links. These established customs clashed, in the nineteenth century, with the tightly managed disciplines of Cuba's new plantations and they were also disrupted by the large-scale arrival of new African slaves. In 1812 these frictions came to a head with the discovery of an island-wide slave plot intended to end slavery. It was led by José Antonio Aponte, who may have been spurred on by the growing colonial mistreatment of those of African descent following the arrival of mass numbers of new

African slaves. He was a free man of colour who, like his father and grandfather, belonged to one of the Yoruba-based mutual aid societies (*cabildos de nación*) famous for enabling Africans to enjoy traditional African social rituals. Such social gatherings were the perfect opportunity for assembling—and plotting. Aponte added an extra, unusual ingredient to this potentially disruptive mix: he distributed a book of pictures of Haitian revolutionary figures and monarchs thought to be sympathetic to the slaves.[12] For slave owners, there seemed to be no escape from the shadow of the years of revolution, from memories of Haiti and the ever-present worry about slave insurgency.

The Aponte rebellion—more a series of revolts and plots than a single attempted revolution—involved slaves and free people of colour who sought an end to slavery and to Spanish colonial rule. Revolts flared across Cuba, but especially in the west of the island, home of the new sugar industry. They were suppressed with characteristic violence—Aponte was captured, hanged and beheaded, and his severed head was displayed outside his house as a warning. But the rebellion proved merely the start of a succession of slave upheavals. The problem was located in the island's booming sugar industry.

The massive levels of Africans arriving

in Cuba transformed the island in the early nineteenth century. Although Cuba's slaves were not restricted to the sugar plantations, it was the emergence of a revitalised sugar industry that fuelled the expansion of Cuban slavery. In 1774 there had been 44,000 slaves on the island. That had risen to 83,000 by 1792. By 1827, however, the slave population stood at 287,000—and it grew to 324,000 in 1846. At mid-century almost half of Cuba's population was enslaved. By then a third of all Cuban slaves worked in sugar, overwhelmingly in the west of the island. (By contrast, Puerto Rico's slave population—again dominated by sugar was only 46,923 in 1854.) [13] Between 1800 and 1866, more than 700,000 Africans were landed in Cuba, and the British were right to see the slave trade as the lifeblood of Cuba's slave system.[14]

Thanks to these massive African arrivals, slavery strengthened its grip in Cuba, despite a number of abolition treaties signed between Spain and Britain (1817, 1835, 1845), all of which were effectively ignored by Spain. The surviving Spanish Caribbean slave colonies were isolated, and Cuban sugar planters developed that laager mentality so familiar throughout the slave islands in the eighteenth century, fearing both revolt by their own slaves and the largely unsympathetic attitude of the imperial homeland. Neighbouring islands had now turned their back on slavery and were not to be trusted either. Both Haiti and Jamaica seemed to Cuban slave owners like enemies at the gate, while, to the north, the growing power of the USA (and the rise of abolition sentiment there from the 1830s) cast an abolitionist shadow across the entire region. There were even fears that southern US planters and their allies were contemplating a military takeover of Cuba to add to their beleaguered world of slave owners. Geographically more distant, but even more troubling because more intrusive, were the British, led by an aggressively abolitionist Foreign Office and the Royal Navy, both nibbling away at Spain's slave trade.

Following the death of Ferdinand VII in 1833, Spanish politicians turned their back on earlier concessions granted to Cuba, and determined to rule their colony in a more draconian fashion. Caribbean representatives were removed from parliament, and the Spanish Captain-General of Cuba was granted new powers to rule the island as he saw fit. The pretext was fear of Haitian-like revolt. Colonial government and sugar planters lived in a climate of anxiety, and the slightest hint or rumour of threatened slave insurrection— or invasion from Haiti—was promptly relayed back to Madrid.

The shadow of Haiti produced some confusing effects in Cuba. While it clearly inspired hope and optimism among slaves everywhere, it also served to worsen their oppression, because slave holders and their political supporters regularly used the Haitian example as a justification to control the slaves harshly, and to punish any slave resistance with severity. Most of Madrid's efforts to ameliorate colonial slavery via new laws and codes were deflected by Cuba's planters and their friends, who preferred to impose their own rules and punishments. And that involved the violence and arbitrary behaviour towards slaves familiar throughout the history of American slavery. Their concerns were exacerbated by the inexorable increase in Africans arriving in Cuba. Like their counterparts in Brazil and the US South, Cuba's old colonial order was worried that Africans would not only become numerically dominant but would rise to social and political dominance. [15] But who were behind the African arrivals? The people who feared the Africans were the very group insisting that the sugar industry could not survive without them.

Cuba's slaves, meanwhile, instead of bene-fiting from the largely ignored reforms from Madrid, found themselves on the receiving end of an increasingly heavy-handed and brutal management by sugar planters and their friends. Cuba in the early nineteenth century was looking more and more like the sugar islands of the eighteenth century: plantation economies that seemed to thrive on severe management of the labour force. Plantation violence was commonplace, with murders of hated managers and suicides among desperate slaves. The verdict of one prominent planter was, 'their state of servitude should be considered as the main cause of their suicides'. Small-scale slave uprisings regularly broke out on plantations, often led by Africans, but wider conspiracies were more threatening.[16]

As the nineteenth century advanced, slave insurgency in Cuba 'became larger, more frequent, and more sophisticated'. There were more Cuba revolts 'than any other place in the Atlantic world'.[17] And they broke out in the sugar region where Africans were arriving in such large numbers. Those rebellions were essentially African, and many of the rebel leaders were from the recently overthrown bellicose Oyo Empire in West Africa. In 1825 (Guamacaro), 1833 (Guanajay) and twice in 1843 (Bemba and La Guanábana), slave revolts were led by slaves from the old Oyo Empire. It was clear enough to contemporaries—especially to sugar planters— that slave resistance was African, and it would continue as long as the slave ships delivered fresh batches to the island.

The simmering discontent among Africans came to a head in 1843–4 in the revolt of La Escalera. The rebellion involved slaves, free people of colour and whites (with support from

271

British abolitionists), and began with a series of slave uprisings in 1843 in the sugar region east of Havana. A plot for a much wider rebellion was betrayed, prompting savage reprisals, with hundreds of suspects tied to ladders and mercilessly whipped. Today, the La Escalera revolt is viewed as the most serious of slave revolts in Cuba's history, though it was more a collection of outbursts that were given a more sinister form by panic-stricken authorities anxious to curb slave unrest.[18] It was crushed with a violence that shocked even contemporaries accustomed to such behaviour.

The cruelty involved and such repeated violent denials of Cuban slave demands were glaringly at odds with the progress in Spain's former colonies in South America. And that may provide a clue. Having lost its mainland empire, Spain (whatever the pressures from slaves and abolitionist friends at large—notably the British) was not willing to concede in Puerto Rico and Cuba. Spanish rule became increasingly despotic, slaves' lives more harshly managed and controlled—and all the while, tens of thousands of disaffected Africans continued to arrive in the island to keep the planters happy.

The tensions in Cuba were accentuated by the fiction, played out in Spain, that the islands were part of Spain and that their residents were progressing to becoming full Spanish citizens.

Madrid viewed the colonies as provinces and their populations as 'Spaniards who would one day enjoy the same political and civil rights'. This prospect, however, was not offered to slaves, nor even to free people of colour: as their fellow Cubans edged closer to full Spanish citizenship, slaves were totally excluded from the political bargain. Here, there was a substantial slice of the population who could have little optimism that their future lay with Spain. This was to have the major consequence, as it had in the South American independence movements, of rallying people in favour of independence. Spain had effectively lost the support of the slaves and of the free people of colour.[19] The outcome was that supporters of independence from Spain also supported freedom for the slaves. Even people who were uncertain about black freedom came to recognise that Cuban independence would inevitably involve slave emancipation.

Serious discussion about slavery and emancipation developed in Madrid in the late 1860s, prompted by the American Civil War and the end of US slavery. Madrid—at last—banned the slave trade in 1867. When Spain refused to extend reforms to Cuba in 1868, some of the planters began to demand independence from Spain. A major war for Cuban independence broke out in the east of the island. The rebellion—what became the 'Ten Years War' (1868–78)—quickly gained control of much of the eastern part of Cuba, but only 10 per cent of the island's slaves lived there: most were concentrated in the sugar region in the west. Carlos Manuel de Céspedes, a major regional planter, launched the move for independence, freeing his slaves at the same time and addressing them as 'Citizens': shades—once again, of Haiti. He urged them to rally to the cause of Cuban independence. In 1869, the rebel leaders (of what was known as *Cuba Libre*) tempted slaves by offering freedom to those who joined the insurgency. Later, they freed all slaves in areas under rebel control.

Slaves now became critical in converting 'a separatist struggle led by white slave-holding elites in eastern Cuba into a war for personal liberation'.[20] In fact, both sides tried to win over slaves to their side—but in the process, slavery itself began to unravel. Slaves, intent on securing their own freedom, joined the rebellion and the rebel ranks—both foot-soldiers and officers—filled with men of African descent. Slaves joining the rebels openly admitted that they had done so to become free, but their opponents tried to spread alarm by claiming that the war had become a war to end slavery. Whenever rebel soldiers of African descent rose to prominence, their enemies spread the rumours that black rebels were seeking a reprise of the Haitian revolt. The rebels were unable to break out of the east of Cuba and in 1878 finally agreed to a truce—the Pact of Zanjón. The agreement granted freedom to slaves who had fought in the conflict—but it produced a bizarre compromise. Rebel slaves were freed, but slaves who had steered clear of the conflict remained as slaves. Even so, the war had fatally damaged Cuban slavery.

The war persuaded Madrid of the need for change, but without alienating the slave lobby or conservative opinion. The Moret Law of 1870 promoted a raft of rights at home and in the colonies and was Madrid's attempt at a move towards emancipation. It banned the use of the whip and the break-up of slave families, and it freed certain categories of slaves, notably the newborn, the old—and those who had fought for Spain. It also freed all Africans landed in the island from impounded slave ships. As usual, these concessions came with a string of qualifications that give slave owners plenty of scope to side-step or delay the measures. The new law was, inevitably, obstructed or simply ignored in Cuba (less so in Puerto Rico) and for years planters and their supporters managed to maintain their traditional control over their slaves.[21] Not surprisingly, the Moret Law faced a hail of criticism from abolitionists. But, despite its limitations and critics, and for all the obvious concessions to slave owners, it signalled the beginning of the end—and it clearly encouraged the slaves. They used the legal provisions that allowed slaves to purchase their freedom, and the number of slaves in Cuba began to decline after 1870. Others simply abandoned the plantations, often encouraged by sympathisers, who sometimes provided the practical assistance required.

Puerto Rico's slaves, now few in number and with their sugar industry of decreasing importance, were more easily helped by both Spanish and local abolitionists, and in 1873 Spain finally freed the remaining 20,000 slaves on the island (Madrid later tried unsuccessfully to revoke the decision), but obliged them to work for their former masters for another three years.[22] The slaves again resolved the matter by simply leaving the plantations.

After Cuba's delegates had returned to the Spanish Cortes in 1880, Spain agreed to abolish slavery (there were still 200,000 slaves in Cuba)—by the technique of renaming both slave holders and slaves. Henceforth, slave holders were to be known as *patronos* (patrons) and slaves as *patrocinados* (apprentices). It was little more than a rebranding of slavery—and yet another sop to the slave lobby. It freed a quarter of the slaves, at three-year intervals, and by 1888 all would be freed. In the meantime, slaves over eighteen could demand wages; food and clothing were guaranteed; slave children were to be educated; and self-purchase was also made easier. Most importantly, perhaps, the grip of the slave owners was weakened by the establishment of a system of supervision. Slaves could bring their owners to account for any wrongdoing.

The Act of 1880 had in effect created a system of apprenticeship, but most slaves were simply unwilling to wait—even for a few more years. They quit the plantations by the thousands. Some negotiated deals with their former owners, working for them on new terms—and for wages. Whatever decision the slaves took, the law was now available to help them: slave owners found themselves being monitored. Throughout the slave empires, it had been an unwritten but golden rule that slave owners were in effect the lords of all they surveyed, unaccountable to anyone. In Cuba, after 1880, they had to answer for their behaviour.

The end of the prolonged Cuban war in 1878 had released a widespread desire to see an end to the entire system. What more did the slaves have to do to prove themselves? They had been vital to the planters in revitalising Cuba's economy and essential in the recent conflict when arguments for colonial independence had become inextricably linked to arguments against slavery. Now they demanded freedom, taking whatever steps were necessary to secure it. They had fought for freedom in the recent conflict; now they simply walked away from slavery or negotiated a personal end to it. After 1880, they exposed and denounced slave owners who broke the law about slavery. Slave owners finally recognised that reality was closing in around them. It had become pointless to delay the inevitable. Full freedom was brought forward, and Cuban slavery ended on 1 October 1886.[23] Once again, slaves had seen off their oppressors. That left only one slave society in the Americas—the biggest, and the one that had started the entire story—Brazil.

# 9

## The Last to Go: Brazil

BRAZIL'S VAST LANDMASS and its ever-changing economy swallowed Africans by the million. North-east Brazil is the closest point in the Americas to Africa, and the trade winds and oceanic currents pushed the slave ships heading to Brazil. Brazil effectively came to dominate the Atlantic slave system: almost a half of *all* Africans shipped across the Atlantic were carried in Portuguese or Brazilian ships, with Rio de Janeiro and Salvador the largest slaving ports of the Atlantic system. Prominent trading houses linked Bahia and West Africa, and Brazilian managers and prominent slave traders regularly moved back and forth between their two trading centres—at home and at ease in both Africa and Brazil. And despite the persistent struggles by slaves themselves and a growing chorus of criticism, both in Europe and the Americas, Brazilian slavery experienced a massive expansion in the nineteenth century.

The demand for tropical produce, conceived and nurtured under the old colonial regimes, was both strengthened and expanded by the massive increase in global populations in the nineteenth century. There were many millions of consumers who wanted commodities which spilled from the tropical economies. Sugar, coffee and tobacco had set the pattern in the seventeenth and eighteenth centuries: in the nineteenth century all three expanded hugely and were now joined by cheap US (slave-grown) cotton. Coffee—production of which was once dominated by St-Domingue's slave plantations—became Brazil's major export, greatly helped and advanced by powerful vested interests which monopolised the economy and held political sway on both sides of the Atlantic.

Slavery in Brazil attracted plenty of critics at home and abroad, but criticisms that rested on philosophy, theology or simple humanity faced the formidable obstacle of economic reality. Slavery and Brazilian economic wellbeing went hand in hand, and Brazilian planters, like their earlier Caribbean counterparts, could swat aside criticism by simply pointing to slavery's economic benefits. That prosperity was based on the millions of African slaves who, from start to finish, were engaged in their own struggle against the system: resisting, adapting and always searching for elusive routes to freedom.

Brazil's slave population was enormous. At Brazilian independence from Portugal in 1822, the population consisted of 2,813,351 free people and 1,147,515 slaves, the latter concentrated mainly in the old centres of slave activity: in the sugar regions of Bahia and the north-east, in the gold-mining district of Minas and in Rio de Janeiro. From the 1820s, however, that pattern began to change, thanks to the development of Brazilian coffee. Coffee planters instinctively turned to Brazil's traditional source of labour—African slaves—to establish the industry. Though slaves worked alongside free labour, it was the slaves who bore the brunt of the heavy field-work. They laboured across Brazil's vast agricultural landscape, became a striking presence in the burgeoning towns and cities, working as domestics, at myriad manual tasks in the streets, and as jobbing labourers and artisans, rented out to provide income for their owners.

The most striking feature of Brazilian slavery in the nineteenth century was the huge numbers of Africans who were landed at the very time the Atlantic slave trade was under growing pressure, especially from the aggressively abolitionist British. Portuguese governments (and the Crown) periodically agreed to restrict their Atlantic trade, but they did little in practice to stop it. After 1822, the newly independent Brazilian state, anxious to secure British help, agreed to implement earlier Portuguese promises to end the slave trade, but, even then, the trade continued. A law of 1831, for instance, ordered the freeing of Africans landing in Brazil, with heavy penalties for illegal slave trading, but the law was not implemented and had little effect. Despite British diplomatic pressure and despite the Royal Navy impounding Brazilian slave ships, Brazil continued to absorb huge numbers of African slaves. In the half-century to 1850, an estimated 2,150,000 Africans disembarked in Brazil, and more than one and a half million of those arrived between 1825 and 1850.[1] In one decade alone, the 1840s, between 30,000 and 40,000 Africans were landed *each year.* A simple explanation for these huge figures might seem to be the enormity of Brazil's coastline, which stretches over 4,500 miles. In fact, most of the Africans (some 1.2 million of them) landed at or close to Rio in the space of a century. These vast numbers of new Africans drove forward the growth of Brazil's slave population. After 1850, however, the overall slave population in Brazil declined, from 1,715,000 in 1864 to 1,540,829 ten years later, thence down to 1,240,806 in 1884. Finally, on the eve of emancipation, Brazil was home to 723,419 slaves.[2] The last years of Brazilian slavery saw numbers decline quickly—for one simple reason: the enslaved fled from slavery in enormous numbers.

Brazil's voracious demand for slave labour in the nineteenth century was made possible by government officials (in thrall to the nation's major economic interests) ignoring the law and turning a blind eye. Brazilian slave traders and slave owners, of course, did not want to end the trade and were usually able to intimidate local juries when rare cases were brought to court. Prosecutors determined to press charges against slave traders ran into the resistant buffer of Brazilian slave interests.

Slavery already had deep popular roots in Brazil. The law of 1831 abolishing the Brazilian slave trade was greeted by a plethora of petitions demanding its repeal, just when the British Parliament was flooded with petitions demanding an *end* to colonial slavery. British politicians, notably their aggressive foreign secretaries, were in no mood to tolerate Brazilian prevarications, nor to worry about the feelings (or the legal rights) of nations who refused to heed British demands to stop the Atlantic trade. The British had been able to enforce favourable trade deals, which flooded Brazil with British goods. And, after 1845, a new British Act authorised the Royal Navy to impound suspected slave traders in Brazilian waters—and try them in British Admiralty courts. Brazilians thus developed an understandable distrust of the British, not helped by the fact that some British residents in Brazil were themselves happy to own slaves. Brazilians were not alone in pointing out that Britain had, in living memory, derived enormous prosperity from its own slave trade. By mid-century then, Brazilian distrust of Britain had curdled into a widespread hostility, which was exploited by the Brazilian slave lobby to its advantage.[3]

The massive expansion of Brazilian slavery in the nineteenth century may have been focused on coffee, but it also fuelled changes in the wider Brazilian economy. The old sugar industry revived with the development of new regions of sugar cultivation (helping to supply the rising global demand for sugar—after the collapse of Haitian production). Brazilian cotton cultivation also expanded, along with other agricultural activities (ranching, for example). No other industry, however, used as much slave labour as the coffee industry.

Coffee had been introduced to Brazil in 1727, and was cultivated, largely for domestic use, around Rio de Janeiro from 1760, but it was the great valley of the Paraíba do Sul River that provided ideal conditions for coffee cultivation. Acquiring land for coffee cultivation was often a matter of brute force wielded by powerful men who could eject competitors and squatters, then legalise their claims through biddable lawyers and judges. With both land and slaves plentiful, it soon became apparent that coffee produced with free labour was unable to compete with the volume and cost of slave-grown coffee, and from the 1830s onwards, there was a major expansion of coffee cultivation in the Paraíba valley, later spreading to large areas of São

Paulo province. By the mid-century, this coffee-growing region was Brazil's main area of slave labour. Though old roads had been established by mining activity, the caravans of mules carrying the coffee sometimes spent days reaching the nearest port. It took ten costly days to reach Santos over the old tracks, and the time accounted for upwards of one-third of the cost of coffee production.[4]

Although coffee production was a relatively simple process, it required substantial investment in slaves. Their work was back-breaking toil: weeding the land, picking and packing the beans, which were then shipped out on mules. In the phrase widely used in governing circles in the mid-nineteenth century, 'Brazil is coffee and coffee is the Negro.'[5] The agents handling the transportation of the coffee beans tended to be British and American, and the prime market for Brazilian coffee was North America, where demand grew at an explosive rate. In 1791 the USA imported 1 million pounds of coffee: by 1844 that had grown to 150 million pounds.[6]

Coffee quickly became Brazil's major export crop and, by the time slavery ended in 1888, it accounted for more than 60 per cent of the nation's export earnings. In the process, it prompted a major process of modernisation: ports and transportation (notably railways) were modernised, and the latest financial and commercial systems were put in place. Yet all this, initially at least, went hand in hand with slavery. It was not unlike the story of cotton in the US South: modern capitalism, the newest banking arrangements and highly industrial manufacturing systems, all functioning smoothly on the back of slave labour.

The Brazilian reluctance to act against the slave trade was driven partly by the widespread ownership of slaves. There were, quite simply, large numbers of Brazilians, even among the humblest of people, who benefited from cheap African slave labour. Tens of thousands of Brazilians owned slaves of their own—albeit in small numbers—and needed those slaves for the income they generated. This was especially striking in urban life. Rio's population of 206,000 at mid-century included 80,000 slaves; 40 per cent of Salvador's population of 75,000 were enslaved; and at much the same time, almost a quarter of São Paulo's 31,000 residents were slaves.[7] As already touched upon, visitors to Brazil were invariably amazed by the ubiquity of slaves on the streets, with slaves transporting every imaginable item, from bags, packs and barrels, as well as their owners in a variety of sedan chairs. Slaves also provided a host of urban services—dispensing food and drink, sharpening knives and working as odd-job men, forming a blur of economic and social activity that was caught in the sketches and portraits by contemporary artists.

Despite the economic dominance of the major plantations—sugar initially, then coffee in the nineteenth century—the typical Brazilian slave was part of a small group owned by people of limited means. Even freed slaves owned slaves: at mid-century, 22 per cent of freed slaves possessed slaves of their own. Brazilians of all sorts and conditions were, then, deeply attached to slavery. Most perplexing of all to modern eyes, we know of Brazilian slaves who themselves owned slaves. One of the slaves working for a Benedictine order in Pernambuco owned eight slaves himself.[8] From the grandest of coffee planters downwards, there were, then, large numbers of people spread throughout Brazilian society who saw no reason to heed the anti-slavery chorus, nor to listen to the demands of the slaves themselves.

This deeply entrenched and widespread dif-fusion of slavery in Brazil made the task of ending slavery more complex than we find in other societies. Where slave ownership was more concentrated and where the demarcations between slave and free were starker and less porous than in Brazil, freeing the slaves posed a very different problem. In Brazil, however, there was a fierce attachment to slavery in all corners of society. Despite domestic and external pressures, Brazilian support for slavery remained largely secure because it was valuable to so many people.

In the years immediately prior to Brazil's formal (but ineffective) abolition of the slave trade in 1831, slave prices were low due to the huge numbers of Africans flooding in, and people hurried to acquire as many as they could afford. Thereafter, and as coffee boomed, slave prices rose and ever more slaves became concentrated in the hands of bigger planters. Poorer slave owners now sold off their slaves to richer planters—often making a good profit in the process. The big planters, with large numbers of slaves, were the bedrock of the unreconstructed slave system. And it was here, on the plantations, that slaves endured the harshest of conditions and where they struggled to secure improvement, let alone freedom.

There were nonetheless growing numbers of Brazilians prepared to consider ending the slave trade: people well stocked with slaves, for instance, could manage comfortably without further supplies of Africans. Moreover, the value of their human property would likely increase if the trade were banned. Many others, however, notably slave traders and planters on recently settled frontier properties, simply could not imagine an economic future without prospective slave purchases. And that meant freshly imported

Africans. But when a new Brazilian law finally imposed serious (and effective) measures against Atlantic slave trading in 1850, the Brazilian trade declined.[9] Unable to buy fresh Africans, many planters finally came to accept the need to improve slave conditions. Better care for their enslaved labour force seemed the only way of ensuring a normal and healthy increase in slave numbers.

Nonetheless, even then the lives of plantation slaves, especially on frontier properties, was stark and brutal. Work was hard and unrelenting, they lived in miserably crude accommodation, clothing was rough and minimal, food simple and monotonous, though sometimes supplemented by home-grown produce and alcohol. Inevitably, the commonplace ailments of poor people were ever-present in the slave quarters: so too were the epidemics that periodically swept across the country. Formal Western medicine was usually far away, and slaves relied on the folk cures and healings which had accompanied them from their African homelands. When Western and folk medicine failed, slaves turned to their sacred beliefs, their saints and spiritual saviours. They needed all the help they could get in a world that offered them very few rewards save for a complexity of personal and communal dangers. Slaves living in the towns generally enjoyed better conditions. There were many more opportunities for slaves to help themselves—to get by—and even improve themselves. In some towns they were helped by city authorities who enforced minimum standards and imposed fines on wayward slave owners. Such regulations had no relevance for the armies of slaves living in remote rural settlements, who endured the lives of beasts of burden.

It seems curious that the arrival of such huge numbers of Africans did not lead to a natural increase of population. Was their inability to increase a consequence of the damage done on the slave ships or perhaps because of the arduous nature of slave life in Brazil? Brazilian planters regularly testified to the high mortality, especially high infant mortality, among their slaves, and though we now know that levels of mortality were not as high as contemporaries claimed, it was more than enough to outweigh the slaves' birth rate. Despite great regional variations, Brazil's slave demographic patterns seem clear enough. The numerical imbalance between male and female slaves, their low fertility and high mortality rates—all helped to undermine the prospects for natural increase, and these basic facts were publicised by planters in order to continue the Atlantic slave trade. Their case was simple: if slaves could not reproduce as required, their owners needed slave labour from Africa.

One problem seemed to be the slave family. Critics (both Brazilian and visitors) often remarked on the slaves' apparent reluctance to form monogamous families. At the end of Brazilian slavery in 1888, only 10.6 per cent of the country's slaves were listed as married (again with great regional variations).[10] What confused observers, however, was the *informality* of slave family ties. Slaves often married according to their own conventions, creating family arrangements that outsiders failed even to recognise as families. The historians' search for monogamous slave families is often misleading, because marriages were informal and were often not sanctified by priests or officials (though that increased after a decree of 1869 ordered that married couples and their children should not be sold separately).

We know that slaves struggled to protect and safeguard their families. They worried that being defiant might bring punishments on their entire family, and their greatest dread was family break-up, with loved ones sold and scattered to distant owners, sometimes hundreds of miles away. Slaves would sometimes flee to avoid this and we even know of tragedies where mothers killed their children, then killed themselves, to avoid separation.[11] In Brazil (as in the US South), the real proof of slave attachment to family lay in the fear of separation—and in the efforts to prevent it—*not* in the formality of marriage documents. Slaves' attachment to loved ones was calibrated by the widespread anguish when slaves were sold and separated from relatives. Parted from families, sold elsewhere and shipped to new locations, slaves howled in distress about their loss and about the heartbreak suffered by everyone involved. If we want to gauge the importance of slave families, we need to look not so much at marriage documents as at the grief-stricken outcries triggered by separation.

For all that, there was also contradictory evidence of kindness and benevolence between masters and slaves; even, at times, of close intimate affection. Children, both enslaved and free, grew up together; devoted nurses and carers; lifelong slave lovers of slave owners; enslaved offspring of master and slave—all and more created a complexity of colours and a confusion of affectionate relationships throughout Brazilian life. That said, the existence of such relationships, and the undoubtedly genuine affection that developed between individuals, cannot mask or deflect the harsh reality of slavery itself. It was a brutal system and most of its millions of victims were not the fortunate beneficiaries of paternal kindness and affection. They remained, from childhood to the grave, items of trade—things— whose purpose was to work for their owners at whatever task the owner specified, in the fields or the bedroom.

Once again, Brazilian slavery raises a problem that continues to perplex modern-day students. How was it possible for such huge numbers of Africans, fresh from the horrors of the slave ships, to be kept in brute plantation subjugation, under such oppressive conditions, for so long? Why did the slaves not overthrow their tormentors? It would be wrong to imagine that upheaval and violent overthrow (on the pattern of Haiti) was the *only* means available to slaves to challenge or resist their bondage. Like elsewhere, slaves devised a variety of personal and collective strategies to subvert slavery— or simply to cope with what life threw at them. Many of their tactics challenged, weakened and undermined slavery itself. But as we have seen, slave resistance came with great risks and dangers.

Brazilian masters, like slave-ship captains and slave owners everywhere, had their own ways of controlling the enslaved and dealing with their recalcitrance. The challenges facing slave masters differed greatly between people who owned a mere handful, and who often lived cheek by jowl with their slaves, and planters on remote plantations who looked across their land to a village packed with hundreds of defiant

Africans. The most common tactic was physical threats and punishment. Slaves were whipped, beaten and struck for numerous shortcomings and failings. Bad time-keeping, shoddy work, foot-dragging, insubordination and insolence: all and more could prompt an angry outburst and assault. Slaves were also permanently at the mercy of the personal quirk and mood of their master or mistress. Slave owners generally disapproved of excessive punishment (and of excessive leniency), knowing that both caused trouble for everyone involved. What they feared above all else was the contagion of slave unrest. In an ideal world, they would have liked to persuade slaves to accept their worldly lot, and they tried anything that might bring that about. Perhaps religion might help?

Britain's planters had been traditionally hostile to converting their slaves to Christianity, but the Brazilian experience was very different. Even before the Portuguese settlement of Brazil, Catholicism had taken root among Africans in Portuguese Angola, though the pattern was for Africans to absorb Catholicism into their own indigenous African beliefs. In Brazil, Catholic missionaries (always in short supply)—notably the Jesuits, who were active among African slaves—faced immense obstacles. There was the simple problem of language, but more fundamental was the chasm in cosmologies between African beliefs and practices and Catholicism. The idea of the Sabbath posed a special problem. On the day when they were free from work, slaves were often reluctant to spend it worshipping as their masters sometimes ordered: they wanted the Sabbath to be a day of rest and recreation.

The Catholic Church felt duty-bound to uphold the world of the slave masters, and its priests sought to inculcate lessons of obedience and application among the slaves. This became especially important after the Haitian slave upheavals. What emerged in Brazil was a range of religious beliefs and practices that blended African and Catholic observances, but all shaped and suited to the slaves' interests and purposes. The structure of worship, from communion to relics, the insignia of Catholic worship, the assortment of saints and holy figures—all and more were absorbed into old African beliefs to produce unique patterns of worship and faith among Brazilian slaves. The result was 'a distinctly Afro-Brazilian Catholicism'.[12] One of the most important practical outcomes was the development of lay brotherhoods, fraternal organisations, which worked to help black people in general, in sickness and death, and in times of stress. The brotherhoods provided slaves with practical help and an escape from the plantations and their owners: a means of meeting other people away from the masters' control. They provided an alternative to the oppression of slaves' labouring lives.

Slaves' beliefs and practices emerged from particular African ethnic groups and were, in effect, a form of African ethnic politics and solidarity transplanted into Brazil. New Africans arriving from the slave ships could find in such gatherings recognisable faces, languages and symbols. In a sense, Africans were at home, even though they were on the wrong side of the Atlantic. But many slaves became Christian, forming churches and holding services with their own preachers. What was preached, and the nature of the prayers offered up by enslaved worshippers, often totally mystified Catholic missionaries and priests. Creolisation took place among all slave communities throughout the Americas, but in Brazil it remained doggedly African in format and expression. Over a period of four centuries, to the mid-nineteenth century, Africa was kept alive through all this by the continuing flow of African slaves into Brazil, which made Brazilian slave religions seem *more* African, less Catholic, than other forms of Christianity we find elsewhere in the Americas at the same time.[13] It was through such religious groups and customs that slaves in effect entered a world of their own making.

The nineteenth-century waves of Africans

consolidated the established patterns of Afro-Brazilian religious culture, but augmented them with the beliefs of new arrivals, notably with the Vodun of Gbe speakers, the Yoruba peoples' Orisa, and the Islam of people drawn from Islamic Africa. In Brazil this became Candomblé (a blend of Vodun and Orisa beliefs). By the mid-nineteenth century, Candomblé had spilled out from slave communities and even local white people turned to it for spiritual sustenance, for practical, everyday support, for medical care and for general wellbeing. These distinctive Brazilian beliefs and practices first took root where Africans landed (Bahia, most notably), but they subsequently migrated, on the back of the country's internal slave trade, to other parts of the country, wherever Africans lived and worked. [14] These nineteenth-century migrations of Africans and their beliefs gradually undermined the influence of the older black brotherhoods, and, though the brotherhoods survived, they lost their importance, undermined too by the growing strength of the Catholic Church, which had begun to exercise a greater influence in the country.

Brazil became notable in the nineteenth century not only for its massive African population but also for the growing number of people who had been freed from slavery. The country had a higher proportion of manumitted slaves than any other slave society in the Americas, largely because manumission was encouraged by the availability of relatively cheap slaves from the slave ships and the natural increase of the population of freed people. (Women and children were freed more commonly than men, local slaves more than Africans.) The outcome, by mid-century, was that there were more freed people of colour than slaves in Brazil. The country's first census in 1872 revealed 4.2 million free blacks and mestiços, 3.8 million whites and 1.5 million slaves.[15]

Manumission, however, sometimes came with strings attached, the most common being the obligation to serve a master until his death. Other slaves bought their freedom, in cash or in kind (proof of the way slaves were able to acquire money and produce during their time free from their masters' demands). Freedom, though, did necessarily bring prosperity. Some freed slaves did indeed improve themselves and some (bizarre as it now seems) prospered by buying slaves of their own. Most freed slaves, however, remained poor, and all freed slaves— poor or prosperous—did not enjoy the social and political rights of other Brazilians. They were not granted citizenship and were rarely treated as equals by other Brazilians: they could not vote or be elected. Even the Brazilian-born had limited social and political rights, in addition to whatever restrictions were imposed on freed people by local authorities (notably on buying property). Being freed from slavery did not bring full social and political equality in mid-century Brazil.

The *promise* of freedom was often used by slave owners as a means of encouraging slaves to be obedient and work hard: toe the line, work diligently and, who knows, freedom might be yours. When freedom came to many Brazilian slaves, it was often bestowed as a reward for years of compliance and industry. Sometimes, though, freedom was conditional, and even rescinded, with the wretched person being plucked back from freedom and once more consigned to the ranks of the enslaved. Freedom was both an ambition for the enslaved and a device in the slave owners' management handbook.

Freed slaves could rarely escape the dangers posed by living in a slave society. Slave masters were often powerful men locally who could bend or defy the law and ignore informal agreements. As long as the slave system survived, the dangers of seizure, capture, re-enslavement and re-sale remained the freed person's perennial nightmare. The system of freeing slaves was not fully secured until the 1871 Free Womb Law. Until then, freed people remained vulnerable and needed to be alert to safeguard their freedom.[16]

Slave masters played cat-and-mouse games with freed slaves, but despite their obvious power, they could rarely dispel their own anxieties about the risks and dangers of living in the company of so many slaves, especially on remote plantations. Brazilian masters regularly resorted to physical punishments of their slaves, and had a tariff of penalties and punishments, with execution and the chain gang at one extreme, the stocks and public whipping at the other, all in addition to whatever punishments were doled out away from the public gaze. It is true that nineteenth-century legislation sought to protect slaves from the worst excesses of arbitrary punishments, but such rules were, generally, in the hands of people and communities for whom violence—the whip hand—was essential and largely approved.

The expansion of Brazil's large population of Africans, and its dispersal to newly opened distant lands, brought a fresh urgency to the perennial problem of slave management. At every point of the Brazilian compass, slave masters were confronted by large numbers of recalcitrant Africans, all of them reluctant workers, and all keen for an escape from bondage. Slave resistance periodically flared across Brazil. It differed from one place and occupation to another, but whatever the nature of their work, slaves devised their own means of resisting and coping, seeking freedom at best, or some form of less demanding accommodation with the system. Everywhere, they struggled to improve their lives, and to safeguard their families.

The centre of slave life consisted of the close ties and networks with loved ones—with family and intimate friends—and they did whatever was necessary to keep them secure. Often, they failed, and family break-up and separation left that emotional desolation that was a refrain in slave life across the Americas. Slaves were involved in permanent negotiations with their owners, striking a complexity of deals and arrangements for small but vital benefits: for land to cultivate and raise animals, with the produce sold and bartered—and the money sometimes set aside for freedom.[17] Wise planters and commentators agreed that slave gardens and plots were important: they benefited slave family life. The pressure for this came from the slaves themselves. Sometimes they had to make threats. When Brazilian slaves' customary rights were denied—when rewards or plots for growing provisions were refused or revoked—slaves reacted violently. They attacked masters and overseers (and their animals), they ran away, and they even stirred up revolt.

Slave rebellions, of various degrees of severity, were commonplace in Brazil, though not always with the intention of destroying slavery. They sometimes broke out to stop local abuses (or abusers) or to demand customary rights that were being denied. Revolts happened in new areas of expansion, where slaves were under severe pressure from the arduous labour. These were regions where heavy concentrations of African slaves were located, particularly young men captured in African conflicts, thence sold into Brazilian slavery. Gangs of African slaves from similar ethnic groups, some with military experience, seemed a recipe for rebellion. Bahia was particularly plagued by such troubles in the early nineteenth century, with upwards of thirty revolts. Most of them were on sugar plantations and were generally led by Hausa or Nago from Yoruba land: men who had arrived in Brazil via warfare sparked by the spread of Islam in their homelands.[18]

By contrast, Rio in the nineteenth century remained much less troubled by rebellion, despite the huge numbers of Africans arriving there. This may have been because the Africans were predominantly Bantu-speakers with no experience of warfare. Moreover, Rio offered little encouragement for slave revolts. Though slaves struck back at oppressive masters, overseers and their property, and although slave owners worried endlessly about revolts, slaves in Rio found it easier, less risky, to run away and even to find other openings for themselves in the city. In many respects, Rio itself was also very different from Salvador in Bahia. It was home to the army, navy, national guard, local militia, mercenaries and police. There were, in addition, slave patrols and 'private armies of armed slaves and informers' employed by slave masters. Slaves in Rio had merely to glance around them to see the forts, the armed ships in the bay, soldiers on parade, the police barracks and patrols, to recognise a complex display of power. Such intimidating force was likely to dispel or curb thoughts of rebellion.[19]

Brazilian slave owners—like slave owners everywhere—had learned their lessons from Haiti. They feared gatherings of slaves on the streets, and worried that they might simply get out of hand. Rio was regularly awash with rumours of plots and conspiracies, but open rebellions were unusual, and slaves took their revenge on a smaller scale: sabotage, theft, attacking and even killing masters and overseers. Though revolts erupted on plantations not too distant from Rio (even the Brazilian Emperor Pedro II suffered a revolt among sixty slaves on one of his plantations), the city did not have the rebellious record of Salvador.

Brazilian officials were all too alert to the problems posed by Africans arriving from war-torn regions of the continent and gave instructions that they should be monitored and prevented from gathering: no drumming or festivities that might provide an occasion to assemble. This failed to prevent slave unrest, which culminated in the Malê (Muslim) rebellion of 1835 in Bahia.

It was planned for the end of Ramadan that year, with Africans parading defiantly in the streets of Salvador wearing Islamic dress and displaying passages from the Qur'an. They were joined by slaves inspired by Yoruba gods of war. Other slave rebellions were also inspired by African deities and religious rituals from the slaves' backgrounds. Catholic slaves were even persuaded to rebel by charismatic priests, and by the slaves' attachment to saints who, they believed, would lead them to freedom. For example, as late as the 1880s, St Anthony became the 'patron saint of slave conspiracies' in São Paolo.[20]

The slave owners' deep-seated fear—and the slaves' inspiration—was, of course, Haiti. As early as 1805, a portrait of Dessalines was worn by black militiamen in Rio. Reports circulated of slaves openly talking about the Haitian revolution, and memories and images of Haiti frequently surfaced in Brazilian slave rebellions and plots: in Pernambuco (1817) and Laranjeiras (1824). Later, the line 'Remember Haiti' appeared in a poem that threatened whites in Recife.

Sometimes, slave disturbances stemmed from much more mundane causes: misunderstandings and disappointments. Brazil's gradualist legislation (offering qualified freedom, or freedom at some distant date) was often misunderstood by slaves who simply assumed that freedom was being granted—but denied or delayed by slave owners. Each new law seemed to prompt a revolt or conspiracy: in Espírito Santo (1831), Minas Gerais (1831 and 1833) and Campinas (1832). The abolition of the Brazilian slave trade (in 1850, rather than the original, ineffective abolition of 1831) and the Free Womb Law (1871) were similarly misunderstood and prompted slave disturbances. Even the last years of Brazilian slavery were pockmarked with revolts, especially in the southern coffee region.

Slave owners viewed slave revolts as the ultimate crime committed by slaves, but there were many, less spectacular crimes that registered slave anger with their lot. Significantly, most slaves committed crimes against free people. As we have seen, the Brazilian slave system was itself a violent system, and its victims regularly turned to violence as their last means of resistance. They killed masters and their agents. (We know of slaves who preferred a life in jail to the life of a slave, handing themselves over to the authorities after committing murder.) [21] Much more commonly, slaves protested by running away. Indeed, what fatally undermined Brazilian slavery in its last years was the flight of slaves from the plantations. As they did during the last throes of other slave societies in the Americas, they simply quit the plantations in their thousands.

Long before then, Brazilian slaves sought freedom by escaping to the wilderness or to the anonymity of town life. In one city after another, police arrested large numbers of runaway slaves. Police records and newspaper advertisements confirm that the largest group of runaways were young Africans, especially in the years of major African arrivals. In Rio in 1826, 86.7 per cent of runaways recorded in newspapers were Africans, the bulk of them aged ten to twenty years old. The evidence also suggests that the fugitives were helped by Africans of similar background.[22] Slaves fled from their masters for a great variety of reasons. They escaped cruelty and punishments, they sought out people who could advise and help, and many set out to find work in towns, perhaps even to find a new master who would treat them better. Others ran away to join the military in Brazil's various internal and external conflicts. Some, living close to national borders, crossed into countries where slavery had already been abolished. Others escaped to join the numerous run-away communities—*quilombos* or *mocambos*—scattered across Brazil's inaccessible terrain, or even those close to towns: communities too remote, too distant, too risky for authorities to bring to heel.[23] Most important of all, however, remained the emotional pull of family. Slaves ran away *to* loved ones, or from the fear of family break-up. The prospect of emotional turmoil forced slaves to escape, sometimes as a family.

The problems posed by Brazilian slavery changed markedly during the nineteenth century, as the largest concentration of slaves shifted from the northern provinces (a legacy of the old slave economies) to the coffee-growing south. By the 1870s, the southern coffee-growing region was home to around 800,000 slaves, creating alarm among local politicians, who pointed to the fate of the US South as a warning of the dangers facing Brazil. They feared that Brazilian slavery was simply decanting from the north into the south, and that northerners would effectively wash their hands of slavery itself, not caring whether it survived or not. The overwhelming fear was that slaves would soon begin to outnumber and overawe local white society, bringing all the physical dangers slave owners had feared for the past three centuries. These concerns about slavery were allied to a debate about the problems of Brazilian agriculture, and the difficulty of persuading free labour to work on the old plantations. Though contemporaries trotted out the lame excuses that Brazilians were lazy by inclination, the truth was different—and obvious. For centuries the plantations and other sections of rural life had been the preserve of African slaves. And who wanted to do slave work? In some places, however, harsh circumstances did indeed force the most wretchedly poor free labourers to toil on the old slave plantations.

After the abolition of the Brazilian slave trade, and as slave prices rose, coffee planters hoped that European immigration (and even Chinese indentured labour) might solve their labour problems. Slowly, the outlook of some planters had begun to change. Mechanisation began to point to new ways of running the economy, in both the sugar and coffee industries. Machines could sort, polish and bag coffee beans—all work previously done by slaves. Even in the old sugar regions of northern Brazil, steam power began to make an impact. Most dramatic of all, some planters started to think that free labour might be better than slave labour.

By 1870 Brazil, along with Cuba, had become the exception. The rest of the Western world had turned decisively against slavery. The US Civil War and the flight of the slaves from the plantations had not only destroyed slavery in North America but had created a post-war society hostile to slavery at large. Brazilians had traditionally looked to the USA as a sympathetic fellow slave society, but all that had vanished with the defeat of the South. Even the Spanish islands turned; Puerto Rico ended slavery in 1873—and Cuba (formally at least) in 1880. Brazil was isolated. To compound the woes of

Brazil's slave owners, they also faced growing pressure from the country's changing political landscape, notably from the rise of Brazilian abolitionism and from the nation's transformed population. There were more and more free people in Brazil, especially the waves of recent immigrants from countries with no attachment to or even awareness of slavery. Government and regionally sponsored immigration schemes had seen tens of thousands of Italians settle in coffee-cultivating districts. Promoters of European immigration to Brazil realised that slavery had become a serious obstacle, because European immigrants seemed reluctant to work alongside slaves, not least because the Western world had spent much of the past few decades demonising slavery as a wicked and sinful institution. To increasing numbers of Brazilians, slavery was both distant and alien.

In the years after the ending of the Brazilian slave trade in 1850, there was little sense of organised abolition sentiment in Brazil. The church was silent, and women remained largely uninvolved at first.[24] But that began to change by the 1870s. Brazilian arguments about slavery were, essentially, debates about the very nature and future of Brazil itself.[25] Abolition emerged as a major issue in Brazilian politics, as abolitionist organisations proliferated in towns across the country and local politicians began to consider the end of slavery in their province. Courtrooms also became a critical forum, not only for arguments about the freedom of individual slaves, but also for a more general legal debate about slavery and freedom. The foundations of Brazilian slavery were being slowly undermined. It was denounced abroad, its former friends (especially in North America) had been silenced, and it was being corroded at home by European immigration and by attack from Brazilian abolitionists. Opinion was shifting, especially in towns. Despite the ubiquity of urban slavery, city dwellers (especially those linked to the nation's modernising industries and finances) were notably abolitionist. These new friends of black freedom were literate, often well educated, well connected and politically savvy.[26] Supporters of black freedom in Brazil's towns created what was in effect an underground railroad, encouraging slaves to quit the plantations, and head for freedom among friends and sympathisers. Brazilian abolitionism began to grow into a broadly based popular movement, but to succeed it had to build support for appropriate legislation in parliament itself. Most crucially, it had to garner the strength of the slaves. Their opponents, Brazilian slave owners, also organised and campaigned to maintain their grasp over their slaves, and even by the late

1870s the prospect of black freedom remained uncertain.[27]

The obstacle was the nature of Brazilian political power, which continued to be dominated by a regime, formed in colonial days, of slave holders and friends—with the Emperor, Dom Pedro II, wielding executive power. It was a political system designed to maintain stability (the Emperor appointed the government) and to limit change. The control of law and administration in the localities lay in the hands of men chosen by the cabinet. Elections were largely derisory, and their outcome unrepresentative of popular feeling. When Brazil's Emperor wanted to gauge the feeling of the nation, he listened not to politicians but to the press and other sources of information. One odd consequence was that the Emperor became a supporter of a free press, and newspapers became vociferous critics of slavery. The most ironic twist to the story of abolition in Brazil is that it became a major national political issue in part thanks to the activities of Emperor Dom Pedro II.[28]

The Emperor was concerned that slavery was damaging Brazil's reputation among other advanced nations. The British—but especially the activities of the Royal Navy—remained a special concern. Although the Royal Navy delivered thousands of Africans freed from impounded slave ships to Brazil (where they were expected to become apprentices, though, in reality, they remained enslaved), they posed an aggressive threat. The Royal Navy blockaded Rio for six days in 1863, for instance. The Emperor also worried that events in the USA after 1860 might be repeated in Brazil. While Dom Pedro looked to Europe for both intellectual inspiration and cultural values, he feared that his country's persistence with slavery was both demeaning and dangerous. He was concerned that Brazil's attachment to slavery impaired the country's aspiration to primacy in South America. He frequently hinted that slave emancipation was being considered—subject to various qualifications—but practical matters always got in the way.[29] The war against Paraguay (1864–70) also complicated Brazil's slavery problems. Slaves were recruited and volunteered for the army (it offered an escape from slavery) and the disruption caused by that war also prompted slave upheavals and large-scale slave desertions from plantations. The war inevitably created huge strains; notably, recruiting slaves for the military led to unease among the old slave-owning class. To some, it seemed like a step towards emancipation, and was viewed as subversive encouragement to the slaves themselves. Once again, the shadow of Haiti was cast across local affairs. (The irony of the Paraguay war was that slaves conscripted for the war were freed, yet they were fighting for a slave state.) The war itself prompted the usual outbursts of slave escapes from the military, of mutinies and various acts of violence.[30]

Victory in the Paraguay war in 1870 enabled the Emperor to bring the matter of slave emancipation before the cabinet (he had first raised it with them in 1867), and a law of limited range but important precedence was passed. The Rio Branco Law of 1871 decreed that all slaves born thereafter should be free, with masters caring for them for eight years. Then the masters should free them in return for compensation, or the slaves could work for them until the age of twenty-one. Henceforth, all slaves had to be registered. If not, they would be seized and freed.[31] The law prompted vehement and widespread opposition among slavery's supporters, and the slave-holding elite fully expected slavery, in reality, to continue into the foreseeable future.

Although slavery was important, in varying degrees, in every corner of Brazil, the *internal* slave trade began to create major problems by the 1870s. Slaves were being moved in huge numbers to the boom industries. They were sold from Brazilian cotton regions, and from the southern ranching economies, to prospering regions of the country, notably to the coffee planters. Some years, as many as 10,000 slaves were traded along these internal slave routes—

some involving enormously long journeys by land and water. The numbers of slaves removed from Bahia, for example, reached a peak in the 1870s. The distress caused by these enforced migrations was profound, both among the people uprooted and among those left behind. That distress became a deep-seated and widespread grievance in the coffee regions thereafter.[32]

The internal Brazilian slave trade was a reprise, on an even larger scale, of what had happened in the USA before 1860. A profound anger settled among the slaves whose loved ones and friends disappeared into the internal slave trade, simply vanishing over the horizon—and this lay behind much of the unrest that erupted from the late 1870s onwards. Angry slaves, allied to other labour problems, were among the factors that began to edge some slave owners, notably coffee producers, to think about alternative sources of labour. This was compounded by concerns about the changing nature of the country's demography, and by the fear of heavy concentrations of slaves in newer areas. And all the while, abolitionist groups began to coalesce.

In 1881 a massive popular upsurge of abolition agitation broke out in Ceará—a north-eastern region stricken by drought—and a notable slave-exporting province. In January, thousands of people flocked to local beaches to block the movement of slaves from Fortaleza and other ports. It set in train a campaign that, by 1883, had not only freed slaves in that city but had inspired abolitionists nationally. The movement was greatly enhanced by the addition and effective work of female abolitionists, and agitation for black freedom began to spread. In the cities, where the power of new voters was undermining the influence of the old slave-owning class, abolition flourished as never before. Newspapers added their voice to the clamour for abolition. Most important of all, it flourished in Rio, where it fed into and was sustained by a much wider wave of popular radical politics about a range of local and national issues.[33] In 1880 the Brazilian Anti-Slavery Society was founded and quickly became a critical force in promoting abolition in the country at large. Prominent abolitionists drew up specific plans—and drafted legislation—to free the slaves. Most striking of all, however, was the astonishing *contagion* of abolition; a veritable groundswell of popular abolition sweeping across Brazil. Ordinary people, of all colours and classes, flocked to public meetings—in theatres, concert halls and public squares—to add their presence, voice and names to demands for abolition. Abolition quickly took on a life of its own, seeping into all corners of the nation and capturing wide public appeal and support.

Popular abolition initially hardened the hearts

and resolve of slave owners and their supporters, but their political power was draining away. Slavery was collapsing locally across Brazil. Popular politics, the concentration on securing freedom in specific localities, legal challenges in courts and, most critical of all, the slaves' growing awareness that the tide was running in their favour, all served to sap the slave lobby's strength. Coalitions of abolition societies came together to form a powerful national lobby, and one Brazilian city after another succumbed to campaigns to free local slaves. In the event, only small numbers of slaves were freed, but the movement developed its own dynamic and language, which was important for the subsequent national discussion about slave freedom.

It was becoming clearer by the month that 'Brazil was no longer totally a slave nation.'[34] Then, in 1884, Brazil found itself with a Prime Minister, Manoel Pinto de Souza Dantas, who was an abolitionist; his son Rodolfo proposed immediate and uncompensated emancipation for all slaves over sixty. The subsequent political crisis propelled abolition centre-stage, with candidates at elections being forced by popular politics to declare themselves on the question of abolition. This was an exact reprise of events in Britain fifty years before. The short-term outcome was that most abolitionists lost their seats, but a new government in 1885 passed a very restricted form of abolition, this time with compensation. By 1886, it seemed that the old order had reasserted itself. In fact, the hard-line anti-abolitionist administration had merely stirred a hornet's nest of slave resentment. Slaves needed little encouragement to add the critical mass of their numbers to the argument. Their desire for freedom had always been there, of course. Now, it had been heightened by the agitation and political successes of recent years. It was as if the slave genie was finally out of the bottle and the slaves took matters into their own hands.

The old pattern of slaves fleeing from their owners now became a veritable epidemic. Slave conspiracies proliferated: some turned to violence against property and people. In São Paulo slave revolts were nipped in the bud in 1882 and 1885. Abolitionists urged fugitive slaves to escape to 'free' territories and, again with royal support, funds flowed in to help. Free slave communities lured slaves across Brazil. Often, slaves left plantations en masse. The number of Brazil's slaves went into a swift, steep decline. In the four years to 1888 it fell from one million to half a million.[35]

The government tried to staunch the flight of the slaves with new laws punishing anyone who helped runaway slaves, but the days of supplicant slaves merely asking for freedom had vanished into the dust raised by tens of thousands of slaves quitting the plantations. In these massive human upheavals, old scores were settled: masters and their helpers were killed by vengeful slaves. In the last years of Brazilian slavery, in places such killings 'became so ordinary that newspapers avoided publishing news about it for fear of creating panic among the free'.[36]

The flight of the slaves was unstoppable and large communities of freed slaves mushroomed outside cities across the country: outside Porto Alegre, Fortaleza, Ouro Preto and Rio. In Bahia, the city of Cachoeira 'became a place of refuge' for fugitive slaves.[37] In Pernambuco, 3,000 escaped along a 'maritime freedom route' organised by local abolitionists. Thousands fled in droves from São Paulo's coffee plantations, heading for the security of free communities in the city of Santos. Everywhere, fugitives flooded Brazil's streets to join friends and supporters in mass displays of popular demands for abolition.

Whole regions became in effect areas of freedom that welcomed fugitive slaves, and Brazil's underground railroad became an over-crowded transit system between slavery and freedom. This underground railroad was more massive and more open than its North American namesake. Sometimes an entire slave population of a plantation fled, many boarding real trains to head for freedom. Local police and military were simply powerless in the face of such numbers, and most refused to intervene. Slave resistance, flight and violence—all and more proved beyond the power of local and national authorities to contain, not least because the public mood had shifted. The abuses of slaves that had once passed unremarked now caused outrage. Slave masters found it hard to believe what was happening. Slavery was collapsing all around them and they lost confidence in the ability of the state—or the locality—to maintain control in the face of such volatility. Many simply threw in the towel. When planters resisted or slaves hesitated, abolitionists converged on the plantations (especially those of notorious planters), urging slaves to down tools and walk away. The proliferation of free communities served to transform local urban politics by giving power to abolition and severely weakening the national government's dogged opposition to freedom. Waves of civil and personal disobedience by slaves and their supporters were bringing slavery to its knees. Even the army was powerless to do anything about this popular uprising—and it refused even to try.[38]

By 1886 planters worried that they would not have enough labour to harvest their various crops, and many began to negotiate their own employment arrangements with the slaves. In Parliament the slave lobby proposed several solutions, trying to secure a compromise between freedom and contractual labour. The last debate revolved around compensation for slave owners (with memories of Britain's £20 million clearly in mind). It was a hopelessly optimistic last throw of the slave owners' dice. And it failed.

This extraordinary black liberation—the loss of half the nation's slave population to a contagion of self-liberation—was now compounded by an unlikely but invaluable intervention by the sympathetic Princess Regent, Isabel (the Emperor was in Europe). She proved a stalwart friend to the slaves, supporting their cause in public and in the face of resistant politicians. She nominated João Alfredo Correa de Oliveira as Prime Minister, giving him instructions, in May 1888, to push through a law for immediate abolition—with no compensation.

Free at last, Brazil's slaves (and many others) embarked on celebrations the likes of which dwarfed all previous Brazilian carnivals and joyous public outbursts. For three days, newspapers were not able to publish: their workers were on the streets celebrating. And at the heart of those celebrations, the crowds of freed slaves paraded images of the heroes of abolition.[39]

African slaves had been the essence of Brazilian history for more than three centuries. They had created wealth and ostentatious living on a lavish scale—all the while enduring a brand of misery like no other. Millions had suffered enslavement in Africa, the hell that was an Atlantic slave ship, followed by the multiple (and repeated) upheavals, cruelties and heartbreaks of Brazilian slavery. In the process, their labour brought into being a society quite unlike any other in the Americas. Now it was gone. Slavery had been the foundations on which Brazil's *ancien régime* had rested, and with the overthrow of slavery, the regime itself tottered. The monarchy had abandoned the slave owners to support the slaves and when, in 1889, the military revolted, the Emperor had no friends to which to turn. The regime fell—dragged down by the death throes of the slave regime that had sustained and enriched Brazil for so long. Slavery ended in 1888 and in the following year Brazil became a republic.[40]

The struggle to overthrow Brazilian slavery had been protracted and bitterly resisted. Its dogged defenders seemed not to care that Brazil became the only surviving Christian country to tolerate it. Though it is true that opinion changed dramatically in the last years of slavery, when swathes of Brazilian life turned against slavery, educated and enlightened Brazilians were ashamed to hear their nation compared to slave-holding Turkey. The decisive factor in the ending of the system was the slaves themselves. As the ideological and commercial justifications for slavery disintegrated, it was the slaves who, to use the words of David Brion Davis 'turned the tide'. They sometimes negotiated, occasionally rebelled, regularly plotted—and periodically hit back—and finally fled in their tens of thousands. Their resistance sapped the resolve of slave owners and their political supporters, who found themselves increasingly powerless in the teeth of massive slave defiance. The slaves toppled the system that for so long had held them in miserable bondage. Their efforts had created Brazil's wellbeing: now, they had brought down slavery in their collective surge to freedom.[41]

# 10

## Abolition in the Wider World

FOR MUCH OF their history, the slave societies of the Americas were sustained by the umbilical cord that was the Atlantic slave trade. But by 1867 that had ended. Twenty years later, the last American slave society fell. This enormous system, of Atlantic slave ships and African slave labour—finally collapsed—to a chorus of political denunciation and moral outrage. Yet for centuries slavery had survived with little criticism or opposition. Now, it was reviled throughout the Western world.

Notwithstanding earlier intellectual and religious roots in France and North America, the political campaign to bring down slavery was British in origin. Throughout the nineteenth century, the British used all their economic and political power (which went from strength to strength as the century advanced) to stop the maritime trade in slaves. But herein lies a curious paradox: had not the British been the dominant slave trader in the North Atlantic before 1807? And had not the Royal Navy (henceforth the scourge of Atlantic slave ships) been the naval guardian of British Atlantic slavery? This British conversion from slavery to abolition was as swift as it was confusing. Not surprisingly, other nations found such a volte-face deeply suspicious. This odd paradox—British zeal for abolition after years of successful slaving—was to become a central feature of British historical remembrance, and forgetfulness, from that day to this. The British like to recall their abolitionist past, but soon became forgetful about their earlier involvement with slavery. Even today, there is a temptation to remember abolition and to overlook what had gone before.

Throughout the nineteenth century, British foreign secretaries (some of them belligerently abolitionist) arrived at diplomatic gatherings determined to negotiate an end to slave trading. Often, they were armed with massive public support: 1,370 petitions and upwards of 1,375,000 signatures accompanied the delegates to the Congress of Vienna in 1815, for example.[1] They made slow progress. It took Europe's major powers thirty years to agree to abolish the slave trade, and a further thirty years to implement those agreements fully. During all that time, the US Navy and the Royal Navy made energetic efforts to intercept the Atlantic slave ships. By 1839, when the Royal Navy had seized 77 slave ships and freed 104,034 slaves, another 2,640 vessels had carried almost two million Africans to the Americas. By the time the last Africans landed in Cuba in 1867, almost three million Africans had been shipped to the Americas as slaves since 1807.

Despite the sluggishness of abolition, the Western world had embarked on an utterly new venture. For the first time in recorded history, major powers came together to end slave trading: a business that had characterised human society for centuries. The first move had been taken at Vienna in 1815 with the assertion that the slave trade was a violation of the rights of man. Though hardly noticed at the time, this was 'the first hesitant step in the direction of the present international human rights movement'. Unconsciously perhaps, that gathering marked the start of a protracted legal and diplomatic struggle that continues to this day: to outlaw slave trading and slavery in all corners of the globe.[2]

The determination to root out slavery became a diplomatic and political obsession of British diplomacy throughout the nineteenth century, and as early as 1830 the 'Slave Trade Dept' had become the largest section in the Foreign Office. It became ever clearer, to diplomats and abolitionists, that slave routes and slavery thrived in all corners of the world. Attacking slavery on a global scale, however, posed very different problems from ending slavery in colonies or in nation states that were friends or allies. The world was laced with slave routes. Africa posed its own complex problems. Trans-Saharan caravans, routes between the Horn of Africa and Arabia, between east Africa and islands in the Indian Ocean, trade linking Zanzibar to the Congo— these and many more generated enormous movements of slaves. India, too, challenged the evangelical British, who began to realise the extent and variety of slave systems on the sub-continent, especially among the myriad princely states.

When western Europe's imperial powers revived their interest in Africa in the late nineteenth century, they faced the problem of how to deal with slavery. Europe's latest phase of imperial expansion ('the scramble for Africa') was fired by strategic and economic interests, but it was disguised and justified by a Christian fervour to bring 'civilisation' to an Africa plagued by widespread forms of slavery. By then, abolition had (in the words of Seymour Drescher) become 'the gold standard of civilisation'. The preferred tactic used by the British was to bring slavery to heel through diplomatic agreement with the guilty state or head of state. By 1890, more than three hundred bilateral or multilateral treaties had been concluded (though all were directed at oceanic slave trading and none against overland routes or slavery itself).[3] When doing this, London made a none-too-subtle distinction between 'agreements' with 'barbarous Chiefs' and international compacts with 'Civilized States'.[4] If Foreign Office diplomacy failed, the Royal Navy was always available to lend a muscular hand. The navy destroyed African slaving posts in the 1840s, attacked Brazilian vessels in 1850 and occupied Lagos in 1851–2, leaving no doubt about Britain's determination to attack slavery when it deemed it necessary.

As the century advanced, what began as a campaign to end the remnants of the old colonial slave systems in the Atlantic became a drive against slavery wherever it existed. Abolition gradually became a truly global campaign. But to be effective, campaigners needed the authority of international legal agreements and, when necessary, military power. In the process, a debate emerged in all Western nations and in diplomatic congresses about human rights. The demand for an end to slavery became a rallying cry for the rights of enslaved people everywhere.

By the late nineteenth century, the focus of attention had shifted from the Americas to Africa, the Indian Ocean and beyond. In India, for example, the British decreed slavery to be illegal in 1860, though enforcing that resolve proved altogether more difficult. There—indeed wherever abolitionist nations looked—they encountered forms of slavery that differed greatly from the slave systems with which they had been familiar in the Americas. Even so, by the late nineteenth century, Europe's major imperial powers had swung into line behind a political and diplomatic abolitionist culture. This represented a major transformation. In the late eighteenth century the instinct of Europe's colonial powers had been to acquire as big a share as possible of the Atlantic slave economy, and to outbid rivals for a share of the Atlantic slave trade. A century later, by—say, 1900—all of them shared a contrary political and cultural outlook. Every major European imperial power defined itself as an anti-slavery nation: their cultural superiority was rooted in an unquestioned opposition to slavery. An abolitionist ethos was now the essence of Western civilisation: slavery had become the mark of a heathen backwardness. As western Europe emerged as a pre-eminent force in world affairs, it left slavery far behind—so far behind that Europeans tended to forget their own intimate and valuable involvement with it. Societies that clung to slavery seemed to offer the West an invitation to step forward and bring it to an end.

A succession of European diplomatic gatherings between 1815 and 1888 had issued a variety of denunciations of slavery, but those high-sounding pronouncements were often little more than diplomatic hot air. Then, in 1888, the tone and the direction of European abolition changed—thanks largely to the Catholic Church. In July of that year the eccentric French Cardinal Charles Lavigerie launched a crusade against the slave trade from the pulpit of St-Sulpice in Paris. Lavigerie had been a missionary in Africa, Archbishop of Algiers, founder of a French missionary order and Primate of Africa. His fierce anti-slavery sermon in 1888 was based on missionaries' reports from twenty years before and portrayed African slavery in the most gruesome and blood-curdling light. He also took aim at Arab slave traders in what looked like a revival of the millennium-old clash between Christianity and Islam. Despite the faded evidence, Lavigerie's apocalyptic tone had a seismic impact, first in Paris, then across Europe. Abolitionist societies proliferated across Catholic Europe and the Pope found himself propelled to the head of a European-wide anti-slavery furore. The outcome was a new international anti-slavery campaign (though it was severely divided by nationality and between Catholic and Protestant).[5]

Following concern about Belgium's rapacious conduct in the Congo, a new treaty of 1885 decreed that both slavery and slave trading were illegal and ordered European powers to bring them to an end in their respective African possessions.[6] Behind the vaunted principles, however, much simpler and more brutal forces were at work. The upsurge in abolition sentiment flourished off the back of Europe's latest zeal for empire, with major powers acquiring a passion for new imperial acquisitions, and all confirmed by diplomatic agreements at the Berlin Congress of 1889–90 to divide Africa into recognisably modern spheres of interest. Europe's major powers had gobbled up vast tracts of Africa to gain access to markets, raw materials and strategic advantages. But the entire process came gilded with the principles of a civilising mission—at the heart of which was the resolve to end slavery.[7]

Cardinal Lavigerie's greatest impact—prompting the pan-European abolition movement—was unintentional. In British eyes, his work was a reprise of the abolitionist tremors that had periodically shaken the country a century before. Anti-slavery sentiment had, at last, become a genuinely *European* phenomenon and had shed the suspicions that had clung to Britain's earlier drives against slavery.

Abolition was also popular. The people of Europe, increasingly literate and well informed, were learning at first-hand about the nature of slavery in regions recently acquired by their own country. They heard about it from missionaries (most famously Dr Livingstone), from the pulpit (notably Lavigerie) and from popular press reports about the activities of military men, diplomats and businessmen. This late-century drift to popular imperialism was widespread and politically influential, and brought together national self-interest, nationalistic fervour and moralising zeal. And all with the aim of bestowing civilisation and removing the scourge of slavery. As enormous tracts of the world—especially in Africa—fell under European control, it was widely accepted as a moral responsibility to purge those lands of slavery.

Revelations about King Leopold's vicious management of what was, effectively, his personal fiefdom in the Congo gave added urgency to European abolition. Under pressure from Britain, the Belgian monarch convened a gathering at Brussels in 1890, which agreed to the first genuinely international treaty against the slave trade and slavery. Though its immediate origins lay in the Congo atrocities, the treaty was the culmination of a diplomatic saga that reached back to Vienna in 1815. The Brussels treaty had its flaws, but it seemed, finally, to be a clear sign that slavery was on the retreat, driven back by the advance of Western nations in regions they now controlled or governed.

The 1890 General Act of Brussels (a treaty of 100 clauses) declared that all parties were 'equally animated by the firm intention of putting an end to the crimes and devastations engendered by the traffic in African slaves'. The same parties also agreed to protect 'the aboriginal populations of Africa and of assuring to that vast continent the benefits of peace and civilization'.[8] All signatories were bound, within the year, to adopt penal laws to punish their own slave traders. The Act also granted the right of search and detention of vessels at sea (though with conditions that avoided friction between the major powers). A major innovation was the establishment of offices in Zanzibar and Brussels (the latter attached to the Belgian Foreign Office), where officials compiled all the available information about slave trading within defined areas.

The irony in all this is there for everyone to see. Many of the Western powers that had grown fat on Atlantic slavery had evolved into the world's leading imperial powers and were using their unrivalled military and diplomatic strength to bring slavery to an end. The poachers of the old-world order had become the bellicose gamekeepers of the new. They also set about ensuring that new international organisations would henceforth be wedded to abolition. All this, like so much else, was swept aside by the First World War. In the diplomatic tumult that followed the war, with the major powers at Versailles reordering the maps of Europe and the Middle East, old concerns about slavery seemed marginal. Even so, a new treaty, of St Germain-en-Laye, in early September 1919, revised earlier agreements about slavery. It revoked the old authorisation of search and detention, and failed to reopen the monitoring offices in Zanzibar and Brussels. Most importantly, however, it bound all signatories to secure an end to slavery 'in all its forms and of the slave trade by land and sea'.[9]

In a world convulsed by the Great War and its aftermath, slavery was clearly a sideshow, and the main priority of international diplomacy was the maintenance of peace via the new League of Nations. In 1926, the League established a Slavery Convention, which was ultimately to outlaw both slavery and the slave trade. The Convention made slavery illegal internationally and established the principle that slavery was a crime against humanity (though there was no means of enforcement).

Although the question of slavery was low on the list of pressing priorities after the war, the 1926 Convention marked an astonishing turn of events. Slavery—which had brought untold bounty to the Western world (and many other societies before that)—was now denounced and outlawed. Henceforth, any nation wishing to be taken seriously in global affairs—especially in the new international corridors of power—had to display their anti-slavery credentials. Nations anxious to catch up with the West, to become modern, democratic and industrial, had to display their disavowal of slavery. The Japanese banned slavery as part of their modernisation and Westernisation. Russia—that huge empire which sprawled from the gates of Europe to the edges of China—had already freed its serfs as part of its own hesitant and troubled passage to modernity. And, of course, all Europe's major powers and the USA proclaimed their civilisation by distancing themselves from their slaving past.

It was as if the world had turned on its axis. What had once been vital, much sought after and fought over (i.e. a share in the profitable business of slavery) had, by the start of the twentieth century, become a global pariah. Slavery was now universally denounced as unethical and illegal. It even seemed, by the mid-1920s, that under the aegis of the League of Nations, the world had finally rid itself of slavery.

Then, in an astonishing reversal of fortunes, slavery enjoyed a major comeback. It did so, not in distant colonies or imperial possessions, but in the very heart of Europe itself. The twentieth century was to see a revival of slavery on a scale and with a ferocity that would have shocked eighteenth-century sugar planters.

# 11

## Slavery in the Modern Age

THE SLAVERY CONVENTION, agreed by the League of Nations in September 1926, was the first time both slavery and the slave trade were defined in international law. Although the Convention accepted the existence of forced labour, it denied the right to remove that labour from its home territory. There remained, however, the perennial problem of how to enforce the rules. Britain argued that slave trading should be linked to piracy, thus allowing navies to board and seize offending vessels. Other member states felt this smacked too strongly of Britain's nineteenth-century gunboat diplomacy, and the matter was left to individual states to strike their own bilateral agreements against slave trading. The League asked two committees, in 1933 and 1934, to report further on slavery, but their efforts yielded no real change. Even so, it is generally accepted that the Convention, and the efforts of the League in the 1920s and 1930s, marked an important diplomatic step forward in the global campaign against slavery. That work was to be picked up, after the Second World War, and incorporated into the new United Nations. By then, however, the problem of slavery had been made even more complex, and much more urgent, by the catastrophe of the war and the widespread use of slave labour by the combatants.

The new Soviet Union had refused to join the League of Nations, had not ratified the Slavery Convention of 1926 and felt no obligation to join the Western condemnation of slavery—not surprisingly, perhaps, because the Soviet regime soon began to use forced labour as an integral feature of the transformation of Russia. The various Soviet economic experiments of the 1930s increasingly relied on forced labour, the most severe, and the most feared, emerging under the supervision of the Soviet secret services. We know of them as the Gulag. From 1928 onwards, the Gulag system's prison camps filled up with prisoners spawned by the various Five Year Plans. Hundreds of thousands of peasants, for example, uprooted by collectivisation, were driven into camps in remote regions where free labour would never tread, to form a new army of servile labour to tap the enormous economic potential of Russia's inhospitable expanses. The Gulag swallowed millions of people: displaced peasantry, conquered peoples and those deemed to be political enemies. About five million peasants and one and a half million Muslims were relocated vast distances in this fashion.[1]

Events in Russia soon attracted outside critics,

drawn by the system's inhumanities—which were well known and widely discussed in the West in the early 1930s. They were debated in legislatures, in the press, and there were even boycotts of Soviet imports produced by unfree labour.[2] Criticisms of the Soviet Union were stilled, however, by the rise of fascism, and finally and effectively silenced by the German onslaught on Russia in 1941. Henceforth the Soviet Union became a vital ally, and the main land-fighting against Germany (with suffering on a staggering scale) was undertaken by Russia.

All the nations drawn into that war imposed tight control over their labour force, but in Russia the war accentuated a process already underway, with a massive increase of penal labour and an expansion of labour camps to cope with the huge numbers involved. The real numbers remain unknown. The 476 known camps formed a formal tip of a massive network of satellite camps.[3] In 1930, there had been an estimated 179,000 people in the Gulag; by 1941 that had increased to just short of two million. Although about one million prisoners left the camps to join the Red Army during the war, the overall number in penal servitude continued to rise. By the time of Stalin's death in 1953 there were almost two and a half million people in the camps. Throughout Stalin's years in power, forced labour—and the Gulag—remained central to his plans for the

Soviet economy, but within three months of his death, 60 per cent of the Gulag's prisoners had been released. Throughout the years of Stalin's dominance—years of domestic revolutionary upheavals, ferocious warfare followed by difficult post-war reconstruction—slave labour had been basic to the Soviet economy.

This story of slave labour in the twentieth century took an even more shocking turn in Germany. A mere decade after the League of Nations had adopted the Slavery Convention, one of Europe's most sophisticated and advanced societies turned its back on all that. Not only did Nazi Germany repudiate all its prior diplomatic commitments to abolition, but it embarked on a violent process of mass enslavement of conquered foreigners, including many Slavs and Jews. In the process—and very quickly—the numbers of people enslaved by Nazi Germany dwarfed the slave systems in the Americas in the previous three centuries.

Even before the outbreak of war in 1939, the pronouncements and theories of Nazi leaders had hinted at what might happen, though the reality that unfolded was far beyond the imagination and understanding of an outside world for whom slavery was viewed as the ultimate evil: something from Europe's distant and forgotten past. Germany's early conquest of western Europe offered the first clues of what might follow, with tens of thousands of prisoners scooped up and transported to Germany as forced labour. What followed in the east, however, shifted the matter to a different level. The 'General Plan for the East' drafted in 1942 was a blueprint for a new and colossal system of enslavement on a scale that far surpassed anything seen before. Alongside schemes for the annihilation of millions, notably Europe's Jews, the plan proposed the enslavement of fourteen million people, and their transportation to work in Germany.[4] In the First World War, Germany's use of enemy civilians (notably Poles and Belgians) as forced labour, especially in agriculture, was to cost Germany dear in reparations imposed by the victors after 1918. But all that seemed trivial compared to what Nazi Germany imposed on its conquered territories after 1940.

Even *before* the attack on Russia in June 1941, Germany was using 1.2 million French POWs and 1.3 million 'civilian workers' (mainly Poles) as labourers. At the height of the war, when eleven million Germans were under arms in conflicts that stretched from Norway to North Africa, the German economy was functioning with the labour of more than thirteen million foreign workers. Without them, the German war effort would have faltered. The Nazi regime had in effect become a modern slave system. This time, it took the largest and mightiest military effort the world had ever seen to bring it down. There is no evidence that the Nazi slave regime would have ended without being crushed by warfare.

Though the Nazis had devised a hierarchy of inferiorities, which defined the nature of their slave labour gangs and the treatment they received, these grand schemes began to disintegrate as the war advanced. As the allied armies closed in on Germany, captives were driven to ever-greater exertions to maintain the flagging war effort. Finally, the captives found themselves either driven from their camps to flee the advancing allied armies—this was the last and most appalling migration of prisoners and slave labour, especially from the east—or deserted in their camps. The abiding images of the Third Reich in its death throes are of millions of skeletal figures, more dead than alive, liberated by the allied armies. These diseased and tormented masses overwhelmed the relief organisations in 1945 and afterwards: there were millions of enslaved survivors of a regime that had used labour systems that the Western world had abandoned in the previous century.

The existence of forced labour in Nazi Germany is beyond dispute. But was it slavery? That question continues to nag critics, largely because of our understanding of what constitutes slavery. Slavery has come to mean the institution that evolved in the Americas. Understandably, perhaps, critics have been at pains to illustrate the *distinctions* between slave labour in the Second World War and African slavery in the Americas. Some regard twentieth-century slave labour as more akin to Roman slavery than American slavery. It is surely important, however, to note that, when peace settled on Europe in 1945, the people most closely involved in securing post-war justice (lawyers, judges, academics) felt comfortable with the label 'slavery' for what they encountered in the ruins of Europe. The historian and critic, Gitta Sereny, spoke of her life, for two years after 1945, 'working with displaced persons, Hitler's slave workers' and other victims. One of the major relief agencies (the United Nations Relief and Rehabilitation Administration—UNRRA) was confronted by five million displaced slave labourers—most of whom simply wanted to go home.[5]

The shadow of slavery lingered over Europe long after the war had ended. Millions of survivors of Nazi slave labour remained locked for years in dispute with German governments (first in Bonn, then Berlin), and with a large number of German industries, demanding compensation for their time as slave labourers. The problems were immense. For a start, the major German industries—the giants of the economy—

were infamous employers of slave labour. By 1943, for example, Auschwitz, in the words of Gitta Sereny, was 'the largest slave-labour camp the Nazis had'. Its enslaved occupants were put to work building and then operating the synthetic fuel and rubber factory built for I. G. Farben. They also constructed the gas chambers at Birkenau close by.[6] But slave labour in addition, was widely scattered across Nazi Germany, from small local bakeries to farms.

The post-war legal, moral and personal complexities involved were enormous, often made worse by the fact that large numbers of victims had no material or written proof of their ordeals. In this legal and moral minefield, one central issue stands out. No one doubted that millions of people had been used as *slaves*. The word itself—slave—was used (though a number of distinctions were drawn between slavery and other forms of penal labour used by the Nazis). Early efforts to agree compensation for the slave labourers failed to resolve the matter and it took a number of class actions in the USA in the 1990s to prompt the German government to establish a foundation and a fund to compensate people forced into slave labour. Billions of dollars were allocated by the German government and by German industries: some 6,500 businesses contributed, though many refused. Even by the early twenty-first century—more than half a century after the end of the war—there were 2.5 million survivors of Nazi slave labour, and many were still pressing their case for compensation. Both at the time and since, the imagery and vocabulary of slavery were widely used to describe these events—although it tended to go unnoticed that in the space of a mere five years the Nazis had enslaved more people than were ever enslaved in the Americas. When the surviving Nazi leadership was called to account at Nuremberg, their actions were deemed to have been 'crimes against humanity'. The term had been inserted into the trials at the suggestion of Professor Hersch Lauterpacht of Cambridge University. After much debate between law officers from all four allied powers, the final charter drafted to govern the trials adopted Article 6(c). This granted the judges of the impending tribunal the power to punish people who had committed crimes against humanity. Those crimes included 'murder, extermination, enslavement, deportation, and other inhumane acts committed against any civilian population, before or during the war'. In the words of Philippe Sands, this clause formed a major shift in legal opinion. It was 'a professional and intellectual leap' that laid the basis for much of the debate not only at the Nuremberg trials, but also, in the years since those trials, about modern slavery.[7]

A major refrain running throughout the trials at Nuremberg was that the Third Reich had imposed a slave system, however complex and inefficient, across its vast, conquered lands. The European heartlands had, in effect, become the site of unparalleled enslavement, all marked by levels of savagery and killings that far surpassed anything we might find in the enslaved Americas.

The widespread revulsion at the atrocities of the Nazi regime was paralleled by horror at the Japanese terror across Asia. There, an estimated 700,000 Koreans and 40,000 Chinese were enslaved by Japan, and perhaps 300,000 Asians died working as slave labourers. This was in addition to the enslaved labour of POWs captured by the Japanese.[8]

The post-war public outrage about these events fuelled a determination that nothing like that must happen again (though much the same had been felt and said after 1918). The European trials after the Second World War saw 5,000 people convicted of war crimes, with 486 people executed.[9] The legal processes initiated at Nuremberg were to have the most profound impact on the subsequent story of slavery and abolition. The concepts of both genocide and crimes against humanity were henceforth securely anchored in international law. Moreover, the concept of slavery itself had been widened to embrace forms of bondage previously excluded.

Debt bondage, serfdom, human trafficking and forced marriages, all were enshrined in the Universal Declaration of Human Rights issued by the new United Nations in December 1948. Article Four simply asserted: 'No one shall be held in slavery or servitude; slavery and the slave trade shall be prohibited in all their forms.'[10]

The United Nations, founded by the major victors of the Second World War, changed rapidly in the wake of the demise of the world's major empires, with the proliferation of independent nations from the 1950s onwards. Colonies and possessions were transformed into independent nation states and the founding UN membership of 51 nations quickly increased. Today it stands at 193. In 1956 the United Nations incorporated an anti-slavery Convention, agreed by the League of Nations thirty years before, into a new 'Supplementary Convention'. To gain admission, each state had to sign up the UN's Charter, and that involves being formally abolitionist. Whatever reservations some of those new nations may have had (and some had been infamous for tolerating slavery at home), they had to agree, in public at least, to abide by the diplomatic conventions of abolition. In a fundamental break with the past, abolition had become a defining characteristic of a modern, civilised state. Not to agree to abolition was to be consigned to diplomatic isolation. Not surprisingly, no nation was willing to accept such a stigma, and by the late twentieth century the universal imperative was to be abolitionist. Abolition had triumphed and had become the globally accepted norm. To be an opponent of slavery had become a definition of civilisation itself.

Freedom from enslavement and slavery was now accepted as a universal human right, and slavery was defined as a crime against humanity. In the nineteenth century, it had been pressure from powerful Western nations that imposed abolition on erring societies: in the late twentieth century, it was the consensus of international law and diplomacy, exercised primarily through the UN, that attacked slavery and slave trading.

And yet, for all the commitments and universal agreements, for all the grandiloquence of moral principles . . . did it work?

In the early twenty-first century, with all the world's sovereign states in agreement that slavery is a crime against humanity, slavery has once again become a source of domestic and international concern. How are we to explain this in the light of everything that had happened at Nuremberg, and of the legal, political and diplomatic onslaught against slavery since 1945?

In what was a remarkable twist in the familiar story, a number of Western societies were shocked to discover that slavery was alive and well—and not merely in distant places. Western

Europe at large and the USA became aware of the existence of slavery *at home*. It was most striking and troubling in the form of people who had been trafficked. Large numbers of enslaved people were being moved long distances by organised gangs of criminals. The slave traders, once an accepted feature of commercial life, were now international outlaws. Their victims sought safety, work and a better life in the West, and often travelled from the far reaches of the globe to find it. Many left home as economic migrants seeking to improve themselves, but many were enslaved people: transported, controlled, and then employed after arrival by complex and rapacious criminal gangs. However different from the world of slavery and slave trading familiar to Western eyes, what was exposed were systems that trafficked unfree people into the West. Once there, the victims were used as enslaved labourers in a number of major industries.

At first, it was tempting to dismiss or minimise the problem by pointing to the obvious differences between, say, the ordeal of plantation slaves and an unfree domestic worker employed in London or New York. But as evidence mounted, as the numbers involved became clearer and as the life stories were teased from the miserable victims, the scale and nature of the problem became indisputable—and more troubling. In the early years of the twenty-first century, researchers had begun to expose a massive global problem of slavery. The most eminent of scholars in the field have persuasively argued that, at the time of writing, there are more than thirty million enslaved people. It is, moreover, a problem that seems to subvert the West's historical efforts to end slavery globally. Alarm about slavery was revived though the realisation that slavery existed not simply in distant or poor countries, but in the West itself.

Slavery in Britain, for example, had not been a serious issue since the late years of the eighteenth century and was abolished in 1834. Now, almost two centuries later, slavery in Britain became a matter of widespread discussion. Today, the news media, political forums and courtrooms are thick with slavery issues. So serious had the problem become in the early twenty-first century that the British Parliament passed the Modern Slavery Act in 2015. It was designed to 'Give law enforcement the tools to fight modern slavery, ensure perpetrators can receive suitably severe punishment for these appalling crimes and enhance support and protection for victims.'[11]

Lending substance to these concerns, some spectacular examples of modern slavery and slave trading regularly surface in the British media. Albanian gangs were jailed for trafficking women into British prostitution (2007); Polish gangs trafficked Polish workers as slave labour into Britain (2017); a Roma gang from the Czech Republic controlled gangs of vulnerable people as slaves in Plymouth; Lithuanian gang-masters imported fellow countrymen as slaves into Sheffield. Finally, and at the time of writing, a family of travellers in Lincolnshire was able to live in some style on the proceeds of eighteen slaves (mainly vulnerable people), controlled with great cruelty, some for upwards of twenty-six years. The severe jail sentences—ranging from five to twenty years—reflected both the seriousness of the offences and the outrage felt by the courts.[12]

In recent years, it has been difficult, in Britain, *not* to notice the discussion about contemporary slavery. Even as I was writing this book, I saw an official notice at Manchester Airport in December 2017:

> Slavery still exists.
> If you suspect it, report it.

The notice was stuck on a wall in a men's lavatory in Terminal 2.

Such anecdotal evidence is unexceptional in modern-day Britain: it litters the press, the airwaves and political debate. Scarcely a week goes by without mention being made of slavery, and especially of slavery in Britain itself, much of it about people trafficked to Britain as slaves to work in prostitution, agriculture, domestic work or catering. It is thought that perhaps 14,000 women and children have been trafficked into Britain in the past twenty years, despite a battery of legislation to prevent such movements.

Though the total numbers seem relatively small, the very existence of slaves in Britain sent ripples of curious doubt through society, with reactions ranging from disbelief to disgust. Such revelations shook some basic assumptions about national identity. After all, it had been the British who had led the attack on slavery for two centuries: they were the people who even defined themselves as the embodiment of anti-slavery. In 2007, for instance, there had been extravagant and nationwide commemorations of the bicentenary of the abolition of the slave trade. Powerful cultural forces remain at work serving to define abolition as part of the British national identity: being opposed to slavery has become quintessentially British. Revelations about slave routes into Britain, and slaves in Britain itself in the early twenty-first century, came as a profound shock to many.

Evidence from the US is even more remarkable, but perhaps not surprising given the geographic and demographic immensity of the States. An estimated 15,000 people are trafficked into the USA each year. In 2004, 49 per cent worked in the sex industry, 27 per cent in domestic work and

10 per cent in agriculture. The largest numbers of people trafficked into the USA come from China, Mexico and Vietnam, and they are controlled (at great expense to the victims) mainly by gangs of their own nationality or ethnicity. Well-defined routes emerged for the movement of trafficked victims from their homelands into the major cities of the USA. Once there, they could easily disappear into well-established ethnic and national communities. Trafficking has clearly become a massive industry characterised by devious illegality, violence—and handsome rewards for the gangs running the systems.[13] The historical incongruity is startling: Lincoln signed the Emancipation Proclamation on 1 January 1863—yet scholars calculate that there are between 100,000 and 150,000 slaves living in the USA *today*.[14]

Despite the initial disbelief the mounting evidence could not be disputed. It was possible, of course, to take some comfort from knowing that the slavery involved was quite unlike slavery in the Americas. But this also created a problem. The types of modern slavery exposed in Britain and the USA differed so markedly from the history of Africans shipped to the Americas that it was hard to persuade many people that it really *was* slavery. Perhaps we needed a different word, a different definition, to describe the bondage that had found a home in the West? An obvious and simple question arises: what do we *mean* by slavery? This is the very question historians have been wrestling with for years.[15]

Modern slavery is now recognised as a global phenomenon. The agencies working against slavery—notably that doughty survivor from the original campaign, the British Anti-Slavery Society in London—regularly investigate and report on slavery in all corners of the globe. To learn, in the twenty-first century, that forms of slavery continue to survive in distant parts of the world came as no surprise. It also fitted the West's sense of superiority and reinforced the distinctions it drew between itself and the wider world: it was much more comfortable with a discussion that focused on slavery as an alien institution, foreign—something found in distant societies. The West had come to believe that slavery was wrong, and had spent a great deal of political and diplomatic capital preventing it. Now, despite the UN, despite international treaties, despite a shoal of national laws, bilateral and multilateral agreements—it was clear that slavery endured, and literally right under our own noses.

For years, anti-slavery campaigners had exposed slavery in various parts of the world, often on a major scale, and always in defiance of international law and treaties. Hereditary slavery had survived in parts of Africa, debt bondage was widespread in South Asia, child slavery—notably in the form of child soldiers—had flourished in conflicts in Africa, Sri Lanka and Myanmar. The seizure of women for forced marriage was widespread.

What became apparent in the twenty-first century, however, was that slavery was remarkably adaptable: it changed contours to suit changing circumstances. It was especially evasive and devious in the hands of those profiting from it. And therein lies a key. Behind contemporary slavery lie some basic economic facts. We now know that the price of modern slaves has fallen worldwide—for simple and obvious reasons. Massive population growth has created armies of poor people desperate for any means of survival. To put it crudely, there is a huge global labour market waiting to be exploited. From a world population of 7.1 billion people, 900 million live below the accepted standard for extreme poverty. For large numbers of people, enslavement is a consequence of poverty. Acquiring slaves thus became incredibly cheap. When we make historical comparisons, the evidence is astonishing. Present-day slaves cost only a fraction of the price of slaves bought in the US South before 1860: a representative price for a modern slave is $90, compared to the equivalent cost of $1,200 for a field hand in the American South in 1850.[16] Conflict and warfare—with the consequent collapse of law and order (sometimes the total collapse of the nation state) can also provide fertile ground for recruiting slaves. This has been the case in parts of Africa, notably Congo, and in Europe after the Balkan conflicts. Slavery has also thrived in countries plagued by corruption, which is itself often a symptom of the decline of law and order. Furthermore, enslaving poor people is almost free of risk for the slavers in societies where law enforcement is poor or sometimes non-existent. The outcome by the early years of the twenty-first century is that, despite a battery of laws, and in the face of formal disapproval of the wider world, slaves were cheap and acquiring them involved little threat of ramifications for those involved.[17]

The existence of modern slavery is, then, beyond dispute, but it is more difficult to be precise about its size. Any persuasive analysis (and programme of action to combat slavery) requires a clear understanding of the data involved, and the increased scrutiny of slavery in the early years of the new century prompted sophisticated analyses of the problem. Previously, discussion had been based on guesswork and hearsay. Now, complex statistical and social analyses have been employed to extract precise data. (This was, after all, the exact route travelled by historians of the slave trade. The guesswork of earlier generations was set aside by pioneering statistical analysis culminating in the Slave Trade Database.) Problems remain, of course, but we can now talk with some assurance about the numbers involved in present-day slavery. In 2013, the Global Slavery Index offered a figure of 29.8 million slaves worldwide.[18] Britain's most eminent scholars of modern slavery recently accepted a figure of 35.8 million. We also know where those slaves live. More than three-quarters of the world's slaves are found in a mere ten countries. (India, with fourteen million, tops the table.) Such massive figures, however, need to be set in the context of a global population of more than seven billion people. Similarly, the estimated annual profits from slavery, of $150 billion, need to be set against a global economy of $87 trillion. In the words of Kevin Bales, the data illustrates that 'while slavery is non-trivial, it is proportionately a very small part of the global population and global economy'.[19] Not only that, but the *importance* of slavery has been reduced over time.

Do such qualifications matter? They can do nothing, of course, to diminish the sufferings of the millions of people who continue to be trapped by modern slavery. Nor do they mitigate the crimes of the modern criminal gangs enriched by slavery.[20] But we are left with a deeply puzzling irony. Slavery is illegal the world over and lacks any moral or religious support. It is confronted by the universal culture of abolition—and that culture originated and developed in the campaign to overthrow the slave empires of the Americas. No one in their right mind would openly support slavery today. But what comfort is that to at least thirty million people who find themselves enslaved?

# Conclusion

WHENEVER SLAVES WERE freed, they joined together in communal and exuberant celebrations, gathering in the nearest town, filling the streets with boisterous delight, and flocking in huge numbers to places of worship to give thanks for their liberation. They danced, sang, drank and gave elated thanks for freedom. In Jamaica in 1838, they crowded their chapels to give thanks. In Washington in 1866, the streets were packed with 3,000 celebrating freed slaves, and similar scenes were repeated in major American cities and in every colonial capital whenever the day of freedom dawned.[1] Freed slaves overwhelmingly celebrated formal emancipation peacefully.

Perhaps the most astonishing feature of these moments of delirious release was their contrast with the bleakness and the suffering that had gone before. This most brutal of systems ended in celebration. It was as if centuries of the brutality and cruelty of slavery had been waved away in the euphoria of freedom. Slave owners expected something quite different. They feared the worst, assuming that their former slaves would seek revenge. Slave owners failed to recognise that their deepest fears were a reflection of their own behaviour: a glimpse into the paranoia that afflicted the masters in all slave societies. Since time out of mind, they had held their slaves in subjugation by formal and informal violence, doling out ad hoc punishments whenever they felt it necessary—or simply when they felt like it. When pressed, they called in help from neighbours, local armed forces and, *in extremis*, colonial armies and navies, to keep the slaves in their place. Their deep-seated fear was that this legacy of oppression would return to haunt and punish them.

Why, then, would slaves *not* respond in kind? Why should they forget the indignities of past? Quite apart from the slaves' commonplace hardships, there were untold numbers of slaves— millions in the case of Brazil and the USA— whose families and loved ones had been torn apart by slavery. For them, freedom prompted a desperate (and mainly fruitless) search to find and, with luck, be reunited with lost loved ones. For them, freedom involved the permanent heartache of family loss, and their lamentations echoed down to modern times. Slave owners were aware of all this. After all, they had brought it about, and they feared that they had built a rod for their own back: slaves' profound grievances all led to the slave owners' door.

Ninety years passed between the overthrow of Haitian slavery and the freeing of Brazil's slaves in 1888, but American slavery itself survived, in one form or another, for more than four centuries. It had proved tenacious and adaptable, creeping from one industry to another, bending and re-forming to the changing demands of American life. It started in the early days of European colonisation and it ended in the age of steam. The first African slaves in the Americas toiled at onerous pioneering fieldwork: America's last slaves worked alongside modern machines, and their products were shipped to distant markets by steam-powered trains and ships. In the USA, Cuba and Brazil, large numbers of slaves escaped from slavery by taking a train to freedom.

Africans and their offspring in the Americas made possible some of the most notable trans-formations in mass consumption in modern history. Europeans learned to love sweet drinks and food (hence their rotten teeth). North Americans consumed coffee on an enormous scale. People everywhere smoked tobacco in staggering volumes, and countless millions, in all corners of the world, dressed in cheap cotton clothing which, like sweet drinks and tobacco, had their roots in the history of slavery in the Americas. But were the world's consumers even aware of what the slaves had made possible? And here lies one of the main problems in trying to understand slavery. Its victims were, in the main, out of sight and out of mind. The metropolitan heartlands—and, later, the rest of the world—enjoyed the benefits of slavery without paying too much attention to the human cost involved.

All that began to change, however, in the late eighteenth century. As the stark realities of slave life dawned on an increasingly literate world, and as slave defiance began to make an impact beyond the boundaries of slave societies, a new kind of awareness, a sensibility, emerged in the West. It germinated and evolved in response to the slaves' ordeals and to their efforts to resist what was happening to them.

Slavery was a remarkably durable institution, and the people who controlled it, at sea and on the American plantations, clung to it with astonishing tenacity. They fought to ensure its survival in the teeth of persistent defiance from the slaves themselves, and despite mounting pressure from growing numbers of people who came to see slavery as an ethical and religious outrage. The ultimate achievement of this powerful slave lobby lay in its commercial success, but that success was rooted in an oppressive culture that relied on punitive threats and sanctions—and inflicted severe punishments on defiance. Most slave owners came to accept that their slaves formed an alien body: an enemy within, which they needed but which was ultimately unknowable.

Some believed they had the trust of the slaves, imagining that their slaves respected and perhaps even held them in high regard or with affection. They were invariably distraught when their slaves turned. Slave favourites, lovers, nannies, cooks, trusted retainers, men and women in responsible positions—all, and many more—turned out to be less reliable, less trustworthy, less loyal than their owners expected. At such moments, it was hard to dispute the bleakest of slave owners' fears: that slaves could never be trusted. Give them an inch and they would take an African mile.

There are many ways of telling the history of slavery. One would be via the recurring hostility and defiance of the slaves themselves. They sought a way out but were normally able to secure little more than small, mundane improvements for themselves. In the most dire of circumstances—on frontier properties in harsh physical conditions—survival itself was as much as they could hope for. Surviving slavery was more important than securing freedom.[2] Most, however, settled into a life of resigned defiance: doing just as much as was required to get by. But there were always some (usually young African males)—angry, dangerous, headstrong—intent on something different; they were the slaves who proved the most persistently troublesome for their masters.

Everything changed, right across the Americas, after the Haitian revolt. Slaves quickly heard of that upheaval (and recalled it fondly many years later), but its most immediate and long-lasting impact was among slave owners. Haiti terrified them and stiffened their resolve in equal measure. It was the most chilling of cautionary tales. At the same time, it encouraged slaves with the awareness of what was possible. Though Haiti was an exception, wherever we look familiar patterns of slave defiance emerged, from one slave society to another: local resistance, runaways, Maroon communities, plots and rebellions, an abundance of individual recalcitrance—all formed a brew of slave discontent that created an endless challenge for the slave holders. Some slaves found personal freedom—in the bush, in the towns, even at sea—but the overthrow of slavery and the arrival of freedom for all came through more uncertain and turbulent times. It was then that slave defiance tipped the balance.

The British tide in favour of slave freedom was turned by the violence of major slave rebellions—and the even greater horrors of their suppression. The wars for independence in South America destroyed both the Spanish Empire and slavery. Slaves joined the fighting and turned the ideology of colonial freedom into an irresistible demand for freedom from slavery. Later, Cuba's slaves similarly joined in the prolonged war against Spanish rule, and the disruption of warfare encouraged other Cuban slaves simply to walk away, in enormous numbers, from the house of bondage. Their withdrawal of their labour, vital to their owners' ability to resist and fight, and the slaves' flight sapped that ability and undermined the self-belief and confidence of the slave owners.

In North America, the US Civil War provided the opening for which slaves had long been waiting. In their eyes, it was their war. They fled the plantations, joined the Union armies, headed north or simply fled on what became a new, and no-longer furtive, Underground Railroad. The South's economic ability to fight the war was fatally damaged by these slave migrations. A generation later, it was the turn of Brazil's slaves to undermine slavery by a massive desertion of the plantations.

In all the drives for slave freedom (in the British Caribbean, the USA, in Cuba and Brazil) slaves were urged to flee by a massive base of supporters and sympathisers. These were people who had themselves turned against slavery due to what they learned about slave life and sufferings. Everywhere, public opinion was roused by a growing awareness of the raw realities of slave life. Slaves, freed slaves, Africans, all and more added testimony and eyewitness accounts of the realities of slavery—and those voices helped to swing opinion against slavery. It was an abolition sentiment that blossomed in the rich atmosphere cultivated by the evidence about slave lives and anguish.

Freedom—emancipation—came (eventually) via legislation, proclamations, constitutional change and declarations. These were usually issued from centres of political power many miles away from the centres of slave life. But none of those official changes would have come to pass exactly when and how they did without the efforts of the slaves themselves. It was slave effort, resolve and defiance that won to their side invaluable political support. Those same qualities served also to weaken their opponents, undermining the confidence and self-belief of the slave owners. Slave owners' power was corroded and weakened, their economic strength ruined by warfare, by revolt, by the regular haemorrhage of enslaved manpower. Finally, slaves everywhere were free. Though freedom was to bring its own tribulations, for the time being, freedom seemed enough.

# Notes

The full citations for the footnotes can be found in the Bibliography. The following notes are designed to help readers locate the relevant evidence.

## Chapter 1

1 Detailed evidence for the slave trade can be found in two related sources: the Trans-Atlantic Slave Trade Database (www.slave voyages.org), and the volume derived from that database: David Eltis and David Richardson, *Atlas of the Transatlantic Slave Trade* (New Haven and London, 2010).

2 David Eltis and David Richardson, *Atlas*, p. xvii.

3 A. E. Lawrence, *Fortified Trade Posts*, Ch. 7.

4 David Eltis and David Richardson, *Atlas*, Maps 9–10, pp. 15–17.

5 David Eltis and David Richardson, *Atlas*, Maps 23, 26, Table 6, pp. 43, 46, 203.

6 David Eltis and David Richardson, *Atlas*, pp. 37–8, 47.

7 David Eltis and David Richardson, *Atlas*, Maps 32–3, 38–40, 41–2, 51, 52, pp. 57–9, 66–71, 85–6.

8 Sir John Hawkins, *First Voyages* (1562), in

Richard Hakluyt, *The Principal Navigations* (London, 1926 edition, 7 vols), vol. VII, p. 5.

9 James Walvin, *Crossings*, p. 77; David Eltis and David Richardson, *Atlas*, p. 98.

10 David Richardson, Suzanne Schwarz and Anthony Tibbles (eds), *Liverpool and Transatlantic Slavery*.

11 David Eltis and David Richardson, *Atlas*, Table 5, p. 90.

12 John Newton, *Journal*, pp. 14, 72.

13 James Walvin, *Crossings*, p. 98.

## Chapter 2

1 James Walvin, *Sugar*, p. 38.

2 João José Reis, 'Slavery in Nineteenth-century Brazil', in David Eltis *et al.*, *Cambridge World History of Slavery, Volume 4*, p. 131.

3 James Walvin, *Sugar*, pp. 120–1.

4 David Brion Davis, *Inhuman Bondage*, pp. 119–20.

5 B. W. Higman, *A Concise History of the Caribbean*, Ch. 4.

6 James Walvin, *Sugar*, pp. 40–3.

7 B. W. Higman, *A Concise History of the Caribbean*, p. 125.

8 Pieter C. Emmer and S. L. Engerman, 'Non-Hispanic West Indies', in David Eltis *et al.*, *Cambridge World History of Slavery, Volume 4*, pp. 75–6.

9 B. W. Higman, *A Concise History of the Caribbean*, pp. 81–7.

10 B. W. Higman, *A Concise History of the Caribbean*, pp. 105–6.

11 Laird W. Bergad, 'Slavery in Cuba and Puerto Rico', in David Eltis *et al.*, *Cambridge World History of Slavery, Volume 4*, pp. 101–5.

12 Seymour Drescher, *Abolition*, pp. 183–5.

13 Laird W. Bergad, 'Slavery in Cuba and Puerto Rico', in David Eltis *et al.*, *Cambridge World History of Slavery, Volume 4*, pp. 107, 110–11.

14 David Brion Davis, *Inhuman Bondage*, Ch. 6.

15 David Brion Davis, *Inhuman Bondage*, p. 156.

16 Richard Follett, *The Sugar Masters*.

17 Stanley L. Engerman, 'US Slavery and its Aftermath', in David Eltis *et al.*, *Cambridge World History of Slavery, Volume 4*, Ch. 7.

18 James Walvin, *Slavery in Small Things*, Ch. 11.

**Chapter 3**

1 For an original and important view of this topic, see the adverts for runaway slaves in Britain, www.runaways.gla.ac.uk.

2 Michael Tadman, *Speculators and Slaves*, Ch. 6.

3 B. W. Higman, *A Concise History of the Caribbean*, pp. 142–3.

4 João José Reis, 'Slavery in Nineteenth-century Brazil', in David Eltis *et al.*, *Cambridge World History of Slavery, Volume 4,* p. 149.
5 Christer Perley, *White Fury*, p. 58.
6 B. W. Higman, *Plantation Jamaica*, pp. 51–2.
7 Rhys Isaac, see Index, 'disciplining workers', *Landon Carter's Uneasy Kingdom.*
8 David Brion Davis, *Inhuman Bondage,* p. 205.
9 James Walvin, *Atlas*, p. 114; Eric Robert Taylor, *If We Must Die*, pp. 67–183.

**Chapter 4**
1 David Geggus, 'Slavery and the Haitian Revolution', in David Eltis *et al.*, *Cambridge World History of Slavery, Volume 4,* pp. 321–2.
2 David Geggus, 'Slavery and the Haitian Revolution', in David Eltis *et al.*, *Cambridge World History of Slavery, Volume 4*, pp. 324.
3 David Geggus, *Slavery, War and Revolution*, Ch. 1; Jeremy D. Popkin, 'Introduction', *Facing Racial Revolution.*
4 David Geggus, *The Haitian Revolution*, pp. xii–xiii.
5 David Geggus, *Slavery, War and Revolution*, p. 25.
6 David Geggus, *The Haitian Revolution*, pp. 15–16.

7   David Geggus, 'Slavery and the Haitian Revolution', in David Eltis *et al.*, *Cambridge World History of Slavery, Volume 4*, p. 324.

8   David Geggus, 'Slavery and the Haitian Revolution', in David Eltis *et al.*, *Cambridge World History of Slavery, Volume 4*, p. 325.

9   Ogé's address, in David Geggus, *The Haitian Revolution*, pp. 48–9.

10  Jeremy D. Popkin, *Facing Racial Revolution*, pp. 44–5.

11  David Geggus, 'Slavery and the Haitian Revolution', in David Eltis *et al.*, *Cambridge World History of Slavery, Volume 4*, p. 332.

12  James Robertson, *Gone is the Ancient Glory*, pp. 134–5; anonymous letter, 18 November 1791, C.O. 137/89, National Archives, Kew.

13  David Geggus, *Haitian Revolutionary Studies*, p. 183.

14  David Geggus, 'Slavery and the Haitian Revolution', in David Eltis *et al.*, *Cambridge World History of Slavery, Volume 4*, p. 335.

15  David Geggus, 'Slavery and the Haitian Revolution', in David Eltis *et al.*, *Cambridge World History of Slavery, Volume 4*, p. 337.

## Chapter 5

1   David Brion Davis, *The Problem of Slavery in Western Culture*, pp. 169–73.

2   Christopher Brown, *Moral Capital*, p. 38.

3   Christopher Brown, *Moral Capital*, pp. 41–4.

4 Brycchan Carey and Geoffrey Plank (eds), *Quakers and Abolition*, p. 2.

5 Maurice Jackson, *Let This Voice Be Heard*, pp. 106–10.

6 Maurice Jackson, *Let This Voice Be Heard*, p. 115.

7 Maurice Jackson, *Let This Voice Be Heard*, p. 117.

8 Christopher Brown, *Moral Capital*, p. 409.

9 Ryan Hanley, *Beyond Slavery and Abolition*.

10 James Walvin, *Slavery in Small Things*, p. 157.

11 James Walvin, *The Zong*, pp. 166, 179.

12 Vincent Carretta, *Equiano*.

13 Vincent Carretta, *Equiano*.

14 James Walvin, *The Zong*, p. 192.

15 Seymour Drescher, 'European Antislavery', in David Eltis *et al.*, *Cambridge World History of Slavery, Volume 4*, p. 375.

16 James Walvin, *The Zong*, p. 197.

**Chapter 6**

1 B. W. Higman, *Slave Populations*, Ch. 2.

2 Michael Craton, *Testing the Chains*, p. 246.

3 Seymour Drescher, *The Mighty Experiment*, Ch. 10.

4 Claire Midgley, *Women Against Slavery*; Moira Ferguson, *Subject to Others*; John Oldfield, *Popular Politics*.

5 Michael Craton, *Testing the Chains*, Ch. 22.

6 Kenneth Morgan, *Slavery and the British Empire*, p. 190.
7 Nicholas Draper, 'Conclusion', *The Price of Freedom*.

**Chapter 7**
1 Stanley L. Engerman, 'US Slavery and Its Aftermath', in David Eltis *et al.*, *Cambridge World History of Slavery, Volume 4*, p. 155.
2 Stanley L. Engerman, 'US Slavery and Its Aftermath', in David Eltis *et al.*, *Cambridge World History of Slavery, Volume 4*, p. 157; Peter Kolchin, *American Slavery*, Table 3, p. 254.
3 Both letters, and thousands more, can be found at www.informationwanted.org.
4 Sven Berkert, *Empire of Cotton*; Stanley L. Engerman, 'US Slavery and Its Aftermath', in David Eltis *et al.*, *Cambridge World History of Slavery, Volume 4*, pp. 152–9; Robert W. Fogel, *Without Consent*, p. 87.
5 Robert W. Fogel, *Without Consent*, p. 258.
6 Robert W. Fogel and Stanley L. Engerman, *Time on the Cross*.
7 Peter Kolchin, *American Slavery*, pp. 180–2.
8 Gwendolyn Midlo Hall, *Africans in Colonial Louisiana*, pp. 344–5.
9 Manisha Sinha, *The Slave's Cause*, p. 58.
10 Manisha Sinha, *The Slave's Cause*, p. 196.
11 Michael Craton, *Testing the Chains*, Ch. 22.

12  Manisha Sinha, *The Slave's Cause*, pp. 406–14.

13  Johannes Postma, *Slave Revolts*, pp. 83–4.

14  Johannes Postma, *Slave Revolts*, pp. 85–6.

15  Peter Kolchin, *American Slavery*, p. 157.

16  Richard Blackett, *The Captive's Quest for Freedom*. The book was published too late to be a major reference for this work.

17  Eric Foner, *Gateway to Freedom*, pp. 152–5.

18  Eric Foner, *Gateway to Freedom*, p. 4; Manisha Sinha, *The Slave's Cause*, p. 382.

19  Robert W. Fogel, *Without Consent*, pp. 254–6: Manisha Sinha, *The Slave's Cause*, p. 256.

20  Robert W. Fogel, *Without Consent*, p. 256.

21  James B. Stewart, 'Antislavery and Abolitionism in the US', in David Eltis *et al.*, *Cambridge World History of Slavery, Volume 4*, p. 406: Robert W. Fogel, *Without Consent*, p. 269.

22  David Brion Davis, *Inhuman Bondage*, p. 259.

23  David Brion Davis, *Inhuman Bondage*, pp. 262, 280.

24  David Brion Davis, *Inhuman Bondage*, pp. 265–6.

25  James Walvin, *Slavery in Small Things*, Ch. 9.

26  David Brion Davis, *Inhuman Bondage*, p. 289.

27  David Brion Davis, *Inhuman Bondage*, p. 302.

28  Eric Foner, *Give Me Liberty*, Appendix A.24.

# Chapter 8

1 Peter Bakewell, *A History of Latin America*, p. 152.

2 K. R. Lohse, 'Mexico and Central America', in R. L. Paquette and M. M. Smith (eds), *The Oxford Handbook of Slavery*, pp. 61–3; Christopher Schmidt-Nowara, 'The Transition from Slavery', in David Eltis *et al.*, *Cambridge World History of Slavery, Volume 4*, pp. 468–9.

3 Peter Blanchard, 'Spanish South American Mainland', in R. L. Paquette and M. M. Smith (eds), *The Oxford Handbook of Slavery*, pp. 68–75.

4 Peter Blanchard, 'Spanish South American Mainland', in R. L. Paquette and M. M. Smith (eds), *The Oxford Handbook of Slavery*, pp. 79–82.

5 Christopher Schmidt-Nowara, *Slavery, Freedom and Abolition*, pp. 90–6.

6 Christopher Schmidt-Nowara, 'Transition from Slavery', in David Eltis *et al.*, *Cambridge World History of Slavery, Volume 4*, p. 468.

7 Christopher Schmidt-Nowara, *Slavery, Freedom and Abolition*, p. 109.

8 Christopher Schmidt-Nowara, *Slavery, Freedom and Abolition*, pp. 111-12.

9 Christopher Schmidt-Nowara, 'Transition from Slavery', in David Eltis *et al.*, *Cambridge World History of Slavery, Volume 4*, p. 469.

10 Peter Blanchard, 'Spanish South American Mainland', in R. L. Paquette and M. M. Smith (eds), *The Oxford Handbook of Slavery*, pp. 81–4.

11 Christopher Schmidt-Nowara, *Slavery, Freedom and Abolition*, pp. 114–15.

12 Christopher Schmidt-Nowara, *Slavery, Freedom and Abolition*, pp. 37, 42, 123–32.

13 Laird W. Bergad, 'Slavery in Cuba', in David Eltis *et al.*, *Cambridge World History of Slavery, Volume 4*, Ch. 5.

14 David Eltis and David Richardson, *Atlas*, p. 202.

15 Christopher Schmidt-Nowara, *Slavery, Freedom and Abolition*, pp. 130–2.

16 Christopher Schmidt-Nowara, *Slavery, Freedom and Abolition*, pp. 136–7.

17 M. D. Childs and M. Barcia, 'Cuba', in R. L. Paquette and M. M. Smith (eds), *The Oxford Handbook of Slavery*, p. 100.

18 M. D. Childs and M. Barcia, 'Cuba', in R. L. Paquette and M. M. Smith (eds), *The Oxford Handbook of Slavery*, pp. 100–2.

19 Christopher Schmidt-Nowara, *Slavery, Freedom and Abolition*, p. 144.

20 M. D. Childs and M. Barcia, 'Cuba', in R. L. Paquette and M. M. Smith (eds), *The Oxford Handbook of Slavery*, pp. 103–5.

21 Christopher Schmidt-Nowara, 'Transition from Slavery', in David Eltis *et al.*, *Cambridge*

*World History of Slavery, Volume 4*, p. 471.

22 Christopher Schmidt-Nowara, *Slavery, Freedom and Abolition*, pp. 148–9.
23 Christopher Schmidt-Nowara, 'Transition from Slavery', in David Eltis *et al.*, *Cambridge World History of Slavery, Volume 4*, p. 476.

## Chapter 9

1 David Eltis and David Richardson, *Atlas*, p. 203.
2 João José Reis, 'Slavery in Nineteenth-century Brazil', in David Eltis *et al.*, *Cambridge World History of Slavery, Volume 4*, pp. 132–3.
3 Emilia Viotti da Costa, *The Brazilian Empire*, p. 131.
4 William Sullivan, 'Brazil is Coffee'.
5 Boris Fausto, *A Concise History of Brazil*, p. 107.
6 James Walvin, *Sugar*, p. 84.
7 João José Reis, 'Slavery in Nineteenth-century Brazil', in David Eltis *et al.*, *Cambridge World History of Slavery, Volume 4*, p. 131.
8 João José Reis, 'Slavery in Nineteenth-century Brazil', in David Eltis *et al.*, *Cambridge World History of Slavery, Volume 4*, pp. 136–8.
9 David Ekis and David Richardson, *Atlas*, p. 203.
10 Emilia Viotti da Costa, *The Brazilian Empire*, pp. 135–6.

11  João José Reis, 'Slavery in Nineteenth-century Brazil', in David Eltis *et al.*, *Cambridge World History of Slavery, Volume 4*, pp. 141, 148.

12  James H. Sweet, *Recreating Africa*, p. 206.

13  James H. Sweet, *Recreating Africa*, Ch. 9.

14  João José Reis, 'Slavery in Nineteenth-century Brazil', in David Eltis *et al.*, *Cambridge World History of Slavery, Volume 4*, pp. 142–3.

15  João José Reis, 'Slavery in Nineteenth-century Brazil', in David Eltis *et al.*, *Cambridge World History of Slavery, Volume 4*, p. 141.

16  João José Reis, 'Slavery in Nineteenth-century Brazil', in David Eltis *et al.*, *Cambridge World History of Slavery, Volume 4*, pp. 145–6.

17  João José Reis, 'Slavery in Nineteenth-century Brazil', in David Eltis *et al.*, *Cambridge World History of Slavery, Volume 4*, p. 140.

18  João José Reis, 'Slavery in Nineteenth-century Brazil', in David Eltis *et al.*, *Cambridge World History of Slavery, Volume 4*, pp. 149–50.

19  Mary G. Karasch, *Slave Life in Rio*, Ch. 10.

20  João José Reis, 'Slavery in Nineteenth-century Brazil', in David Eltis *et al.*, *Cambridge World History of Slavery, Volume 4*, pp. 150–1.

21  João José Reis, 'Slavery in Nineteenth-century Brazil', in David Eltis *et al.*, *Cambridge World History of Slavery, Volume 4*, p. 146.

22 João José Reis, 'Slavery in Nineteenth-century Brazil', in David Eltis *et al.*, *Cambridge World History of Slavery,* *Volume 4*, p. 147.

23 João José Reis, 'Slavery in Nineteenth-century Brazil', in David Eltis *et al.*, *Cambridge World History of Slavery,* *Volume 4*, pp. 147–8.

24 Seymour Drescher, *Abolition*, p. 354.

25 C. T. Castillo, 'Abolition and Its Aftermath in Brazil', in David Eltis *et al.*, *Cambridge World History of Slavery, Volume 4*, p. 488.

26 Emilia Viotti da Costa, *The Brazilian Empire*, pp. 161–2.

27 C. T. Castillo, 'Abolition and Its Aftermath in Brazil', in David Eltis *et al.*, *Cambridge World History of Slavery, Volume 4*, pp. 493–5.

28 Seymour Drescher, *Abolition*, p. 353.

29 Seymour Drescher, *Abolition*, p. 355.

30 Seymour Drescher, *Abolition*, p. 356.

31 Seymour Drescher, *Abolition*, pp. 356–7.

32 Seymour Drescher, *Abolition*, pp. 360–1.

33 C. T. Castillo, 'Abolition and Its Aftermath in Brazil', in David Eltis *et al.*, *Cambridge World History of Slavery, Volume 4*, p. 497.

34 C. T. Castillo, 'Abolition and Its Aftermath in Brazil', in David Eltis *et al.*, *Cambridge World History of Slavery, Volume 4*, p. 499.

35 C. T. Castillo, 'Abolition and Its Aftermath

in Brazil', in David Eltis *et al., Cambridge World History of Slavery, Volume 4*, p. 501; Seymour Drescher, *Abolition*, p. 365, n. 88.

36  João José Reis, 'Slavery in Nineteenth-century Brazil', in David Eltis *et al., Cambridge World History of Slavery, Volume 4*, p. 146.

37  C. T. Castillo, 'Abolition and Its Aftermath in Brazil', in David Eltis *et al., Cambridge World History of Slavery, Volume 4*, p. 501.

38  C. T. Castillo, 'Abolition and Its Aftermath in Brazil', in David Eltis *et al., Cambridge World History of Slavery, Volume 4*, pp. 501–2; Seymour Drescher, *Abolition*, p. 366.

39  C. T. Castillo, 'Abolition and Its Aftermath in Brazil', in David Eltis *et al., Cambridge World History of Slavery, Volume 4*, p. 503.

40  Christopher Schmidt-Nowara, *Slavery, Freedom and Abolition*, pp. 146–55.

41  David Brion Davis, *Slavery and Human Progress*, p. 297.

## Chapter 10

1  Seymour Drescher, *Abolition*, pp. 228–30.

2  Suzanne Miers, *Slavery in the 20th Century*, pp. 10–15.

3  Silvia Scarpa, *Trafficking in Human Beings*, pp. 42–3.

4  Robin Law, 'Abolition and Imperialism', in Derek R. Peterson (ed.), *Abolitionism and Imperialism*, Ch. 6.

5 Thomas Pakenham, *The Scramble for Africa*, p. 396.
6 Silvia Scarpa, *Trafficking in Human Beings*, p. 43.
7 John Iliffe, *Africans*, Ch. 9.
8 Silvia Scarpa, *Trafficking in Human Beings*, p. 43.
9 Silvia Scarpa, *Trafficking in Human Beings*, p. 44.

**Chapter 11**
1 Anne Applebaum, *The Gulag*, pp. 276–7.
2 Anne Applebaum, *The Gulag*, pp. 74–5.
3 Anne Applebaum, *The Gulag*, p. 179.
4 Michael Geyer and Adam Tooze (eds), *The Cambridge History of the Second World War: Volume III: Total War.*
5 Gitta Sereny, *The German Trauma*, pp. xi, 26.
6 Gitta Sereny, *The German Trauma*, p. 139.
7 Philippe Sands, *East West Street*, pp. xxi, 111–14.
8 Kevin Bales, Zoe Trodd and Alex Kent Williamson, *Modern Slavery*, p. 15.
9 Tony Judt, *Postwar*, p. 53.
10 www.un.org/en.
11 www.gov.uk/government/collections/modern slavery-bill.
12 *Daily Mail*, 12 February 2018; *Guardian*, 27 January 2016; *ITN News*, 30 May 2017; *Manchester Evening News*, 15 February 2007.

13 Kevin Bales, Zoe Trodd and Alex Kent Williamson, *Modern Slavery*, pp. 22–5.

14 Kevin Bales, *Understanding Global Slavery*, p. 186.

15 Kevin Bales, Zoe Trodd and Alex Kent Williamson, *Modern Slavery*, Ch. 2.

16 Kevin Bales, 'Contemporary Coercive Labor Practices', in David Eltis *et al.*, *Cambridge World History of Slavery, Volume 4*, p. 660.

17 Kevin Bales, 'Contemporary Coercive Labor Practices', in David Eltis *et al.*, *Cambridge World History of Slavery, Volume 4*, Ch. 28.

18 Kevin Bales, 'Contemporary Coercive Labor Practices', in David Eltis *et al.*, *Cambridge World History of Slavery, Volume 4*, p. 663.

19 Kevin Bales, 'Contemporary Coercive Labor Practices', in David Eltis *et al.*, *Cambridge World History of Slavery, Volume 4*, p. 674.

20 Kevin Bales, 'Contemporary Coercive Labor Practices', in David Eltis *et al.*, *Cambridge World History of Slavery, Volume 4*, Ch. 28.

## Conclusion

1 *Harper's Weekly*, Vol. 10 (12 May 1866), p. 300.

2 Randy Browne, *Surviving Slavery.*

# Bibliography and Further Reading

For the most recent annual bibliography on slavery see Thomas Thurston, 'Slavery: Annual Bibliographical Supplement', *Slavery & Abolition* (December 2018).

## Databases

Trans-Atlantic Slave Trade Database, www.slave voyages.org

Legacies of British Slave-ownership, www.ucl.ac.uk/lbs

Runaway Slaves in Britain, www.runaways.gla.ac.uk

Last Seen: Finding Family After Slavery, www.informationwanted.org

## Publications

Anstey, Roger, *The Atlantic Slave Trade and British Abolition* (London, 1973). Applebaum, Anne, *The Gulag: A History of the Soviet Camps* (London, 2003).

Bakewell, Peter, *A History of Latin America: Empires and Sequels, 1450–1830* (Cambridge, MA, 1997).

Bales, Kevin, *Understanding Global Slavery: A Reader* (Berkeley, 2005).

Bales, Kevin, Zoe Trodd and Alex Kent

Williamson, *Modern Slavery* (Richmond, 2009).

Beckert, Sven, *Empire of Cotton: A New History of Global Capitalism* (London, 2014).

Blackburn, Robin, *The Making of New World Slavery* (London, 1997).

Blackburn, Robin, *The Overthrow of Colonial Slavery, 1776-1848* (London, 1988).

Blackett, Richard, *The Captive's Quest for Freedom: Fugitive Slaves, the 1850 Fugitive Slave Law, and the Politics of Freedom* (Cambridge, 2018).

Blackett, Richard, *Making Freedom: The Underground Railroad and the Politics of Slavery* (Chapel Hill, 2013).

Brown, Christopher, *Moral Capital: Foundations of British Abolitionism* (Chapel Hill, 2008).

Browne, Randy, *Surviving Slavery in the British Caribbean* (Philadelphia, 2017).

Burnard, Trevor, *Mastery, Tyranny, and Desire: Thomas Thistlewood and His Slaves in the Anglo-Jamaican World* (Chapel Hill, 2004).

Burnard, Trevor, *Planters, Merchants, and Slaves: Plantation Societies in British America, 1650-1820* (Chicago, 2015).

Carey, Brycchan and Geoffrey Plank (eds), *Quakers and Abolition* (Chicago, 2014).

Carretta, Vincent, *Equiano the African: Biography of a Self-Made Man* (Athens, Georgia, and London, 2005).

Craton, Michael, *Testing the Chains: Resistance to Slavery in the British West Indies* (Ithaca, 1982).

da Costa, Emilia Viotti, *The Brazilian Empire: Myths and Histories* (Chapel Hill, 2000).

Davis, David Brion, *Inhuman Bondage: The Rise and Fall of Slavery in the New World* (Oxford, 2006).

Davis, David Brion, *The Problem of Slavery in Western Culture* (Ithaca, 1966).

Davis, David Brion, *The Problem of Slavery in the Age of Revolution, 1770-1823* (New York, 1999).

Davis, David Brion, *Slavery and Human Progress* (New York, 1984).

Devine, T. M. (ed.), *Recovering Scotland's Slavery Past* (Edinburgh, 2015).

Draper, Nicholas, *The Price of Freedom: Slave-ownership, Compensation and British Society at the End of Slavery* (Cambridge, 2010).

Drescher, Seymour, *Econocide: British Slavery in the Era of Abolition* (London, 1977).

Drescher, Seymour, *The Mighty Experiment: Free Labor Versus Slavery in British Emancipation* (New York, 2002).

Drescher, Seymour, *Abolition: A History of Slavery and Antislavery* (Cambridge, 2009).

Eltis, David, *The Rise of African Slavery in the Americas* (Cambridge, 2000).

Eltis, David and David Richardson, *Atlas of the*

*Transatlantic Slave Trade* (New Haven and London, 2010).

Eltis, David, Stanley L. Engerman, Seymour Drescher and David Richardson (eds), *The Cambridge World History of Slavery, Volume 4, AD 1804–AD 2016* (Cambridge, 2017).

Fausto, Boris, *A Concise History of Brazil* (Cambridge, 1999).

Fogel, Robert W., *Without Consent or Contract. The Rise and Fall of American Slavery* (New York, 1989).

Fogel, Robert W. and Stanley L. Engerman, *Time on the Cross. The Economics of American Negro Slavery* (Boston, 1974, 2 vols).

Follett, Richard, *The Sugar Masters: Planters and Slaves in Louisiana's Cane World 1820–1860* (Baton Rouge, 2005).

Foner, Eric, *Gateway to Freedom: The Hidden History of the Underground Railroad* (New York, 2015).

Foner, Eric, *Give Me Liberty: An American History* (New York, 2005).

Geggus, David, *Haitian Revolutionary Studies* (Bloomington, 2002).

Geggus, David (ed.), *The Haitian Revolution* (Indianapolis, 2014).

Geggus, David, *Slavery, War and Revolution: The British Occupation of Saint Domingue, 1793–1798* (Oxford, 1982).

Geyer, Michael and Adam Tooze (eds), *The*

*Cambridge History of the Second World War: Volume III: Total War* (Cambridge, 2015).

Hall, Catherine, *Cultures of Empire: Colonisers in Britain and the Empire in the Nineteenth and Twentieth Centuries—A Reader* (Manchester, 2000).

Hall, Catherine, *Civilising Subjects: Metropole and Colony in the English Imagination, 1830–1867* (Cambridge, 2002).

Hall, Catherine, *Macaulay and Son: Architects of Imperial Britain* (New Haven and London, 2012).

Hanley, Ryan, *Beyond Slavery and Abolition: Black British Writing, c.1770–1830* (Cambridge, 2018).

Higman, B. W., *A Concise History of the Caribbean* (Cambridge, 2011).

Higman, B. W., *Plantation Jamaica, 1750–1850: Capital and Control in a Colonial Economy* (Kingston, 2005).

Higman, B. W., *Slave Populations of the British Caribbean, 1807–1834* (Baltimore, 1984).

Iliffe, John, *Africans: The History of a Continent* (Cambridge, 1995).

Isaac, Rhys, *Landon Carter's Uneasy Kingdom. Revolution and Rebellion on a Virginian Planation* (Oxford, 2004).

Jackson, Maurice, *Let This Voice Be Heard: Anthony Benezet, Father of Atlantic Abolitionism* (Philadelphia, 2009).

Judt, Tony, *Postwar: A History of Europe since 1945* (London, 2007).

Karasch, Mary, *Slave Life in Rio de Janeiro, 1808–1850* (Princeton, 1987).

Kolchin, Peter, *American Slavery, 1619–1877* (London, 1995).

Lawrence, A. E., *Fortified Trade Posts: The English in West Africa 1645–1822* (London, 1969).

Midgley, Clare, *Women Against Slavery: The British Campaign, 1780–1870* (London, 2016).

Midlo Hall, Gwendolyn, *Africans in Colonial Louisiana* (Baton Rouge, 1992).

Miers, Suzanne, *Slavery and Antislavery in the Twentieth Century: The Evolution of a Global Problem* (Lanham, 2003).

Morgan, Kenneth, *Slavery and the British Empire* (Oxford, 2007).

Morgan, Philip D., *Slave Counterpoint: Black Culture in the Eighteenth-Century Chesapeake and Lowcountry* (Chapel Hill, 1998).

Newton, John, *The Journal of a Slave Trader*, ed. Bernard Martin and Mark Spurrell (London, 1962).

Pakenham, Thomas, *The Scramble for Africa* (London, 1991).

Paquette, Robert L. and Mark M. Smith (eds), *The Oxford Handbook of Slavery in the Americas* (Oxford, 2010).

Peterson, Derek R. (ed.), *Abolition and Imperialism in Britain, Africa and the Atlantic* (Athens, OH, 2010).

Petley, Christer, *White Fury: A Jamaican Slaveholder and the Age of Revolution* (Oxford, 2018).

Popkin, Jeremy D., *Facing Racial Revolution: Eyewitness Accounts of the Haitian Insurrection* (Chicago, 2007).

Postma, Johannes, *Slave Revolts* (Westport, 2008).

Rediker, Marcus, *The Slave Ship: A Human History* (London, 2007).

Richardson, David, Suzanne Schwarz and Anthony Tibbles (eds), *Liverpool and Transatlantic Slavery* (Liverpool, 2007).

Robertson, James, *Gone is the Ancient Glory: Spanish Town, Jamaica 1534–2000* (Kingston and Miami, 2005).

Sands, Philippe, *East West Street: On the Origins of Genocide and Crimes Against Humanity* (London, 2016).

Scarpa, Silvia, *Trafficking in Human Beings: Modern Slavery* (Oxford, 2008).

Schmidt-Nowara, Christopher, *Slavery, Freedom and Abolition in Latin America and the Atlantic World* (Albuquerque, 2011).

Sereny, Gitta, *The German Trauma: Experiences and Reflections, 1938–2001* (London, 2000).

Sinha, Manisha, *The Slaves' Cause: A History of Abolition* (New Haven and London, 2017).

Sullivan, William, 'Brazil is Coffee and Coffee is the Negro', *Historian* (Dept of History, New York University, 2014 issue).

Sweet, James H., *Recreating Africa: Culture, Kinship and Religion in the African-Portuguese World, 1441–1770* (Chapel Hill, 2003).

Tadman, Michael, *Speculators and Slaves: Masters, Traders, and Slaves in the Old South* (Madison, 1989).

Taylor, Eric Robert, *If We Must Die: Shipboard Insurrections in the Era of the Atlantic Slave Trade* (Baton Rouge, 2006).

Walvin, James, *Atlas of Slavery* (London, 2013).

Walvin, James, *Crossings, Africa, the Americas and the Atlantic Slave Trade* (London, 2013).

Walvin, James, *Slavery in Small Things* (Chichester, 2017).

Walvin, James, *Sugar: The World Corrupted, from Slavery to Obesity* (London, 2017).

Walvin, James, *The Zong; A Massacre, the Law and the End of Slavery* (New Haven and London, 2011).

# Acknowledgements

This book is a concise study of a complex and far-reaching historical story. Its purpose is to offer a distinctive explanation of the way slavery in the Americas ended. It is a book that engages with many other interpretations of the same issue, and has grown out of my long-standing interest, both as a teacher and as an author, in the history of slavery and abolition. That interest has been influenced and shaped by the work of many other scholars whose arguments, often advanced in substantial scholarly volumes over the past fifty years, have transformed our understanding of the history of slavery and its demise. I could not have written this book without that rich scholarship or, indeed, without the generosity and help of many of the historians involved. My intention here, however, has been to write a book that, while remaining loyal to the scholarly findings of others, seeks to appeal to a non-specialist audience. This is, then, a book for that elusive general readership: people keen to learn more about this critical historical experience without having to confront the fine detail or technical structures of more scholarly presentations. Those same readers can follow the arguments of other historians by using my guide to further reading in the notes and bibliography. Academic readers will know where to look without any help from me.

This book has emerged from work in a number of libraries, mainly in the USA. I first began to think about the ending of slavery when working in the Huntington Library in California. The Gilder Lehrman Institute of American History enabled me to work in the rare book room of Columbia University. Yale's Beinecke Rare Book and Manuscript Library generously supported research in their remarkable holdings. Much of my reading of secondary sources took place closer to home in the J. B. Morrell Library of the University of York, and on regular visits to the Swem Library at the College of William and Mary in Williamsburg.

My ideas about slavery and its abolition have been greatly influenced not only by the published scholarship of other historians, but by a professional and personal friendship with many of the people whose names dominate the bibliography. What follows therefore runs the risk of appearing to be a roll call of old friends. The late Michael Craton first launched me into the world of slavery in the mid-1960s. Since then, Gad Heuman has proved an invaluable supporter and friend. So too, more recently, has John Oldfield. In Barry Higman I have been lucky to have a colleague whose remarkable scholarship guided me (and many others) through the complexities of Caribbean culture and history. David Blight has been a steadfast ally and host at a variety of academic events at Yale and in New York City. Caryl Phillips has never failed to be a much-valued friend and helper. Three historians deserve special mention. Seymour Drescher has, almost single-handedly, transformed our understanding of the ending of slavery, while David Richardson and David Eltis have created a monumental study of the Atlantic slave trade. All three have also been unfailingly generous to me with their time and ideas. Though this book is not solely about British slavery, it has evolved from work on the history of the role of slavery in British history. For that, I am greatly indebted to the work of Catherine Hall. In addition to her major publications, the research project that she and Nicholas Draper have inspired and guided at UCL has thrust the question of slavery back to where it rightfully belongs: at the heart of our understanding of modern British history.

One historian above all demands special and respectful acknowledgement. The major volumes by David Brion Davis devoted to the various problems of slavery stand as a unique intellectual achievement. I hope his influence is clear, even in the necessarily truncated and crisp version I have used in my broad approach to this complex issue.

My thanks also go to Duncan Proudfoot for trusting me by commissioning this book, and to Howard Watson, whose excellent copy-editing greatly improved the final text—and, once again, to my agent Charles Walker.

As a young, inexperienced historian speaking to a group of historians meeting in Hull, I tried to make the case that slavery belongs at the centre of recent Western historical and economic experience. My remarks (doubtless too simple and naive) received a hostile response. This book might stand as my answer—fifty years late—to what, at the time, was a disheartening experience.

**Center Point Large Print**
600 Brooks Road / PO Box 1
Thorndike, ME 04986-0001 USA

**(207) 568-3717**

**US & Canada:**
**1 800 929-9108**
www.centerpointlargeprint.com